# This Life In Death

Volume II

'The Madness'

By Howard Hodgson

# This Life In Death



Published by
Chipmunkapublishing Ltd
United Kingdom

http://www.chipmunkapublishing.com

Cover Image design by Sam Harper

## This Life In Death

# This Life In Death

# This Life In Death

Foreword

There are stories, and then there are sagas. Some books entertain, others educate, but every so often, you come across a tale so compelling that it does both. *This Life in Death Vol. 2* is one of those books. It is not a work of fiction—though at times, you might think it is. The twists, the betrayals, the power struggles, and the relentless pursuit of something greater—it has all the makings of a legal thriller, minus the courtroom, but with stakes just as high —a journey through the highs of empire-building and the depths of near-ruin, where every triumph comes at a price and every setback demands reinvention. It reads like a thriller, but make no mistake—every twist, every triumph, and every downfall is real.

Howard Hodgson is not your typical businessman. He didn't inherit a gilded empire, nor was he handed a golden key to success. He built it. Brick by brick, deal by deal, funeral by funeral. His battlefield was not a boardroom but the delicate and often cutthroat world of deathcare—an industry few dare to look at too closely, let alone master.

This book picks up where the first left off, with Howard at the pinnacle of success, celebrated as "Mr. Death" in the press. But as every good story goes, the higher the climb, the greater the fall. Boardroom betrayals, economic downturns, and corporate politics threatened to unravel everything he had worked for. The deals got bigger, the opponents tougher, and the risks—both financial and personal—deadlier.

But Hodgson is no ordinary protagonist. He fights back. He adapts. He reinvents himself. And just when it seems like he's lost it all, he finds a way to turn the tables once again.

I first met Howard in 1971. With two colleagues and the backing of a millionaire Manchester merchant banker, we had built a thriving investment brokerage across the North of England and were looking to expand into the Midlands. A manager of mine, Joe, mentioned he'd met a young director of an investment business in Stoke-on-Trent who could be a great candidate.

"What do you know about him?" I asked.

"Well, not much," Joe admitted. "He's very young, sounds like Prince Charles, and looks a bit like Robert Redford."

## This Life In Death

Although Joe's assessment was entirely unhelpful my curiosity was piqued. A few days later, I met Howard in a cramped, run-down office in Stoke-on-Trent, a town then struggling under the collapse of the pottery industry and high unemployment.

Howard was utterly out of place, an undeniable force of charisma and optimism. His "can-do, will-do" attitude was electric. It brought to mind a favourite poem, Rudyard Kipling's *If*, particularly these lines: *If you can force your heart and nerve and sinew To serve your turn long after they are gone, And so hold on when there is nothing in you Except the Will which says to them: 'Hold on'*

We hit it off immediately. By the end of our meeting, he wasn't just going to develop the Birmingham area—he was taking on the entire South of England. I looked at my watch. It was 4 a.m. Three days later, Howard and his team arrived at our offices in Altrincham, where they were duly impressed by the brand-new office block and the two yellow Lamborghinis parked outside. Over the next year, Howard didn't just meet expectations; he shattered them. London, the South East—every target was conquered. He had the unique ability to inspire and motivate an audience of two or three or 500 without missing a beat.

Looking back on that first meeting, I can still see the raw determination that would define his incredible business journey.

Howard pulls no punches. There are no sacred cows, no hidden agendas. Every scene in this account is presented through the eyes of a cast of bystanders and insiders who share one thing in common: they were there. This book is fast-paced, thrilling, and rich in forensic detail, balancing the precision of a business manual with the heart-pounding momentum of a true-life drama.

If you've ever dreamed of building a business, navigating corporate power struggles, or reinventing yourself after a fall, then this is more than a memoir—it's a masterclass in resilience, strategy, and entrepreneurial survival.

As you turn these pages, consider the lessons embedded in Howard's journey:

**Spot the Opportunity** – Success begins with recognizing an underserved market. Howard saw an industry ripe for change and seized the moment. What industry are you looking at? Where are the gaps?

**Build a Brand, Not Just a Business** – Customers don't buy products; they buy trust. Howard understood the power of branding, ensuring that every service, every location, and every employee reflected a unified identity. Are you thinking about the long-term perception of your business?

**Master the Art of Negotiation** – Deals are won and lost on the strength of relationships. Howard's career is a testament to knowing when to push and when to compromise. Are you playing the long game?

**Survive the Setbacks** – Every entrepreneur faces betrayal, bad deals, and economic storms. The question isn't if you'll fail—it's how you'll recover. Howard's ability to pivot, adapt, and reinvent himself is a lesson in long-term thinking.

**Leave a Legacy** – True success isn't measured solely in profit. Howard's commitment to dignity and service ensured his impact extended beyond financial gains. What legacy will you leave behind?

Beyond the boardroom battles, beyond the financial highs and lows, lies a deeper truth: life is about more than wealth and power. This book closes on a philosophical note, reinforcing the idea that death is not an end but a transition, both personally and professionally. The love we give, the dreams we pursue—these are what endure beyond the final curtain.

So, take a deep breath. Open the first page. And prepare for one heck of a ride.

But be warned: once you start, you won't put it down. Howard Hodgson's journey is more than a business memoir—it's a testament to the extraordinary resilience of the human spirit.

Your next big idea starts now. Let's begin.

David Meakin.

# This Life In Death

# This Life In Death

## Dedication

Below is the Memoria Mission Statement. It was written by me in 2009 as we started Memoria MK II. I dedicate this 2nd volume of 'This Life in Death' to all the wonderful men and women who were engaged by Memoria to live and breathe these words and make them become a reality for hundreds of thousands of bereaved families in the following fifteen years and will no doubt for years to come – long after I have gone.

## Our Mission Statement

Memoria has a mission to provide exceptional standards of service, facility and products to the bereaved families that use its funeral directing services, crematoria, cemeteries, gardens of remembrance, financial & legal services or online retail store. This is because it is not only commercially sensible to do so but also because it is an essential act of human decency towards people who have just lost a much-loved member of their family or friend. Bereavement is the price we must all pay for the joy of loving and being loved. The loss of a loved one is the most stressful, unhappy and traumatic experience that we will face in life. We at Memoria realise that we are unable to eradicate such pain, but we also know it is our responsibility and duty to be as efficient, kind, respectful and polite as humanly possible to our clients at their time of grief, and thereafter when they need to conclude estate matters for their cherished relatives or friends. Therefore, it is our aim to provide immaculately clean and tidy facilities in tranquil and beautiful surroundings attended by people who are sincerely dedicated to our mission, and who take a great pride in their work as a result.

Most people go to work every day for the money they receive. Instead, you go on a saintly mission every day to show man's humanity to man; to do unto others what you would have done unto you.

I know each of you, respect and love all of you. Thank you for your exceptional dedication to making the 'Mission Statement' a reality. I am extra-ordinarily proud to have known you and led you into commercial battle and witness you smash the opposition.

## This Life In Death

# This Life In Death

## Acknowledgements

I received huge amounts of encouragement to consider actually perceiving and then writing both volumes of 'This Life in Death' – and then got a lot of additional help especially regarding this second volume.

Firstly, I must thank all the characters who appear in these pages and play their part as this colourful life tumbles down crevasses before climbing up mountains again. Whether, they have been good, bad or ugly, they are really vital ingredients, because without them the read would be much more dull and nothing like the rip-roaring true yarn that you are about to discover.

Secondly, I must thank my son Jamieson and co-Memoria director, Michael Hackney, for remembering the last ten years of, at times, complicated events involving the technical details of planning issues, which they were both closer to than me.

Thirdly, I would also like to thank Jason Pegler and Andrew Latchford, my publishers at Chipmunka Publishing, for their support and encouragement, and my first wife, Marianne, eldest son Howard, and all my other children and grandchildren for their enthusiastic reception of each draft that I shared with them.

And lastly, I must acknowledge the tireless labours of three women: my wife Christine and Executive Assistant Jane Hayes for their proofreading, corrections and help with the 50+ photographs contained herein; and the independent reading by Anja Jorgensen, who read each chapter as it was completed as someone who had not known me over the years of either volume and therefore could give me the independent and fresh view of a reader who had never met me. This was invaluable on so many levels.

So a wonderful thank you to you all – sent with great love and gratitude.

## This Life In Death

# This Life In Death

## Introduction

The words of the song 'Happy Talk' from the Rodgers & Hammerstein musical 'South Pacific' of 1949: 'You gotta have a dream, if you don't have a dream, how you gonna have a dream come true?', explain my life and especially the successes wonderfully. I really believe that real wealth and satisfaction can be made by anyone with drive, determination and a dream. For it is these qualities and not academia which made me successful, despite my other several failings. I said so in the press at the height of 'Mr Death' mania by the press and I have remained constant to that view for the last fifty years.

We saw in Volume I of 'This Life in Death' how I recorded a life of turbulence and emotion in a fight to recover lost wealth and love from an idyllic childhood, through a hectic journey of much happiness, but also hurt, extreme tragedy, pain, before ultimate success and victory. There were also births, marriages, deaths, love affairs and flirtations galore, as well as the odd fight and corporate battle along the way. Now in Volume II the rollercoaster ride continues.

I have been around for many years and could, like any of us, face the 'final curtain' unexpectedly. Therefore, I have taken this opportunity to share my experience of life and the challenges it has held, so that it might help others realise that they can overcome life's slings and arrows – even when sometimes these are self-inflicted.

I hope you really enjoy this second volume of a rollercoaster ride of willpower set against adversity amid a family life, love affairs and the workings of an industry that deals in life's greatest taboo – death.

This is because in the frantic and manic life I have led there is adequate proof that much can be achieved if you believe in yourself, your values and your dreams.

You really don't need to be an 'Einstein' to be either successful or just to win when the odds are stacked against you. In fact, most successful entrepreneurs are not academic and are, perhaps, more like you than you think.

I am no psychological expert, I realise that all people are different, that no two lives are the same and that I have no right to preach to anyone about how they should feel or what they should do to cope with their life's problems or deaths affecting them.

However, I also know that we all have our inner demons and secrets and our individual external challenges, hopes, and fears. So, I have decided to share mine in the hope that we both can draw something from you reading them and me writing them.

Therefore, please enjoy my second volume of memoirs about my life among the twilight machinations of the funeral directing world and draw from it what you will without using it as a road map to recovery or salvation as I'm not qualified to give to you such direction.

Nevertheless, I really do hope that I can show you how much is achievable with a positive attitude of mind and a little realisation that whatever our experience, others have been there before us.

Throughout time each generation thinks it is wiser than the last. However, the truth is that while we all benefit from invention and discovery, we hardly ever learn from previous generations' experiences and apparently almost never from their mistakes.

This is because wisdom is gained by experience and experience is gained with age and then we die, and the next generation must learn from personal experience too just as their fathers did. Such is life and such is our stupidity to put our trust in youth as a guide to the future. It usually disappoints for these reasons.

So, this is a continuation of the tale of a young man becoming an older man who, still constantly, had learned from his own mistakes having believed, like many a man before or since, that he was the first person to tread that particular path through life.

So, now in Volume II we see I still have a lot to learn as the explosive and hectic ride through life continues.

I'm pleased to report that writing both volumes have also been cathartic experiences for me. I have been forced to ask myself some questions which I had never delved into before and have come up with answers which have helped me to understand why all that you are going to read happened – for there is an identifiable recurring theme. I suspect that is probably true with all of us. However, I could not always see it as clearly then as I can now.

So, I think I know me much better now due to the writing of these works. My life has been a continual rollercoaster of troughs to peaks and back again and again. These have been usually driven by my own internal Piscean swings between pleasure-seeking indiscipline to obsessive drive, determination, and fanatical discipline. I must be a psychiatrist's dream.

Therefore, this volume, like the last, is all about what has been my road from failure to success and my route to happy recovery from bleak despair.

## This Life In Death

# This Life In Death

Chapter I

Climb Every Mountain

1989 – 1991

We left this tale of high-octane success at work and self-inflicted problems at home on the exceptional 'high' of the much-acclaimed Hodgson Holdings and Kenyon Security merger in 1989.

I was now the undisputed 'King of the British funeral industry.' Moreover, with a couple of exceptions, the press still loved their 'enfant terrible' known as 'Mr. Death', and so Volume I ended in an orgasm of self-congratulation centred around a Swiss educated, beautifully spoken toff, with a tough Brummie 'Peaky Blinders' attitude, who had fallen on hard times but had bounced back to become 'USM Entrepreneur of the Year in 1987' and a high-profile millionaire in the process.

However, no one should under-estimate that the task which I now faced was mountainous for many reasons and the first was the fact that the Prudential and some other Hodgson institutional holders were not altogether happy.

The reality behind the scenes after the merger was that, as with all major takeovers and mergers, not all shareholders were happy.

The French company, Pompes Funèbres Generales, had insisted on a one-for-one deal in the shares between Hodgson and Kenyon. Some of the Hodgson shareholders, who had subscribed two years earlier for shares at Hodgson costing 240p to fund the Ingalls acquisition, were not happy with the 180p at which they were going to be merged. And when Kenyon's latest results were announced on 26th July 1989, the Times highlighted further objections:

'Kenyon Securities has produced disappointing results for the year to end March with earnings per share dropping 7 per cent to 10.8p. The decline makes the merger terms look increasingly unbalanced. Several Hodgson shareholders are suggesting they may oppose the deal when the offer document is published.... Kenyon says its poor performance is the result of a fall in the death rate in the south of England where it has most of its branches.

'These results, however, contrast sharply with Hodgson Holdings' interim figures, announced with the merger last week, which showed earnings up 13 per cent to 9.3p. Yet Hodgson and Kenyon shareholders are being offered the same one-for-one share swap in the merged company, PHK International, with a part cash alternative at 180p. The terms value Hodgson at less than 11 times historic earnings, but Kenyon at more than 16. It is believed that the one-for-one terms were insisted on by Pompes Funèbres Generales which holds a 29% stake in Kenyon and is taking a 25% stake in PHKI'.

All of this is true. However, as we saw at the end of Volume I, Hodgson Holdings really needed to do this deal in order to get its hands on Kenyon's considerable annual funeral numbers, so that it could apply the much more successful Hodgson formula to the same.

This way Hodgson would not only raise earnings per share, but generate enhanced profits to pay down bank debt, which it could no longer repay by a rights issue or pre-emptive placing due to market conditions.

In any event, after the hectic expansion of the previous three years, when Hodgson and Kenyon had been buying as many independent funeral directors as they could – and in Kenyon's case, sometimes without checking thoroughly enough whether they were worth the price being paid – there clearly needed to be a period of consolidation to allow the Hodgson magic to work on the Kenyon numbers.

Moreover, what would happen if the merger was blocked by Hodgson shareholders? What would be the circumstances that faced the Prudential and their schoolboy advisors then?

My arguments were soundly made to all the Hodgson institutional investors, the revolt never materialised, and the merger was accepted by a large majority of Hodgson shareholders consequently – even if not quite as a high a percentage as the Kenyon holders' acceptance for obvious reasons.

## This Life In Death

My points, happily, had not fallen on deaf ears. We really did now need a period of consolidation to ensure that we could get a Hodgson performance out of the Kenyon funeral numbers and it was 100% true that external general market conditions and the shell-shocked stock-market climate were not vaguely conducive to the galloping expansion that the mid-80s bull market had encouraged.

Indeed, most quoted companies were now forced to mark time as the fashionable growth by acquisition of those years was a thing of the past. However, we had the benefit of a very profitable internal consolidation to work on as an alternative to growth by acquisition.

The external doom and gloom thinking was because the British economy was taking longer to respond to high interest rates than had been originally anticipated, and in the autumn of 1989 a smouldering row between Premier Margaret Thatcher and her once close ally, Chancellor Nigel Lawson, erupted in the press with his resignation and replacement by John Major.

Major continued with the harsh medicine of the Premier's prescription for a cure to inflation of high interest rates, and so business thinking was directed towards survival and away from expansion.

However, we had just stocked up with a big fat dose of Kenyon fat which we could trim off to increase profits. My status by having pulled off this deal was increased in the financial press as a result.

Moreover, PFG Hodgson Kenyon International, or the necessary abbreviation to get away from such a silly name, PHKI, was also ideally suited to such conditions. Why? Because people do not stop dying just because interest rates are high, or the economy is in a 'slow down'.

As a result, by early 1990 financial commentators were fairly, if not euphorically, bullish about PHKI. The Investors Chronicle wrote: 'The shares have long-term growth potential and should be bought.'

County Nat West added: 'We have raised our 1990 forecast from £13.32 million to £14.5 million because of a surge in the death rate in January which has got the year off to a good start'. Clearly, the writer had about as much understanding about death rate trends as Russia's President Putin does about the morality value of murder.

However, the ICI Stock-market letter picked this up and under the heading 'Signs of a good start to 1990' noted that Great Southern had stated that 'Trading levels since December 1989 have increased significantly.'

As a result, they continued to recommend PHKI as offering 'strong defensive characteristics and long-term growth potential.'

Therefore, so far so good. The merger with Kenyon was a logical development for Hodgson and had been recognised as such.

Moreover, it had taken courage, skill and foresight to push it through, particularly in the light of gradually worsening economic and stock-market conditions as her ministers, the Conservative Party and, to a much lesser extent, the country, were falling out of love with 'The blessed Margaret.'

Mrs Thatcher had been in power for over decade. She had resurrected a bankrupt UK economy to one of international renown; negotiated much better terms for Britain's financial contribution to the EU, defeated the Argentinians in the Falklands War; crushed the politically motivated trade unions; sold ordinary folk their council houses at knocked down prices; de-nationalised state monopolies and sold the shares in them to millions of people who had never owned shares in anything ever before.

Since Churchill's contribution to saving Great Britain, and as a result, the world, from the genocide of the Third Reich, in the 1940s, no Prime Minister had ever been considered more successful or had stood so tall on the world stage.

Yet, now at the turn of the decade, and in her increasing isolation she was starting to become suspicious, unobjective and unwilling to listen.

Whereas, by the good fortune of my calling being about the death rate as much as my own skill, my stock had never been higher, and my opinion was sought on many issues and I was invited to write articles for many magazines.

One of these was the 'Director' magazine and the subject was 'The Thatcher Decade'. I wrote a four-page article and 95% celebrated the huge successes that Margaret Hilda had enjoyed over this period.

However, I did also venture, that in my opinion, more should be done to generate industrial investment in the northwest, or I could not see who would be staying in the scores of new hotels being built in that region as it was a horrid holiday destination.

The article was published and was becoming fish and chip paper for the rich, when I was due to have lunch at the Savoy Hotel with John Gummer, a pleasant government minister and great supporter of the Prime Minister.

Gummer was late. When he arrived, he apologised and told me that he had been delayed by Mrs Thatcher. She had asked him where he was going for lunch, and he had told her.

"She's very angry with you," he concluded.

"Me? I'm surprised she has even heard of me," I countered.

"Oh, but she has, and she has a message for you. She told me to tell you that she doesn't tell you how to conduct funerals – so don't you tell her how to run the manufacturing base in the north-west."

This comment made me suspect that her time was up and so it was three months later.

xxxxxxx

The merger also had a considerable effect on our homelife too. The French had been keen to mend fences with the Kenyon directors in general and Michael Kenyon in particular. I think they also preferred flying into London rather than Birmingham.

Therefore, they asked me to support their idea of establishing the new PHKI head office in Kenyon's Freston Rd offices, Shepherd's Bush, London, rather than the Hodgson head office in Sutton Coldfield, which would become the finance centre for the new group. I readily agreed.

This meant that we had to sell our Evelyn Gardens apartment on the Fulham Rd, London as well as our beloved Eden Wood.

The financial cost was zero. I even made enough extra money on these property transactions to buy a 5-bedroom house in Canford Cliffs, Dorset – so we could sail every weekend as I kept 'Fat Girl' at the RMYC in Poole Harbour.

This was because I managed to sell the Evelyn Garden apartment for a fortune and didn't overpay for the five-floor house in Wilton Place Belgravia.

However, leaving Eden Wood where Charles had spent two of his three years with us was very emotional. This was made all the worse as we had to have Kelly put down around this time as she had become riddled with cancer.

She was a grand little dog who had been an important part of our lives for nearly thirteen years. She doesn't get as much coverage as Scamp did in Volume I – but that was because Scamp was with me through those very bleak years as my only lifeline to my childhood.

So now Howard must think about taking his A' levels at the Lycée French school on the Cromwell Rd in Knightsbridge, while Jamieson, now aged six, started at the Hampshire School near Hyde Park.

However, before all of this, Marianne, had agreed to my request to remove her coil as it was 'biting William' and that can be very off putting in a moment of passion. Nevertheless, she couldn't go back on the pill as she had become allergic to it.

So, she consulted her gynaecologist and one of our very best chums, Joe Jordan, for many years. He listened carefully to her situation and pronounced that perhaps to do nothing is the best course of action.

He explained that he can't imagine that we indulge in a lot of sexual activity as I'm often away; I still have my young PR mistress to see; that Marianne had had two affairs with Michael Hackney due to my extra-marital sex activities and despite all of this, he doubted, as I worked so hard, that I would get her pregnant even if we got round to making love.

# This Life In Death

Marianne explained his prognosis to me over dinner in London not long after the merger. I was furious. I'm thirty-nine years of age and have come to think of myself, rather arrogantly, as 'the complete cocksman.' Moreover, how could I possibly know as I had never seen another 'cocksman' in action?

Whatever! But now one of my dearest friends has written me off as a 'has been' incapable of making his wife pregnant. I can't wait to get back to Evelyn Gardens and into bed.

It was a 'one shot goal' and we conceived Davinia Clementine Marianne, who was born some seven and a half months later as she was delivered early by Joe in order to save her life.

Marianne had struggled to keep Jamieson seven years earlier and the Davinia pregnancy was even more difficult as it was Marianne's fourth and she was now approaching forty.

Davinia, or 'Dinky' as she became known due her birth size, was to be my fourth child out of an eventual six and the only girl. She is beautiful and intelligent, and no man ever had a better daughter as I was proud to announce at her wedding nearly thirty years later.

Marianne had wanted to call this longed for girl Clementine, after Winston Churchill's much-admired wife. However, her French family were not very keen on the idea as 'Clementine' is best known as a brand of tangerine in France.

Therefore, even as the date of birth approached Marianne had not got a first name.

The night before the birth, I was watching the 1990 World Cup match between England and Belgium. Things were not going well and then just before the final whistle a Gascoigne free kick floated into the box and a magical bicycle kick by Aston Villa's David Platt saw England steal the game and get England into the last 16 of the competition.

I was delighted. England were still in the World Cup and a Villa man had saved the day – just like another Villain, Ollie Watkins, did thirty-four years later against the Netherlands in 2024.

David Platt had given England a divine result. David and divine combined in my head to make 'Davinia.'

I went upstairs to see how Marianne was feeling. I told her I had thought of a name for our baby. It was Davinia. She thought it was a wonderful name. I did not tell her how it had come to me. She was only to find out later when she read it in a magazine interview I had given, by which time I had forgotten that I had never explained to her mother that Davinia had been named after David Platt.

Davinia had to remain in the Queen Elizabeth Hospital in Birmingham for over a month because she was born so prematurely. However, once she was released, we all moved to 19 Wilton Place, Belgravia, London SW1.

Moreover, with the birth of Davinia, I decided that, as a father of four and now forty-years of age, that I really needed to grow up and give my marriage the respect it deserved and become a faithful husband.

My long suffering and delightful long-term lover became a casualty of this decision, and it is not to my credit that she had devoted over 3 years of her life to me only to be cast aside.

Nevertheless, away from self-inflected domestic pain at home, and the external market pressures of running a plc at a very difficult time; the late '80s and early '90s always saw us enjoying extremely happy summers in France.

We had a beautiful home next door to Joan Collins in Port Grimaud. We sailed, or sped on my Sunseeker, after I had returned 'Fat Girl' to Poole in Dorset, which is a place better suited to sailing, over the Gulf to Tahiti Plage for lunch or ventured further to places like Cannes or Cap d' Antibes.

We were nearly always accompanied by either Marianne's brother Alex, his lovely wife Beatrice and their son, William, who is also my godson – and was born not long after Davinia - or by my buddy Simon Draycott, with his very intelligent wife Rukhsana and their three daughters, Natasha, Charlie and Camilla.

## This Life In Death

And of course, there were also the usual adventures to break up the tedium of drinking four buckets of rosé daily at four-hour long lunches.

Two worthy of note spring to mind here:

One day, when Simon and I were anchored with our children in my Sunseeker between the two islands off Cannes, the kids were throwing each other's trainers into the sea as part of a very silly game.

Of course, the trainers floated and were recoverable. However, one of Simon's daughters had a pair of gym shoes and they didn't. So, when the first was flung into the water several metres away from 'Red Rose Speedway' (named after the McCartney album), it sank.

This was a signal for Simon to sink into a dismal moan about how much they had cost. Simon could blow hundreds of pounds on booze but counted every penny spent on anything else. It was such a painful whinge that it prompted me to offer to dive down and recover it if he would stop moaning.

I swam over to where I was told it had 'gone down' and indeed I could see a small black speck on the sandy seabed beneath me. I took a deep breath and duck dived down. It didn't seem to get much closer, so I pulled on down and again and again several times.

I thought my lungs were going to burst. But I was determined to get the bloody thing. Eventually, I did and pushed very hard on the sand to get back into breathable air before I blacked out.

I got back on board with the retrieved gym shoe. Howard noticed that there was blood coming out of my left ear. I glanced at the depth sounder. The water was 11 metres deep and I had just burst my left ear drum.

The next morning Simon found me sitting in a bar in the 'Old Port' in Cannes drinking a very large cognac. I was in agony.

"A bit early to get started isn't it?" he questioned.

"Fuck off Si." My reply said it all.

## This Life In Death

Then there was the gunfight that Alex and I got into. Gunfight? Yes gunfight. And a very one-sided affair it was too as he and I were unarmed but our opponents were.

We were staying in the Port Grimaud house and had decided to go out to dinner in the beautiful village of Grimaud, which was about 3 miles away in the hills, almost mountains, behind the Port.

We went there in Alex's car and for some reason, which now escapes me, we drove past the restaurant and ended up having to go to the bottom of the village to turn left on to the main road to make the 'circuit' back to the restaurant.

Alex turned into the road, but because it was a very tight turn to the left, he had to reverse and have a second go. At that moment, a car full of inebriated French young men, came round the corner from the left. Alex was blocking the way. They were forced to stop, and all were clearly were very angry about it with audible threats heard above the driver sounding the horn in one long burst.

Alex, having completed the manoeuvre, opened his window to ask them what the problem was. An exchange of very rude and insulting French followed between their driver and Alex, which resulted in Alex opening his door forcefully to smash the other guy in the face.

A roar of blood-curdling threats could be heard in response as Alex sped away with this hornets' nest of anger, having done a hand-break turn, in hot pursuit.

Marianne was in the front, in the back was Michele (Marianne's elder sister), who had the tiny baby Davinia on her knee, Beatrice, and me.

Beatrice was calm, the other girls were screaming. Somehow Dink continued to sleep. Alex asked me what we should do as we fled at high speed along the main road below the village and back towards Port Grimaud.

It was clear to me that our pursuers, who were clearly drunk, were catching us up fast and perhaps would ram us when they did; and besides anything else, we had a baby on board, and I already knew only too well how easy it was to lose a precious little life.

So, I told Alex that he should pull up on the large gravel forecourt of the local wine cooperative, which was round the next bend and where I would get out and go to talk to them.

He did as I suggested. Surprisingly, our pursuers skidded to a halt a distance from us. I got out and started to walk towards them. A guy got out of the back of their car on the driver's side. To my complete disbelief, he raised his left arm to shoulder height as if he was going fire a pistol. Then there was a loud crack. He had fired a pistol.

I dived back into my seat as a second bullet whistled over my head and must have only just missed the car.

"Let's get out of here!" I suggested in as calm a voice as I could muster.

Alex didn't need any encouragement as his car sped off the forecourt with the wheels on opposite lock and gravel flying everywhere. Somehow, we managed to escape and made it through the narrow streets of Grimaud and to the restaurant, who called the police. The trigger-happy Frogs were never caught but I had used up another of my nine lives in the adventure.

xxxxxxx

Meanwhile, things had got off to a good start at PHKI. Initially, the French kept their distance and Michael Kenyon, despite his understandably prickly start, became a friend and an ally in the boardroom who often supported me against the sillier ideas that the French occasionally came up with.

Clearly, Michael disliked the French more for giving his company away than he did me for wanting to run it.

Moreover, I was only just forty and still missing my father, who had died five years previously. So, I was content to respect his wisdom of age and consider his opinions accordingly.

## This Life In Death

Initially, the relationship between myself and the French was cordial. I liked Hervé Racine very much and his number two Jean Nerve was a decent chap. Neither were spoilt Parisians, and both shared my desire to offer excellent standards of service and facility to the bereaved families who required our services.

Hervé and I could see that PHKI was a vastly better company than the bureaucratically run and vastly incompetent PFG.

This was because PFG ran a funeral company that survived on monopolistic local government contracts and did not have to perform in a competitive market such as the one that I had built Hodgson Holdings in the UK.

So, we asked Sandy Frazer, who had by now left UBS to join PHKI as an in-house corporate finance advisor, to see if it was possible for us to organise the funds to achieve a reverse take-over of PFG as we were convinced we could make it a major success when these local monopolistic contracts were abandoned in favour of private enterprise and open competition, which the French government announced that it would bring about within two years.

The three of us met in August 1989 at Nice Airport to see what could be done. However, Sandy advised that raising the sort of funds required in the current bear market, plus the belief needed by any institutional investor to shell out the cash required while holding on to the idea that 'Mr Death' could deliver a 'Hodgson solution' in a foreign market was a bridge too far.

This was perhaps our only chance of keeping the band wagon rolling and with me at the 'real' helm of the ship. But it was not to be.

As we learned in Dennis Amiss's foreword to Volume I, I was to try for another big international deal some 9 months later in Canada, but by then I was starting to have to look over my shoulder rather than just concentrate on moving forward as one united unit.

Soon after this, and not that long after the merger, Hervé was offered and took the Chairmanship of the French famous brand Hermes. He deserved the opportunity, but it left me to have to deal directly with the bureaucratic Parisians. Of course, I still had Jean with me, but he had zero influence over his Parisian masters and was petrified of them, while Hervé never had been.

However, all in all, things weren't going too badly in the autumn of 1989.

Moreover, PFG, for some strange and completely illogical reason, had a few years earlier bought a funeral company doing some 1,000 funerals per annum in Singapore.

They decided that it would be better suited under my management rather than theirs as it was in a free and highly competitive market and the people of Singapore respected the British more than the French.

However, I also think that the fact that Lyonnaise des Eaux had decided that the PFG directors could not travel out to visit the firm twice a year on Concorde, had had something to do with their decision too.

Hodgson Holding rules, which PHKI now operated by, only allowed for international long haul business class travel.

Therefore, one Sunday in October 1989, Marianne, Howie, J and I left Eden Wood, having seen Aston Villa beat Manchester City 2- 0 at Maine Road on TV, bound for Heathrow, where we met up with Jean Nerve and all of us went from there by BA business class to Singapore – with me paying personally for Marianne and the children.

It was a memorable trip. Not only was there a huge difference in the various funeral cultures of the diverse religions there; but Marianne bought me a Cartier watch, that I still wear today; I caught pneumonia; and we had a bizarre experience with an elusive snake.

On the first day, Jean Nerve took me to a large Chinese cemetery. We went into the long grass and walked some 200 metres off the path. We surveyed the scene. I noticed an old lady tending a grave some yards away.

"She will die soon," pronounced Jean.

"How do you know?" I asked.

"Because this place is riddled with deadly poisonous snakes," he replied in a matter-of-fact kind of way.

"Oh great. Why are we standing here then?" I questioned.

However, my British Empire upbringing did not permit me to show fear. Nevertheless, I was very pleased when we reached the path again.

Later that day my 'Mr. Death' celebrity status saw Marianne and me as the guests of honour at a dinner thrown by Lyonnaise des Eaux to welcome us to Singapore.

I recounted the cemetery scene. The guy in charge of Lyonnaise des Eaux Singapore said that Jean had been correct and that only the previous week a friend of his had stepped into his bath in his hotel suite and trod on a flying tree snake, which had flown into the bathroom by mistake though the open first floor window and landed in the bath. The man had died within the hour.

Marianne was horrified and, on the way back to our hotel, did not even want to walk near a tree. Once in our room and in bed, she shook me to alert me to the fact that she could hear a snake hissing in the room.

I hate snakes, but I had a petrified wife asking me to do something and two sons asleep in the adjoining room.

I put the lights on and got up, selected my tennis racket as a weapon, and started to look for the snake. I took courage in both hands and searched under our bed and all the furniture. Now I thought that I could hear the hissing too.

Then it occurred to me that the guy that had died had been in a first-floor room, whereas we were on the 27$^{th}$ floor!

I got back into bed while pointing out to Marianne that no flying snake, created by either God or the Devil, could manage to get up to the 27$^{th}$ floor as I made fun of her assertions that she had heard a snake.

The next day we met the previous night's host for lunch as Lyonnaise des Eaux were clearly on a charm offensive. I laughingly told him the story about the supposed snake in the room.

However, he didn't laugh. Instead, he went a whiter shade of pale and told us that snakes made it to any floor by coming up via the air conditioning passages.

Throughout 1989 the Lyonnaise des Eaux charm offensive continued. My family and I were invited to spend Christmas with their CEO and his family. I politely declined on the basis that we had already agreed to spend it in France with Marianne's family.

This was perhaps the first nail in the entente cordiale with the French.

However, unabashed, Lyonnaise then invited me on to the PFG board to see how I could improve profitability.

This was a very strange experience. The board meeting was completely scripted in advance and read out by various members as directed. It was therefore like a Soviet Union 'rubber stamp' operation and there was no discussion about anything whatsoever.

However, I didn't mind that much, as PFG was not my concern. Nevertheless, the next thing that happened saw me put my foot down and was my first crossing of swords with my French shareholders.

Philippe de Margerie called me to say that PFG intended to bill PHKI £100,000 per annum for advice that they were giving.

I pointed out that PHKI was an independent London quoted company; that no advice had been received from PFG; in fact, the advice was going from PHKI to PFG; that PHKI was four times as profitable as PFG despite only conducting around 25% of their funeral numbers per annum; and that as CEO of PHKI, it was my job to protect all shareholders' interests and not promote PFG's only.

"But you are a good Lyonnaise des Eaux man Howard" said de Margerie in a beseeching voice.

"No, I'm a good PHKI man" was my reply, given through clenched teeth, in my best Clint Eastwood voice.

This was then the second of many nails that would be driven into the entente cordiale's coffin over the next year.

Nevertheless, the press followers of PHKI were naturally oblivious to this growing tension and were still fascinated by 'Mr Death.' They continued to adore the 'rock star or footballer looks' as they were still frenzy feeding on their image of one who looked like a member of the 'Rolling Stones' but was a funeral director.

Indeed, in 1989, the Daily Mail took 2 pages to describe 'And Here's Howard's Day' – a play on the then current Sunday night soap 'Howard's Way'. The article started with, 'Howard Hodgson is typical of the new breed of self-made millionaires. He often works 18 hours a day,' before listing a typical day.

They included a giant half page graph which listed that Hodgson was formed in 1850; that it was only conducting 400 funerals in 1975; that this had increased to 5,600 by 1986; to 23,000 in 1987; to 40,000 in 1989; and a truly huge leap to a predicted 70,000 in 1990, which was never achieved although over 60,000 was.

However, even though the press, except for Jason Nisse, were still very nice to me, I was amazingly, given some of my very stupid future behaviour, capable of seeing the dangers of being still up on a British press pedestal for over 4 years.

Indeed, in a sensible interview with the Director Magazine, I'm quoted as saying that, as I was searching for acquisition opportunities abroad, I would welcome a lower profile in the UK.

'"That's probably a good thing", he muses, as otherwise he may fall victim to pedestal bashing by a media that tires of him. "The secret", he says, "is to get off the train before they blow it up. One interview quoted me as saying that 'death was the great Crewe Junction of life' – I've never even thought of that line."'

This was observant of me. Within a couple of years, I was not only to not 'get off the train' but to invite the media assassins on board in an orgy of self-destruction which was to ensure I would keep as low a profile as possible for the rest of my life.

At around the same time, the Investors Chronicle did a major feature, which contained a whole page shot of me with what can only be described as an awfully long haircut worn by a man in a city pin-striped suit.

'An undertaker is supposed to be an oily, obsequious character whose face mirrors the horrors of the open grave. By that exacting standard, Howard Hodgson doesn't make it. The country's foremost funeral director, who's cremated more people than he has had hot dinners, looks more like a refugee from the Bee Gees than a master mortician.

'That doesn't worry Hodgson. He is primarily a businessman and completely rejects the idea that undertakers should smell of freshly turned earth.

"Funeral directors don't have to be elderly men with ulcerated alcoholic noses who rub their hands saying, 'There's been a fair few in at the general this weekend'. My managers are normal young men or women who are very dedicated."

'Some observers describe Hodgson as flamboyant rather than normal, but he defends his long hair and trendy suits vigorously, "I'm a fifth-generation funeral director who has spent most of his life with a short haircut and a top hat. Now I don't have to and I'm going through my second childhood. I have always wanted to look like Paul McCartney when I have had to look like David Copperfield."

'An undertaker who looks like Tranmere Rovers' star winger ought to make Dickens turn in his grave. It hasn't stopped Hodgson's cheeky verve and hard-headed business skills from propelling Hodgson Holdings (now PHKI) into death's First Division' (this was before the creation of the Premier League).

I was never sure, as usual, if I liked the article as it didn't portray me in the way I wanted to be portrayed. However, I had to accept that a lot of that was my own fault for being so outwardly open and not emphasising enough that I was a person who had conducted 1,000s of funerals to the most exacting standards.

Moreover, as usual I had to grin and bear the headline 'Rave from the grave' although I did approve of the sub-headline, 'I care vastly more about funeral directing than anyone I've ever met.'

## This Life In Death

This was an accurate quote from me and as true today as it was in1989.

Nevertheless, I will make two further comments from the various articles of 1989: firstly, upon reflection now, I am profoundly fed up that I was always described as a Bee Gee or 2nd or 3rd Division footballer! Why couldn't I have been a Beatle or George Best or even an Aston Villa footballer? Outraged now yes – but I didn't even notice it then!!

Secondly, I came across this quote from me in the press in 1989.

"Some people just want a disposal service. I'm against providing that through all our traditional funeral activities. I'm more inclined to have a national name – perhaps Serenity – that would accompany the presence of an established funeral director. It would have one vehicle that went straight to the hospital and then to the crematorium. If you want a cortege, a chapel of rest, and all the works, then you would go to a traditional funeral director. There isn't a half-way house on this. You either have the 40-man hours work and the hundreds of thousands of pounds of working capital for administration and arrangement – or you don't."

When I penned Volume I, I was pleased by my vision and fortitude to escape from poverty and build Hodgson. However, I did not expect to be too impressed by any thought that I might have had in Volume II.

However, this quote talks about 'direct cremation' over thirty years before its advertisements were to come to dominate ITV 3 and ITV 4 channels all day and every day.

However, despite the continuing media obsession with 'Mr Death,' I knew the 1980s party was over. I knew that I had to consider those adorable mid-1980s years as but fading memories. I knew that I had to adapt to the much less 'immediate' idea, yet one I was to use so effectively with Memoria over a decade later, of organic growth by brand recognition, backed by all the other ancillary services that bereaved families needed.

Indeed, having listened intently to my comments, Andrew Yeo, the very bright analyst at UBS then, headlined his analysis at the end of 1989: 'Now It's All About Added Value.' Underneath he wrote:

'PHKI offers investors the opportunity to hedge against recessionary pressures in the economy whilst benefitting from the Hodgson/Kenyon merger which we expect to produce operational cost savings of £2 million a year. In the long term, the development of ancillary income from pre-paid funeral plans and monumental masonry will ensure strong earnings growth moving into the 1990s.'

In addition, and while Hodgson was the much more efficient and effective funeral director of the merger, Kenyon was bringing divisions to the merger that Hodgson did not have.

Director Magazine noted, also in December 1989, that 'Hodgson is very enthusiastic about Kenyon's additional services.' This was true as they already existed and enhanced our development into a complete 'one stop bereavement service.'

Kenyon boasted a major disaster unit, a repatriation unit, stronger monumental and floristry sales than Hodgson and, most importantly, was just about to open its first crematorium.

Therefore, my plans to develop PHKI away from straight line growth by acquisition towards increased market share by organic brand growth, backed by a complete array of ancillary services, was forming nicely and that message was even getting out to the investors.

So far so good as this was largely music to their ears. They knew as well as I did that the glory days of high bank debt and multiple rights issues to fund growth by acquisition had fried on the fire of excess during the 1987 crash which had brought an end to all of that.

Early in 1990, I secured French support for my plans by writing to them:

'The development of 'Dignity in Destiny' and of post-funeral financial services will be a gradually accelerating profit generator in the 1990s. 'Dignity' will not only generate additional profit, but it will guarantee future funeral market share and enhance the company's image.

## This Life In Death

'With a good percentage of the UK population over forty-five, and therefore to be increasingly likely to be interested in pre-arrangement plans, the growth started in 1988 will continue and then expand more rapidly in the next century. At that time the death rate will also increase.

'Therefore, now, and given the current economic constraints, it is important that PHKI focuses on growth brought about by additional ancillary services and organic funeral growth brought about by the introductions to our funeral division that these services, in time, will bring.

'However, and even more importantly, the organic growth that will be achieved by the recognition we will receive in the funeral division by ensuring a rigid branding policy is even more important.

'This must apply to colour, words, typeface and design which must be applied to all vehicles, livery, external and internal decoration, and funeral home and shop frontages.

'If we are to replace growth by acquisition with organic growth these plans must be followed without hesitation or deviation.

'Much of the management's effort and the shareholder's money has already been put into this programme which commenced at Hodgson Holdings before the merger. This is already providing excellent and uniform standards of service, facility and image.

'We are in the process of now applying the same branding to the Kenyon operation. By the end of 1990, the whole of PHKI will have midnight blue Volvo hearses and limousines. All office staff will have midnight blue uniforms, all chauffeurs Portland grey livery and every staff member will have 2 corporate ties or scarves (for women) each.

'There is also an expensive capital investment programme afoot to convert all funeral homes and branches to the same uniform corporate colours.

'The introduction of a brand name is essential, as the cornerstone of this investment programme and the route to organic market share growth.

'I suggest we choose one of these two: 'Dignity Funerals' – as it identifies with our pre-arranged plan; or 'Oak Funerals' – as it identifies with our established logo. Of course, you may prefer another name. However, we should not consider using PHKI as it does not lend itself well to the purpose.'

The French bought 100% into this strategy at this stage and said they would consider which of the two brand name choices offered they preferred.

So, despite, the huge amount of work and considerable potential problems to overcome, mainly concerning Kenyon's ill-disciplined and truculent staff, as well as the very difficult economic climate, things were going as well as could be expected.

We now had over 500 outlets in the UK. This was more than many household brand names, but due to the use of local trade names, nobody knew who we were.

Moreover, local independent funeral directors started to use our use of local funeral names against us by saying things like, "That isn't really Ann Bonhams, but a huge funeral company owned by the Frogs."

This and the fact that they could and did continually bribe matrons at old people's homes to recommend them to bereaved families, where we, as a fully listed London Exchange public company could not even contemplate the same, meant that we were likely to lose market share if we continued with this policy.

"Oh, I always recommend Mr. Jones. He is our local family funeral director," would be the sort of thing the matron might say.

"But what about Ann Bonham?" a family might reply.

"They are not local funeral directors but owned by a very large French water company," might be her reply.

Naturally, she did not add ".... And Mr. Jones will bung me a £100 if you use him instead of Ann Bonham" or perhaps, "... and give me one on a Saturday night in gratitude."

Indeed, private independent funeral directors had become so paranoid about PHKI since the launch of Dignity in Destiny that they had formed the 'Society of Allied & Independent Funeral Directors' which was run by men who were convinced that PHKI had stopped acquiring funeral directors because we believed that our pre-arranged funeral plan sales had taken away our need to acquire market share growth. You and I now know that it was the 1987 stock market crash and the following economic downturn that had stopped us from using a policy of growth by acquisition.

However, they didn't understand this and started a war of attrition to blacken PHKI's name and promote local privately owned funeral directors.

This campaign was so successful that even the Bishop of Norwich told me that, "Your funeral directors can't be as dedicated as a private local funeral director."

"Oh, why is that?" I replied politely.

"Because they don't own their own business," was his indoctrinated reply.

"Gosh sir! I had no idea that your clergy owned their own churches," I retorted.

End of conversation and game, set and match to Mr. Death.

However, this point about 'local trade names', in the forthcoming branding debate between PFG and me that was to follow, was to become central to it.

The realisation that a branded image was necessary for the future originally came in 1987. It was because Hodgson Holdings had realised that it was paying 'top dollar' for funeral businesses; spending money on them to improve their standards of service and facility; and applying the economies of scale to improve their profitability; but wasn't receiving the national recognition for it – which we deemed to be very important following the crash in that year. This was the year when the Volvo deal was struck as I wanted to have a national fleet of unique vehicles.

However, before I could launch my brain into this idea, matters forced me to decide upon a course of action more quickly than I had intended.

The catalyst for the Volvo deal was that our Ford limousine coach builder, Coleman Milne, sent a decent man, named Malcolm Dewar, down to see me in Birmingham. He informed me that I could no longer expect 15% off new Dorchester hearses and limousines we ordered each year. In addition, Coleman Milne would only accept one part exchange for each new order. This was an important announcement by him as rationalisation of acquisitions meant that we were always selling more part-exchange vehicles than we were buying new ones.

Malcolm then concluded his statement with the message he had also been told to tell me that as Daimler or any other coach builder could not meet my demand, I had no choice but to except their terms.

Oh dear. This is not the kind of message you send a 'peaky blinder' who had come up the hard way.

He asked me for my 1988 order. I replied that there would not be one. He left empty handed and dumbfounded.

I picked up the phone to Volvo. I had for some time felt that the Volvo 740, as it was box rather than wedge-shaped, would look attractive as either a hearse or limousine.

Initially, they didn't seem very interested but vaguely asked about the numbers I might be interested in.

"I want to place an immediate order for 127 and that will become well over 1,000 over the next five years," I replied.

Two days later I was on the Volvo chairman's private jet to Malmo in Sweden to negotiate the deal.

This was followed by a second trip with Bob Gray of the British coach builder Glenfrome Engineering, and my number two, Graham Hodson, to work out production details.

## This Life In Death

The three of us enjoyed a brilliant evening out on the town which turned into a very entertaining night with the Mayor of Malmo's daughter – for which I ought to thank Coleman Milne I suppose.

Volvo had chosen Glenforme, famous for their Range Rover conversions, to carry out the conversion work. The value of the initial order was £4 million and Glenforme agreed to take 150 vehicles in part-exchange for £2 million. All new vehicles were to be in midnight blue.

Glenforme's Bob Gray was duly invited to PHKI's huge annual conference at the NEC in Birmingham just before Christmas 1989. This had been organised so that the Hodgson and Kenyon senior staff could unite behind the new company plans, which were explained to them over two sessions, before a grand banquet for over 500 managers that night.

Gray introduced the new midnight blue fleets at a presentation during the afternoon session and stayed on for the banquet.

Bob was a large jovial man who sadly died when still relatively young. He loved life and practical jokes. Indeed, he was great company but not always the best judge as to when a practical joke might be inappropriate.

The main theme of the day had been to drum into the Kenyon staff heads' that PHKI was to be 100% dedicated to providing excellent, kind and professional service. Then they could relax at the banquet.

After dinner, before the disco, and completely unscheduled, a Father Christmas appeared on the stage with a sack of presents and I was invited to join him.

I was taken completely by surprise. This wasn't on the agenda. However, not wishing to appear truculent, I obliged.

To my horror Father Christmas discarded his beard, disrobed and in a flash revealed himself to be a herself and a stripper, who was halfway through her act. The look of horror as well as surprise is plain to see on my face in the photograph herein.

Someone tipped off the 'red top' press and they had a field day of reporting how Mr Death had organised a 'funeral workers' bash' that involved strippers!!

xxxxxxx

Having now developed a plan for our corporate image, and despite the stripper, I continued to turn my attention to ensuring our staff were second to none in the quality of service that they offered. In the long term, I knew that consistency of good service could only be achieved and maintained by effective and continuous training.

This was even more necessary in the case of the Kenyon staff. The Hodgson staff who had been acquired by acquisition had arrived and immediately been trained to do things to the Hodgson standard. This was not true of the Kenyon staff, who had been bought and by and large left to their own devices. Consequently, they thought they had a job rather a vocation.

Hodgson executives were initially shocked by how unprofessional, uncaring and uneducated in bereavement care Kenyon staff were with the except of a few good men, like Sam Kershaw and Peter Kenyon, at the top of the operation.

To be fair, Michael Kenyon had recognised this problem before the merger and readily agreed with me that we needed to think about training after it.

Together we set up the Acorn training programme and situated it in one of Hodgson Holdings large Blackpool and now redundant, due to rationalisation, funeral homes. A very decent chap, whose father's business I had acquired in the area, called Geoffrey Horsefield, was put in charge of developing the programmes and running them.

At the official launch of the Imperial Training Centre, with a large company of press there, it was emphasised that training was now a must, and no longer something which was optional. To progress, PHKI must have an improved rate of referrals, and increased sales of ancillary services, a more consistent standard across the whole group and lower turnover of staff at the London Kenyon offices.

The Guardian summed up the launch, and it showed that it was not only PHKI employees that would benefit:

'The funeral industry yesterday laid to rest its heritage of spasmodic preparation for eternal farewells by unveiling its first comprehensive training package, covering everything from coffin presentation to the dos and don'ts of the flip chart. Courses will be offered to the 1,500 employees of PHKI, which has invested £500,000 in an open-learning where students advance at their own – in this case respectful – pace. By January 1991 the whole industry is expected to be able to benefit from courses and eight supporting seminars. These include 'monumental memorial services'; 'the full range of coffins in a professional and caring manner' and a discussion about 'hygienic treatment, and what you should tell the client.'

This piece might have ended with a typically tongue in cheek press comment, but they were there in force to see PHKI breaking new ground and the story was being read and digested by the nation.

Then in January 1990, we launched the 'Bereavement Support Service' and this received a huge welcome from the media, helped by Michael Kenyon's brilliant idea of co-opting the popular comedian and former 'Goon,' Sir Harry Secombe.

We consulted Cruse Bereavement Care, solicitors, Social Services and other organisations. Then we had Sir Harry record eleven useful topics on tape which could be listened to over the phone by dialling a separate number for each. They all lasted about three minutes and gave essential information and contact details.

Calls were charged at BT normal rates, PHKI didn't make a profit from the calls but instead made donations to Help the Aged, who had also been granted, as you will recall, shares in Dignity in Destiny and received commission on each plan sale too.

Help the Aged Chairman, John Wheatley, invited me to meet HRH the Princess of Wales in gratitude. I duly attended a magnificent black-tie dinner with him, where the guest of honour was Princess Diana and she was making the main speech.

She clearly had not written that herself and delivered it without passion in a very flat monotonous voice. Indeed, it was one of the worst speeches I have ever had to endure – and that includes some awful ones from dull National Association of Funeral Directors' presidents.

Nevertheless, it didn't really detract from the occasion because the guests had come to see the beautiful Princess of Wales and just enjoy being in her presence rather than listen to her speech. Everyone knew that her husband was the committed, dedicated and brainy one; she was the fashion icon and celebrity part of the partnership.

Nevertheless, I was horrified that, when the time came for me to be presented, Wheately rather stiffly announced, "Your Royal Highness, might I present to you the country's most famous funeral director, Mr. Howard Hodgson."

Happily, she ignored such an uninspired introduction, and I was delighted when Princess Diana replied, "Well he looks the spit of Robert Redford to me," which was accompanied by one of her famous coy smiles as her eyes met mine briefly before she gazed down at the floor and her face turned a matching pink to her magnificent ball gown.

For that moment, I thought that I was probably the most important man on the planet. The heady cocktail of her flawless beauty, vulnerability, discreet but definite flirtation and girlish sex appeal made me understand in an instance how men loved her, and women admired her.

In addition, I could also see how such qualities could be manipulated to promote a completely false impression of who she really was.

xxxxxxx

## This Life In Death

So, things were going quite well under extremely difficult circumstances until about June 1990 and the birth of Davinia. However, by then, some tough decisions needed to be made to save money in order to secure profits growth because there would be none coming from acquisitions.

First and sadly, Dennis Amiss had to go. The economic climate would not allow us to make acquisitions and that was his sole job.

I had really liked Dennis for years; he was my friend; and before that he had been a childhood hero as he had battled his way through the ranks of Warwickshire County Cricket and into the England Team at the age of just twenty-three.

Moreover, he had been an extremely successful Hodgson Holdings plc Acquisition Director, not only on the mainland, but also in Northern Ireland – where we had shared a couple of adventures together.

You must remember that in the late 1980s, 'The Troubles' as they were known, had been raging in Northern Ireland for over 20 years. Indeed, at Christmas 1988, when asked by the Sun to record the news story that had made the biggest impression on me that year, I had replied that it was man's inhumanity to man as two British soldiers came across an IRA funeral cortege. They had declined to shoot their attackers in defence of themselves but their humanity had seen them dragged from their car, stripped naked, beaten and shot dead on film.

The Sun told me that they wanted a pleasant story instead. I declined saying that that was it and I wasn't in the mood to choose a light-hearted story. It was true, I had been horrified by the whole event and had even had nightmares about it.

We had started by that time to buy funeral businesses in Northern Ireland and even look at others in Southern Ireland as acquisitions on the mainland were becoming harder to find.

On one of many trips to Belfast, where we always stayed at the Dunadry Hotel outside Belfast, as the Europa Hotel in Belfast, which was known locally as 'Bomb Hotel' was considered too dangerous.

## This Life In Death

On this occasion, Dennis, Graham Hodson and I flew from Birmingham early in the morning to Belfast. Dennis and I were going to seal a deal to buy a business in Lisburn, south of Belfast in the morning, have lunch back at the Dunadry with Graham, before the three of us would go to the north of the city in the early evening where I was to make a speech to the local National Association of Funeral Directors, before returning later to have dinner with the Massey Brothers, who were Dublin funeral directors that we were tempting to sell to us.

The visit to the funeral director in Lisburn went well and the deal was agreed. On our return trip to Belfast, I asked the taxi driver to show us where the two soldiers had been killed.

Dennis was horrified and asked me why the hell I was trying to get both of us killed. However, we survived this slight detour, but the traffic was bad – so I told the driver to take us over the top road back to our hotel.

He replied that he would, but it could be a bit risky as around the next corner one was never sure if we were going to be flagged down by a patrol. If it was the British Army patrol, we would be fine. If it was an IRA patrol, we could be in serious trouble.

Dennis went white. I told him not to worry as the IRA didn't like cricket and didn't read the Financial Times. Therefore, as they wouldn't know who the hell we were, we would be fine.

We got back to the hotel safely, and I told Dennis not to be such a wet, after all he had faced vicious bouncers from Lillee, Thompson, Garner, Roberts, Marshall and of course Holding in his illustrious cricket career. Nothing had happened this morning, and nothing would.

Dennis took this on board. The three of us left for the NAFD meeting. It was a beautiful evening in this very pretty but troubled land. I delivered my speech, which was well received by funeral directors who were grateful that I had come all that way to speak to them.

Then we left to travel back to the hotel. As we approached the Dunadry, Dennis now wonderfully relaxed and reassured by my earlier assurances, was pointing out to Graham and me various beautiful properties as we suddenly turned off the main road just before we were due to arrive. Dennis wasn't concerned. Graham and I were. The taxi driver was suddenly speeding down a very narrow lane. He must know that a vehicle wasn't going to come up the other way.

Shit! Perhaps, we were being abducted. Perhaps, we were just about to end up in a field surrounded by a ring of hooded IRA gunmen. I glanced back at Graham. He was thinking the same thing. Dennis was still waxing lyrical about the lovely mansions. Graham put his hand through between the seats to grab the handbrake while I clenched my fist to smash the driver in the face. We were just about to action this improvised plan when we drove into the back entrance of the hotel car park. The driver had taken a short cut. So, were Graham and I any more secure really than Dennis about being there?

This was followed by dinner with the Massey brothers, Rom and Connor. Rom was a loveable rogue and Connor could recite English poetry like only an Irishman can. It was an enjoyable evening and ended with some horseplay in the corridor late at night. Suddenly, we were surrounded by armed security guards who thought the hotel was being attacked by the IRA.

The next day at lunch a waiter dropped a tray of glasses with a great crash. The whole restaurant froze instantly. I made the light-hearted comment "Missed."

A waitress serving me said over my shoulder coldly, "If it had been the IRA they wouldn't have."

On our arrival back in Birmingham that evening, I was stopped by security as we arrived back at the Airport. It must have been, in the very clever minds of the security services, that a man in a brown fedora and an off-white double-breasted overcoat must be a gangster and therefore, as he had arrived on a flight from Belfast, a member of the IRA.

I smiled and whipped out my passport with the comment, "Oh I can see my disguise didn't fool you guys."

## This Life In Death

A guard looked at me and then, in a thick Brummie accent, declared, "Hold on that's Mr. Death and he supports the Villa."

It really wasn't that easy going to, being in, or coming from Northern Ireland in those days. However, it was much harder for those folk who had to live there permanently.

Mrs Thatcher had beaten the Argentinians, the trade unions and stood up to both Protestant and Catholic Northern Irish terrorists. However, she hadn't beaten either.

The sound of bombs going off was very common. You would hear that telling 'boom' almost daily. The worry was always about the one you didn't hear – because it had got you.

I hope I have made it clear to you, in Volume I of these memoirs, how close we all were at Hodgson Holdings, and while life was tougher and less fun at PHKI, we all remained very close.

I loved Dennis dearly and wanted to give him every chance to survive with us. So, initially, I had tried to buy him a little time by asking him, and his assistant Timothy Penrose, to start a '5-star luxury executive limousine service', but the take up was slow despite it being both a first-class service and had low overheads since we had all the midnight blue Volvos and Portland grey liveried staff already engaged in the funeral division.

So, this was a classic marginal cost operation. However, plc life was tough, and I dared not give it too much time as the French would be expressing their concern very quickly that I was purely trying to save a friend's job.

Nevertheless, before closure, Dennis did get an order from me to take my close childhood friend Simon Draycott QC and my two sons to see Sir Paul McCartney appear in Liverpool Docks and a sizeable order from PHKI itself, to supply 14 limousines for a charity event at the NEC's Metropole Hotel to ferry star quests like Denis Waterman, Jimmy Tarbuck, Jasper Carrot, Kenny Lynch, and Robert Powell of Jesus of Nazareth fame, and many more stars from Birmingham International Station to the hotel and back.

PHKI had sponsored the event which had been organised by Jasper Carrot. Dennis and I had discussed what was needed with Jasper in the 'Bon Viveur' restaurant in Sutton Coldfield a few months earlier. Jasper had appeared very morose and nothing like the funny guy that the nation saw on his very successful TV shows.

Dennis and I just thought that, like most comics, Carrot was probably bi-polar, and this was a bad day.

Dennis tried to lighten the mood by asking me about skiing as he was going to start to ski now that he had retired from professional cricket. JC said nothing and appeared to me to be in another world.

So, we were both surprised to hear a ten-minute monologue, which was very funny, on his next TV show entitled 'Ski Bores.' He had lifted our conversation and converted it into a discussion between a toffee-nosed expert skier (me) and a Brummie 'all the gear but no idea' novice (Dennis).

On the night in question, all the stars were very grateful for this VIP service. However, Tarbuck wanted more. When he left the dinner, he gave me a hug and took his limousine in time to catch the last train to London.

But once comfortable on the back seat he informed the chauffeur that I wanted the limo to take him back to London instead. The chauffeur duly obeyed and didn't get back to his Erdington garage until it was time for him to go on the first of the following morning's funerals. He had driven all night, had no sleep and didn't even get a tip.

I was not pleased when I found out. I didn't bump into Jimmy again for twenty years until we were both invited to a party at the 'La Famiglia' restaurant, just off the King's Road in London. He took one look at me and threw up his hands in surrender and we both burst out laughing. We became quite good friends, and I must say he is great company to be around.

Secondly, and even more sadly, the growth of the company and the need for a comprehensive regional director level of management had made John Taylor's job redundant.

## This Life In Death

You will recall that I had met John at Tri-Star Investments in 1971 – nearly twenty years earlier. He had been with me at NWM, Hodgson & Sons Ltd, Hodgson Holdings plc and now PHKI.

John was by no means overpaid. However, we just could not afford to carry anyone given the need to produce profit growth without acquisitions.

'A pound saved is worth ten in the till', was my father's expression and in 1990 it had never been truer. But this was painful indeed, for John had not only helped me every inch of the way but had on one occasion, saved my life.

This had been in the late '70s. Next door to the Oaklands Funeral Home on the Soho Road in Handsworth, there was a large Asian wholesaler of ladies' Asian clothes. It was owned by a brusque Pakistani man, who had proven to be a difficult neighbour.

One day, I was drinking a cup of coffee in between funerals in my morning tails and looking out of my window to see the busy Soho and Holyhead roads merge, when I noticed my neighbour swerve across the road in his Merc and onto his forecourt. He then leapt out and ran into his warehouse. As he did so a second Merc swerved on to the forecourt and four men got out in hot pursuit. It was obvious to me that they meant him harm.

I jumped down the elegant Oaklands staircase four steps at a time, shouting to Beryl Smith to call the police. I sped through the reception, across both our and his forecourts and into his warehouse. I managed to lodge myself between him and his four assailants just as one of them had picked up a huge pair of tailor's scissors and was intending to stick them under my neighbour's chin. Instead, they were now under my chin.

"Get out of the way please. This has nothing to do with you," said the assailant holding this deadly weapon.

"I won't and if you kill me as well as him you can say goodbye to your lives too. Whatever, he has done to you four, is it really worth paying the price you will pay?" I managed to get out despite the scissors sticking into my throat.

There was a pause. They looked at each other and then the police sirens were blaring as I announced that I had called the police before I had burst in.

The four scarpered and were away before the Bill could get through the busy traffic on the Soho Road.

It wasn't until I thanked Beryl and she replied that she was relieved that I was OK, but that she hadn't called the police, because she hadn't heard me ask her to.

John Bruce Taylor had called them. He had noticed the car scene from his window and had seen me dash next door.

Both Dennis Amiss and John Taylor were fine Hodgson Holdings men and good guys. I remain eternally grateful to both.

xxxxxxx

However, looking back, and despite the pain of losing these two wonderful chaps, things were still going in the right direction in that summer.

Moreover, I can now appreciate more than ever, that the Hodgson Holdings team of Graham Hodson, Stevie Gould, David Bonham, Harvey Hewitt, Arthur Abraham, Dennis Amiss, John Taylor, Cliff Summerfield, Timothy Penrose and many others at PHKI, as well as David Meakin and Steve Fox for Dignity, worked their 'balls off' to make this essential, very sensible and totally achievable plan work.

In addition, they were joined by some very capable Kenyon executives, namely Peter Kenyon, Michael's son, and Sam Kershaw, who was to go on to build the hugely successful company 'Funeral Partners' post the Millennium.

However, while the plan was spectacularly advanced thinking for its time, and has been vindicated since by the eventual events that occurred over the next thirty-five years; and was economically sensible, even essential, at that moment, given the circumstances of the economy then; it needed everyone to pull together to make it work.

And here cometh the problem. Circa 40% of the company consisted of very poorly trained and undisciplined Kenyon staff. They didn't like the Hodgson Holdings executives, whom they considered to be like Hitler's SS with their rigid rules, discipline and demands that the clients always came first whatever the circumstances. To Kenyon personnel these guys became known as the HH SS.

For example, the new PHKI Freston Road head office sat above a large Kenyon funeral garage that serviced most of north London. It was out of control and run like a mafia operation, where union thinking ruled the roost and the garage foreman/union representative even had a gun in his office safe.

This was reported to me by the new PHKI regional director, and Hodgson Holdings stalwart, Harvey Hewitt, while I was away in Scotland on a tour of our sites there. I told him to go into the foreman's office and demand to have it off him.

"Call me Harry in future Boss," he said.

"What?" I replied.

"Cos, I get all the dirty jobs" was his obvious reply.

Then, and quite suddenly, the French started to get cold feet about the thrust of the plan, mainly I suspected, because I controlled it.

This was because they were increasing frustrated by my determination to continually tell them that they only had a large shareholding in an independent London quoted company of which I was CEO and that I would not allow them to syphon off cash from it against the interests of other shareholders.

So, now I appeared to them to be a worse devil than Michael Kenyon had ever been. I might be delivering to them a more successful company, but I would not allow them to rape the same to enhance PFG profits.

Therefore, their attitude became increasingly like one of a private equity holder as a result and through the second half of 1990 relations between me and the French became increasingly strained as a result.

Then there was Graham Barber, the ubiquitous villain of this chapter.

Sir Roger Moore wrote in his memoirs that his father had always told him that if you can't say anything nice about anyone, then don't say anything at all. So, I will write very little about Graham here – just the essential facts.

Graham Barber's father's company in Norwich, was bought by me, when we were still Hodgson Holdings.

Graham had a high regard for himself, but was a man of limited ability, as proved a few years later, when he sold Westerleigh a crematorium owned by Dignity, as PHKI was to become, worth some £16 million today and at least £5 million then, for circa £600,000.

He was also a vindictive chap. He dismissed, some years after I had left, the very genuine, dedicated and hard-working Harvey Hewitt, with the words, "This is bad news for you, but great news for me. You're sacked."

Some years after that, Dignity was subject to an extremely damaging TV investigative exposé on the machinations of their funeral operation, and Graham hung his very decent son Matthew out to dry rather than face up to the responsibility of these awful failings himself.

In the second half of 1990, the Machiavellian Graham started alerting the French to the fact that, in his opinion and that of several Kenyon executives, the branding plan was flawed and designed by me for my own glorification.

At first PFG were reluctant to listen, but then relations between them and me became more and more frosty, to the point that I started to serve Italian wine at board meeting lunches, through the autumn months.

Then in November, they threw a cocktail party in my honour in Nice, France. I, most unforgivably rudely, failed to turn up in protest at their continuing attempts to move cash out of PHKI. Now they started to listen to Graham.

This was not because they had lost faith in the plan. Only morons would have done that – as history has proved – but because I had become their 'Thomas Becket' and they needed to be rid of me.

Then Michael Kenyon retired. He should have been replaced on the board by a person of my choice to rebalance it but wasn't – a bad mistake by me. This gave the French a chance of winning a board vote as a result.

Next Ronnie Middleton, the PHKI and old Hodgson Holdings Finance Director, decided to change the PHKI budget numbers and issued the same to PFG before I had seen them as the French were sticklers for accounts and board packs being delivered on time.

Indeed, the French might have had limited entrepreneurial or management skill, but they were fine administrators, and I learned a lot from them in that regard.

Now they demanded Ronnie's head. They had a point. It is a cardinal sin to change budgeted figures. They are cast in stone. Actuals against budget year to date equals the year's ongoing forecast. That is the accepted principle.

I agreed and spoke to Ronnie. However, the French got in touch with him too and promised to reprieve him if he voted with them to take me off the board. He agreed. They also approached Graham Hodson, but he refused to vote with them.

Philippe de Margerie called me and told me the same. He said that I must now recognise their board control going forward and fall into line or I would be out.

I said I would fly over to Paris to discuss the issue face to face, which I did the next day.

Once there, PFG told me that they wanted to slow down the branding programme as it was too expensive, that there was no guarantee that it would work and that PHKI had paid a lot of money for these local trading names which I was proposing to ditch.

I said that I was not proposing to ditch them but introduce uniform colour, wording, design and typeface with the local name still as the major billing with 'part of Oak Funerals' underneath and then switch this round over a five-year period to 'Oak Funerals' with 'Incorporating whoever' underneath.

There was no debate. They just countered my argument by stating that I would do as I was told, or they could remove me as CEO.

I reminded them that while they might be able to fire me, I could call an EGM if they did; that while they had 18.4% + of the PHKI shares and I only had 12.5%, the majority of the other 69.1% were British institutions who had invested in 'Mr Death' in the first place and that there was a good chance that I would win any vote as a result.

This stopped de Margerie in his tracks.

"OK Howard, what do you want?" he asked in his thick Parisian French accent as he dragged deeply on his Gauloises cigarette.

"We are not going to see eye to eye going forward. I can't afford to buy your 18.4%, but you can afford to buy me out."

And that is what happened. We negotiated a deal. I wanted a premium to the current market price as I was selling 12.5%. Philippe didn't want to pay that claiming that the share price was bound to fall, perhaps even sharply, on the news of my resignation.

However, he was willing to pay me the equivalent price that I had asked for as long as the addition was made up by paying up my contract in full and giving me a golden goodbye.

I was somewhat puzzled, nevertheless, I agreed.

It was only on the flight home that it dawned on me why he had done this. Of course! PFG, would have to buy my shares with their own cash, but PHKI would have to pay up my contract and bonus.

Good old Philippe was still doing his best to swindle the other PHKI shareholders even now!

So, my fifteen-year career from that awful starting day of a bankrupt Hodgson & Sons in August 1975, to that awful finishing day in January 1991 had run its full course and I had sold my corporate baby both for the sake of my real family and because I had come to realise, in that last six months, that trying to make PHKI work with the French was like trying to push water uphill.

Moreover, I was exhausted by trying to achieve this while also captaining a team of unprofessional Kenyon staff who had zero concern for bereaved families and refused to buy into the concept that they should.

Then the realisation that Graham Barber was secretly no more than a Hodgson Holdings 'Judas' was just the last straw that broke my back.

Working when you and your team are standing together against the world is exhilarating. Working when you know people working in your team are working to destroy you is not.

So, here ends the first part of my life in death. It had seen me buy a serious loss-making 400 funerals a year and turn it into a national public company making millions each year and which conducted 60,000 funerals per annum in the process.

I had gone from a determined twenty-five year old on a mission to the well-known entrepreneur 'Mr Death' aged forty in the process and had more than recovered our lost family fortune on the way.

I had also dragged the sleepy Victorian funeral industry into the 20th century in the process and started trends which were to shape it for the next thirty-five years and beyond.

However, when I started to think about the PHKI chapter of this story, I did so without much enthusiasm, as I had pushed this period of my life to the back of my mind.

It had been an extremely unhappy and stressful episode and it seemed to be a fruitless failure of an end to an otherwise exciting story of success.

Moreover, I knew that my own lack of political skill and stubborn attitude when dealing with the French had aggravated issues and turned them into conflicts and, that in the end, PFG had outmanoeuvred me in the ensuing board room battle.

Therefore, maybe I should have listened to Graham Hodson who had cautioned me against the merger in the first place saying that my entrepreneurial and their bureaucratic styles were bound to clash. And yes, he had been proved to be right.

In addition, the 'PHKI' of then went on to become 'Dignity' and, by not adopting my policies but sticking to the PFG policies instead, until forced to change some 25 years after my departure, the company did not cover itself in any professional glory over that period.

But that was not my fault. How could it be? They were not my policies, and I was not there to run the company.

So, when I came to write the PHKI story, I was forced to remember that we had had little option but to do a merger that we had sought due to the 1987 crash in the first place.

Moreover, and, as a result of re-living those years, I also came to realise that PHKI was the vehicle that had shaped the British funeral market of today every bit as much as Hodgson & Sons Ltd or Hodgson Holdings plc had done before it. Indeed, when I look at current market trends, perhaps even more so.

So, I now realise that the PHKI years were ones when I worked very hard and was extremely successful in my invention of a new and low investment cost direction and that I had given, at home, an extended longevity to my marriage, by being dedicated and focused at work and faithful to my wife when not.

Therefore, this was not a bad period of my life. More one where I had tried to be very good, if not great, and had continued to do my best in every direction.

So why had I shunned it and made it a bad memory in my mind? I suspect that this was because my master plan had not been accepted and therefore had failed to save PHKI from what was crass French ignorance and stupidity by a group of bureaucrats that knew less about funeral directing than the little finger on my left hand might forget.

## This Life In Death

I had led my shareholders and staff into the merger and thus had owed it to them to put my head down, roll up my sleeves and make this essential deal, and therefore PHKI, work.

I had tried my hardest, but I had lost out to French bureaucracy and political scheming and therefore, in my head, I had failed because I had always needed to win, and I always had, but on this occasion, I had lost and lost my baby in the process.

## This Life In Death

Chapter II

'The King & I'

1991

The immediate effect on the financial press and the stock market on reading the announcement was one of complete disbelief. Mr. Death retiring and abandoning his creation seemed to them to be quite unbelievable.

Philippe de Margery was right; the share price did go down. However, much more than he had ever anticipated.

Thank God that I had concluded my exit deal before the announcement was made as the fully listed share price dived below its USM flotation price of five years earlier to an all-time low and continued down after that, made worse by press comment that the ship would be rudderless without me.

The French and I had signed mutual gagging orders to prevent either of us from slagging off the other after the announcement had been made.

I honoured this agreement and was quite clear to the press as to why I had resigned in the countless press interviews I gave at the time.

I am only now telling you the real story thirty-three years later.

There were a few silly headlines about me 'passing' from papers like the Daily Mail, but, in the main, the headlines were factual and sensible because this was very surprising news for the newspapers' readers to wake up to on January 19$^{th}$, 1991.

The Times led with a big article written by Jonathan Prynn under the headline 'Hodgson resigns as PHKI chief and sells 12.5% holding.'

Having reported the sale details, the fact that I had bagged £6m (big money in 1991) as well as a fully paid-up contract, it went on to report:

'Mr. Hodgson rescued his father's undertaking firm, then known as Hodgson & Sons, from the brink of receivership in 1975. The company expanded through a policy of aggressive acquisitions and the development of innovative financial packages under the brand-name 'Dignity in Destiny.' In 1986 it was floated on the USM, moving to the main market two years ago. In 1989, it merged with Kenyon Securities, a rival, becoming Britain's largest firm of funeral directors with a market share of 11%.'

It went on:

'Mr Hodgson has attracted publicity throughout his career because of his refusal to conform to the sober images usually associated with funeral directors or the heads of quoted companies.'

It then quoted me:

"Being a chief executive of a plc is a very arduous task. I seem to have been working an 18-hour day since I was aged 18."

And concluded by:

'He added that he hoped to write biographies of famous figures who had been badly treated by history.'

These, the article stated, included Richard III, Charles II, Napoleon, Ian Botham and HRH Charles the Prince of Wales.

Furthermore, I wanted to write an account of the relationship between John Lennon and Paul McCartney.

This article, as well as the other articles on the day, now brought a host of folk beating a fast track to my door in Wilton Place, Belgravia, London SW1 to get their hands on my cash.

The first was the head of Pavilion Books, who persuaded me to sign up to write a business book, largely to be written by a ghost writer, under the awful title, as dictated by him, of 'How to Become Dead Rich,' as he would allow me to write 'The Walrus was Paul' – about Lennon & McCartney if I agreed.

I readily agreed because I wanted to write the Lennon & McCartney book and because I liked this guy called Colin Webb and was impressed that his business partners were two men I admired – Sir Tim Rice and Sir Michael Parkinson.

I got to know both over the next few years because of agreeing to the suggested deal, and both were very likeable chaps – who will appear again in this chapter and later in this volume.

However, the next guys to appear in my drawing room were the private secretary of HRH Prince Charles, Tom Shebbeare, and the head of the Prince's Trust fund raising, a man called, I believe, Manny Cohen.

They wanted me to consider donating to the Prince's Trust. I admired Prince Charles greatly and had huge respect for the work the Trust had done with the under privileged and largely ignored youth in Britain's inner cities since its foundation some twelve years earlier.

Nevertheless, I declined their invitation politely with the explanation that I had nearly killed myself with hard work for over twenty years to restore the family fortune and that I had not done so to give it away.

However, I added that, as I now had time on my hands, I would be delighted to help the Trust raise cash.

A month later, in February 1991, the telephone rang. My secretary, Lynn, answered almost wearily as it hadn't stopped since I had retired. Newspapers wanting to write articles about how Mr. Death was going to spend millions; Pavilion Books about their book on how Mr. Death was going to teach normal folk to make millions; and lots of people wanting just to tell me how to invest millions – which, as you have no doubt already guessed, was with them.

It was in the middle of the afternoon and I was in bed – not because I was now living the life of the idle rich or wooing a new sexual interest; but because two of my discs in my back were by now shot to pieces by years of fast bowling cricket, horse riding, coffin bearing with the dwarf Harry White (as reported in Volume I) and, in particular, lifting 1,000s of heavy dead bodies incorrectly.

I had been told by my surgeon Mr. Crockard that intense and complete bed rest was the only alternative to having these discs removed as my right leg had become paralysed.

It was the urgency in Lynn's step as she thundered up the never-ending staircase of this typical Belgravia house that made me think that this call might be something different. Eventually, she arrived breathless at my door.

"Guess what?" she panted and then continued before I could 'guess what.'

"I've got St James's Palace on the phone and the Prince of Wales wants to have dinner with you at Kensington Palace. What shall I say?"

"What do you mean, what shall I say?" I asked. "Say yes and be quick about it before they ring off. He may never invite me again."

"But what about your leg?"

"Sod that. Don't even mention it. Just accept."

And before she had even descended the mountain back to her office, I was already on the phone to my doctor.

"Well Crockard won't like it one little bit", Doctor Anthony Ashe, warned.

Of course, Anthony was right: Crockard would have had a fit if he had known what I had in mind.

"But he won't know. Look, you shoot some morphine into my arse, and I'll get by for the night. I have a dinner engagement in the House of Commons the night before so we can have a trial run then."

Lynn White, who was as pristine, pure and virginal as I was not, told St James' Palace that I would be delighted to attend the dinner, and Anthony duly obliged with the injections when the time came.

Thank the Lord that I had suggested the House of Commons trial before meeting the future King of England. This practise run was not altogether a success.

I just about managed to stumble through a conversation with Tony Blair, whom I had had lunch with previously when he had first become a young shadow cabinet minister.

Then I made it, with some difficulty, to my table in the main dining room. I was in no pain whatsoever, but the dose was a little too strong and I felt very sleepy. The first glass of claret, which admittedly I'd been advised by Anthony not to have, put me to sleep.

This was most embarrassing for me and incredibly boring for my host, Anthony Bevan MP, and made all the worse by the fact that he had been a chum of my father.

So, the next night, Doctor Anthony Ashe arrived and duly administered a smaller dose to prevent a reoccurrence of the previous evening, as to fall asleep at dinner with the Prince of Wales might be considered more than just bad form.

Then I took off in a car, which had been sent for me, resplendent in my dinner jacket and supporting myself on an antique cane with a beautiful silver top in the form of a crucifix. This was hardly as practical as the crutches the hospital had provided, but more elegant and fitting, I felt, for an occasion that I was determined to enjoy even if I suspected that I was only going on the strength of my newfound disposable wealth.

The car sped up the rather narrow drive of Kensington Palace and was waved on by a single police officer, before stopping in a dimly lit yard. The chauffeur opened the door and I gingerly got to my feet to be greeted by a charming young man and invited to follow him into HRH's apartment.

I struggled up an unimpressive flight of stairs that opened into an even less impressive hallway which reminded me of one you expected to enter when visiting your headmaster rather than the Prince of Wales. My overcoat was placed on an old church pew on top of several others already there.

This was nothing like the royal splendour that I had expected. Indeed, it lacked the elegance of the Ritz Hotel that I had visited several times with my father as a child.

I was impressed that it appeared that the Wales family lived much like any other well-off British family and nothing like the way that the public imagined.

Then I was shown into a cozy and tasteful, if not regal, drawing room, where I joined a dozen or so similarly dressed men. There were no women present – as one might expect there to be today over thirty years later.

A butler offered me a drink from a tray he was carrying, and I accepted a glass of champagne with some difficulty and some mental caution that I should not even sip it in case it put me out before I managed to make it to the dinner table.

Next, the charming and long-serving Tom Shebbeare made his way over to me and explained the form. When the Prince arrived, he would mingle with his guests before dinner, and we would then proceed to the adjoining dining room, where I would find my place by name card. I should address Prince Charles as 'Your Royal Highness' on the first occasion, and thereafter as 'Sir'.

He added that he was sorry to see me in such a bad way but reminded me that nobody could sit until Prince Charles did. I proudly replied that I had been presented to Her Majesty the Queen and several other more minor members of her family and that I appreciated the form. He smiled, as I suppose spiders do when inviting a nice juicy fly into their parlour.

This was the well-worked format. The Prince had amazing pulling power: captains of industry the world over were willing to pay a fortune for the privilege of being in his company and basking in the reflected glow of his royal image, perhaps for just a day or, if their shareholders could afford it, for several. They relished the chance to become associated with, if not a friend of, this genial man who would become King Charles III one day.

The future King had a reputation for being charming – and he needed to be if he was to undo the purse strings of those multimillion-dollar corporations. He needed that money for his good works and used his considerable charm and royal glamour to get it.

Tom and his crew worked the room as warm-up acts before the main man entered, and when he did you knew about it. The crowded small drawing room attendees parted, as if the biblical Red Sea, before him as he moved across it, trying to look happy with a nervous smile on his face, but an unmistakable kindness twinkling in his warm and friendly eyes.

# This Life In Death

He played with his right cufflink as he looked knowingly at people that he was supposed to recognise and skilfully managed to avoid the glance of those that he didn't for fear of upsetting the planned introductions which were to follow.

He had clearly done this thousands of times and, like a seasoned cabaret star, he looked very good at it. However, it was obvious to me that confidence was an important ingredient in his performance as he appeared to me to be frail in that regard, despite his undoubted determination to see his task through and ensure that the Prince's Trust was, as Tony Blair came to declare later when Prime Minister, 'one of the most successful voluntary sector organisations in the world, never mind this country.'

However, pain now interrupted these contemplations as I started to hope that these introductions would speed up. They were seeming to take forever as guests naturally wished to savour their moment with the Prince of Wales.

By now I had been standing for over fifty minutes and still there was no sign when dinner was to be served, and therefore when I might sit down. The lower dose of morphine had prevented me from falling asleep, but at the cost of not killing off the pain as it had on the previous night. The antique stick was now bending under my weight, its silver top was digging into the palm of my hand, and I began to feel faint.

"You mustn't pass out in the Prince of Wales's drawing room," I kept impressing upon myself. Drastic measures were called for, so I threw caution to the wind and knocked back all the contents of the large champagne flute that I had been holding, rather than sipping, for an hour.

Eventually it was my turn. The champagne seemed to have had a good effect and I felt a little better – or maybe the fact that the Prince of Wales was shaking my hand and talking to me made me forget about the pain.

He was not as tall as me, but nevertheless taller than I had expected. He was tanned and looked very fit for a man of forty-two. He congratulated me on the success of Hodgson Holdings plc, cracked a couple of funeral jokes, which were no worse than any others I had heard, and then asked me why I looked as if I had been 'in the wars.'

I told him about my back, and he told me about his and how he was forced to take a supporting roll to put behind the base of his spine whenever he was sitting down.

Then he was off, but a couple of paces away, he stopped, half turned and looked back deeply into my eyes before saying, "We need men like you. You'll not get away from us now, you know."

Well, that was it. I had grown up a royalist, always a cavalier, never a roundhead and later had come to share, as a compassionate capitalist, Prince Charles's concerns for the nation's underprivileged youth and so admired his work.

Nevertheless, Shebbeare and co still might find it hard to divert my hard-earned cash from going to my children: but after that statement and intense stare that burned into my very soul, if Charles Windsor wanted me to go to Moscow in a blizzard and walk there with that bloody awful stick as my only form of support, I was his man.

The effect was amazing. I was almost able to march into dinner, enjoyed the meal, despite the appalling nut cutlets that were served for the main course, as HRH was going through his vegetarian phase, and ended the night by going off to Annabel's Nightclub with Tom Shebbeare and some of the other guests. My miraculous recovery wasn't enough to allow me to dance, but I chatted to Tom until the small hours before returning to Wilton Place a very contented man. It had been a fairytale evening.

The next morning, I received a call from a member of the Prince's staff. The Prince hoped that I had enjoyed the previous evening. I replied that I had. He then asked if I would agree to serve on a new steering committee chaired by Richard George, chairman of Weetabix, that was being assembled to guide the Prince's Trust's future? Naturally, I agreed. Could Tom and Manny come back to Wilton Place and explain the form (and no doubt try again to tap me for some cash)? I agreed.

"Er, one last point", the chap stammered rather nervously. "When cigars were offered last night after dinner, you declined."

"Yes, I did. I prefer a cigarette", I replied, not then the non-smoker that I am today.

"Well, that's the point. HRH has asked me to inform you that you are the first person to smoke a cigarette in that room for the last fifteen years and he'd prefer it if you were to be the last person for the next fifteen. If you get my meaning." I did.

Tom and Manny duly came a week later. I offered them shares in a new company that I was investing in as a compromise to the cash they were seeking. They accepted, knowing that it was likely to be all that I would offer them and, if the company floated, they would receive a windfall (it didn't).

I joined the committee and at the first meeting we designed the now famous 'Jump' advertising campaign featuring heads of industry jumping off the ground. I enjoyed these meetings over the coming months, although felt that Richard George tended slightly to restrict debate in favour of a rubber stamp that he required from us for his views.

Over this time, I was also sent on various assignments. The first of which, and I was personally chosen for this by HRH, was to Birmingham. The reason that I had been 'hand-picked' was because I knew my old mentor Doug Ellis, Chairman of Aston Villa, better than anyone else connected to the Prince's Trust.

'Deadly' had been promising a Villa Park concert in aid of the Prince's Trust to HRH for some time but it hadn't materialised. So, the Earl of Shrewsbury and I were dispatched to a charming little restaurant in Chad's Square, Edgbaston to have lunch with the amiable Doug and secure an agreement.

Shrewsbury was a charming fellow and 'Deadly' was on great form as he regaled us with many amusing stories. Indeed, he might not have smoked a cigarette in HRH's dining room like his former pupil, but he had laughed at one of Prince Charles' jokes, in that very room, to the point when the dining chair, which was supporting his not inconsiderable weight, had broken and deposited the Villa Chairman on the royal carpet.

According to Doug, HRH was more concerned about the chair than he was about 'Deadly' as it had been borrowed from Princess Margaret's apartment next door for the dinner.

Then, it was down to business and after a little cajoling from the two of us, Doug promised to get both Elton John, someone whom he said owed him a lot, as 'Deadly' had taught him everything he knew about football, when the tantrum-throwing star first became Chairman of Watford; and Nigel Kennedy, who was a fanatical Villa fan whom 'Deadly' had entertained on his yacht in Majorca. He would get on to it tomorrow and fix a date.

The Earl and I returned to London very pleased and were more than a little flushed with the success of our first mission when Shebbeare duly praised our efforts.

However, I was soon to learn that HRH was less impressed when he learned that no date had been fixed and had moaned that we had brought back from Birmingham no more than exactly the same story that 'Deadly' had told him during that chair breaking dinner party.

The Prince of Wales was right. 'Deadly' did not deliver. Perhaps, he could not hold the two stars to account. Shame on them if this was the case. Perhaps, the price of an empire medal or even a knighthood was simply too high. After all, Aston Villa was still a private company, largely owned by him, in 1991, and all the financial risks associated with such an event would have rested on his shoulders, rather than the Prince's Trust, if the event had not been a success.

Ellis was a man made good from a modest background and clearly was impressed that his former pupil now was on speaking terms with the heir to the throne, loved his own association with HRH, but was, understandably, perhaps more risk adverse than anyone appreciated at the Trust. Hard won cash is certainly not 'easy come, easy go' money.

## This Life In Death

Some twelve years later, in 2003, on a visit to the then new Prince's Trust HQ in Regent's Park, a young female graduate informed me that, "A struggle between a donor's desire to keep his cash and have a title is still going on today."

However, 'Deadly' must have coughed up something because in the 2005 New Year's Honours, he was awarded, quite rightly, for his services to football and the West Midlands' community, an OBE.

This was jokingly, and without any intended malice, described to me by my great friend, the former Aston Villa and England Manager Graham Taylor, as being remarkably apt in Doug's case.

"Howard, if the OBE stands for 'other buggers' efforts' then this was never truer than in the case of 'Deadly."

Graham, like me, could see through Doug, but we still loved him. 'Deadly' was a self-promoting man often with a cock-eyed vision of events surrounding his involvement in them. However, he was extremely likeable, and, in my case, he had plucked me out of the gutter in 1971, something that I will remember until my dying day. Although, we were to cross swords over our beloved Aston Villa in 2003, this was quickly forgiven on both sides.

This appreciation of Doug wasn't always true of other Villa managers. My friend and a guy I really liked around this time, Ron Atkinson, once described 'Deadly Doug' as a lovely man "when he is asleep."

My next assignment was far worse than my trip to Birmingham. I was sent to Cardiff, instead of HRH, to hand out various awards to young folk who had turned their Prince's Trust grant into a small but successful business. As I entered the room, I noticed that all of them were looking through and beyond me to see where the future King of England was; this was followed by hardly disguised expressions of disappointment. I realised there and then how difficult it must have been for Prince Charles when the crowds on his side of the street groaned upon realising that Princess Diana was to walk down the other side.

In early summer of 1991 came my third assignment. I was asked to go to Highgrove to help entertain guests at a cocktail party that was being held in aid of Macmillan Nurses. As Marianne and I arrived we were astonished by how slack security was – we were hardly checked by anyone before entering the hallway where we were introduced to Lord and Lady Zetland, served with a glass of champagne and offered delightful little canapes by Princes William and Harry, who were identically dressed in blue and white striped shirts, pale blue chinos and dark brown loafers.

The Prince of Wales, when all the guests were eventually assembled, made his entrance. He looked very smart in a dark grey double-breasted suit, pale blue shirt and red tie. Like many women before her, Marianne was immediately taken by his presence, warmth, kindness and charm. She thought him to be very attractive.

We chatted about various things before he remarked upon my back. "You're looking a lot better than the last time I saw you."

He obviously hadn't read my letter to him. But then why should I have expected him to have – given that he receives thousands each week. Nevertheless, I was surprised that he didn't know that my trip to Brum had been delayed until I had recovered from my operation.

Following our previous meeting and my carefree trip to Annabel's with Shebbeare et al, I had been rushed into the Wellington Hospital and both protruding discs had been removed in an emergency operation to prevent them severing the nerve serving my right leg and causing permanent paralysis.

"I had both discs removed, Sir. I wrote to you about it. Mr Crockard did it in the Wellington. I made a TV series for the BBC, travelling all over Europe three weeks later and I'm already playing cricket and riding horses again. You should consider having it done, Sir," I told him enthusiastically.

However, my enthusiasm was immediately dampened by his uncharacteristically arrogant reply, "Oh, I don't think so. I have a room full of suggested cures sent from all over the Commonwealth."

This man was my future king, and I loved and admired him, but I was not going to let this reply drop without a response. "Well, you should be so lucky that your subjects love you so well," I replied, hurt by his dismissal.

HRH was taken aback. He stared at me in almost disbelief. The Zetlands looked down into their champagne glasses. Marianne looked at me. I looked at the Prince. And then suddenly, after what Marianne described as a 'minute' but was probably about two seconds, Charles's glare evaporated into a kindly smile as he added, "Of course, you are right."

A couple of weeks later, I received this letter from him:

19th August 1991. Highgrove.

Dear Mr. Hodgson,

I am afraid it has taken me a very long time to find your kind letter and I heartily apologize, but with so much going on at present I can never get to my letters! I was very touched you should bother to write, and I have since seen you at Highgrove when I could see for myself that you were a new man! However, my back is now considerably better, owing to the endless exercises recommended by the physiotherapist, and I will do anything to avoid an operation!

Yours sincerely,

Charles.

I believe this short but sincere letter shows the real reason for his pompous remark – understandable fear of the knife – and it further shows him to be a man of a good and generous nature. There is no other explanation as to why he had sought out my original letter and then taken the trouble to reply to it. This was, perhaps, the closest one was ever going to get to an apology from royalty and, in my mind, it enhanced my regard for him.

I don't know if it was this frank exchange or because he simply wanted to talk about the workings of the Prince's Trust, but after we had finished our champagne, we set off on a tour of the wonderful Highgrove gardens with fifty or more guests in tow but the Prince kept Marianne and me by his side and wanted to talk.

What did I think about the fund-raising activities of the Trust, he asked. I replied that I believed that they were uncoordinated. This set us off on an hour's conversation.

He listened, thought, questioned, listened again and then became quite excited. Eventually, he told me that what I was telling him was quite right. Things could be better organised and yes, we should do something to move away from the current fund- raising activity.

He went on to say that he appreciated what I had said about the dangers of raising money for the Trust by granting 'gongs' for cash.

I had told him that, when I was CEO of Hodgson Holdings plc, it had been put to me by a very high-profile CEO of another public company that a gift from Hodgson Holdings to the Trust would, as long as I never mentioned it, gain me great recognition. He then showed me a list of PYBT contributors, and how much they were donating. He advised me to look at the next honours list and see who got what. At the bottom of the list was written 'Anonymous - £500,000'. He had pointed to this and said, "Howard, that guy will get a knighthood."

Then I had explained to HRH that I believed that there were dangers here for the Trust. I said that while I had absolutely nothing against 'king's patronage' in bygone years when a merchant might financially support the crown and in exchange be granted a title, this was because it had been his money to give.

However, I pointed out that CEOs of publicly owned companies didn't own them and were giving away other shareholders' money in order to buy a title for themselves. I told Prince Charles that, in my opinion that this was morally wrong and that if the press got to hear about it a scandal might ensue.

He took my point. He looked concerned and was pensive for a few moments. Then he looked happier again and asked me to write to him about how I thought things might be organised.

So, I did as commanded. However, this didn't turn out quite the way Prince Charles and I had expected. The next time I met Richard George he hardly passed the time of day with me. Then I got a call from someone on his behalf.

Apparently, Mr. George was not happy with me. How dare I go down to Highgrove and give HRH my private advice? These were my own views and not those of the committee. Didn't I realise that with Prince Charles it was the last storyteller who always told the best story. Had I no idea of the disruption I had caused? People who had been courting individuals for ages were now in danger of having these donations endangered thanks to me. It would take a lot of time and effort to get the Prince calmed down.

I replied that I wasn't vaguely sorry and stood completely by what I had told HRH. This was before Princess Diana and the Duchess of York had plunged the British Monarchy in turmoil and marital scandal. The House of Windsor's status was high and, despite some adverse comment about the Prince of Wales' views on climate change, which were then wrongly thought to be 'loony', the work of the Prince's Trust was universally acclaimed.

I pointed out that a 'somebody else's cash to buy a title' scandal could alter that. Therefore, the caller could inform Mr George that I would have to beg to differ with him as I believed that I had done HRH a favour and if that had caused problems for those who worked on fund raising, I was sorry but stood by my opinion, nonetheless.

I hold that opinion still and believe that a tabloid press more concerned with rooting out true stories than inventing titillating ones would have picked up on the fact a public company CEO had promised that his company would donate £300,000 to the Trust. He duly received a CBE. However, the company went into receivership during those stormy economic waters of the early 1990s and the Prince's Trust never saw a penny.

I remember years later, in 2003, Tom Shebbeare told me how angry he had been when that had happened and that the Trust had been lucky that the press had missed the story altogether.

Anyway, I was no longer Mr George's favourite committee member, and my phone stopped ringing. Moreover, as we shall see in the next chapter, I was to push the self-destruct button, in both my personal and business life, so hard that my hands were completely full trying to undo the serious damage that my own stupidity had caused, and so I no longer had time to worry about how the Prince's Trust raised its funds as I was very busy trying to save my own.

However, that is for the future, and looking back on that beautiful summer's late afternoon in 1991 as HRH and I walked round the extensive Highgrove gardens, I observed many things about Prince Charles that were quite at odds with the image of him that his wife was surreptitiously starting to promote through some of her media associates.

He explained to me, for example, how he had grown a hedge so that Princess Diana could sunbathe on a terrace free from the prying telescopic lenses of the press. We now know, but were only just starting to suspect then, that their marriage wasn't going terribly well. However, he referred to her several times, always fondly and with a tone of genuine care in his voice.

He then asked me about my children and expressed genuine sorrow on hearing about the death of my son Charles, before speaking very warmly about his own sons.

On the way through the walled garden, suddenly several Macmillan lady guests behind us squealed as a salvo of rotten apples rained down on them and dislodged at least one hat. HRH turned to Marianne and me and said "Little devils" with a warm smile of amusement at such mischievous exploits.

Then, in the wooded area, where Charles had constructed a tree house for his sons, we watched as the two princes clambered up a ladder before descending again by a rope and their father roared with laughter when Prince Harry asked, "Papa, shall we do it again in case the back people didn't see."

A little later, Prince Harry was tugging so hard at his father's sleeve that the Prince of Wales's shoulder was bouncing up and down and his head rolling from side to side. "Papa! Papa!" He shouted, "Don't listen to him. Listen to me!"

A few minutes after that the boisterous Harry snapped the stem of a flower. His father rebuked him before gently explaining that Harry had shortened the time of that flower's beauty in the garden. Harry looked down and said, "Sorry Papa." HRH smiled at his youngest son, who then beamed back.

Children who have cold, distant and unloving fathers, as Diana had been briefing elements of the press that Prince Charles was, don't behave like that. Harry's behaviour towards his father, as much as Prince Charles's reaction to it, told any parent that this was a warm and loving relationship.

This observation has been completely borne out ever since by King Charles III's patience and kindness towards his youngest son, despite the latter's imbecilic, selfish, irresponsible and half-witted behaviour since his marriage to a minor actress, the scheming and attention seeking Meghan Markle.

As we were nearing the end of our epic walk, the same could be said of the affectionate way HRH cuddled Prince William as we neared the house, and he cracked another funereal joke for my benefit. He pointed up to the stone balustrade running along the roof. It was interspersed by urns. "Those were not there when I bought the place. I suppose I should have asked your advice before erecting them."

As we looked up at them people passed us on their way back to the house and a welcome cup of tea. The Macmillan ladies were gaily chatting as they went down the path but were not keeping to the paving stones. Instead, they were trampling on his delicate little flowers which he had planted in between.

"I suppose these women think that they are trampling on colourful weeds" he seethed under his breath. Then and out of the blue, he asked me if I had any siblings. "A brother and a sister, Sir" I replied somewhat taken aback.

"Are they older or younger?" he asked.

"Both younger, my brother by six years, my sister by two."

"Ah," he sighed, "A sister two years younger. I imagine she could be bossy." And then he laughed. There was no reference to Princess Anne, and I did not presume to mention her name, especially given our little spat concerning cures for bad backs an hour or so earlier.

Upon our return to the drawing room, via French windows that lead into the house and the rear hallway, I left Marianne chatting to HRH about his watercolours painted in her native Provence, to get something that I had been asked to give him from my car.

Prince Harry asked if he could come with me. Prince Charles smiled his permission. As we entered the car park, Harry pointed to a gleaming cobalt blue Jaguar XJS convertible, with its hood down to expose cream leather seats.

"Is that your car?"

I nodded.

"Wow! Can I drive it?"

I got in and put Harry between my legs and we set off around the car park. He steered while I operated the accelerator and brake.

Then Prince Harry announced, "We could go out on the road if you like?"

Not only would this have been against the law, but no doubt there probably were some security men present in the grounds, despite their not obvious visibility, and one of them might have thought that I was kidnapping the third in line to the throne and might take a shot at me through his telescopic lensed rifle as a result.

"Oh, I don't think so" I replied as I terminated Prince Harry's first driving lesson. Then having delivered my package and safely returned Harry to the care of his father, in the delightful but surprisingly small drawing room, we took our leave of their Royal Highnesses and attended a dinner with the other Highgrove guests in Tetbury. Once there, I was horrified to listen to Lady Prior, wife of Tory wet and former Cabinet Minister, Sir Jim Prior, launch into a vengeful, untrue and unobjective attack on Mrs Thatcher.

I was horrified and launched into the rather large lady with a string of facts and figures. I convincingly won the argument. Later that year, Lady Prior's daughter, Sarah Jane, approached me at a party thrown by a mutual friend.

## This Life In Death

"I hear you beat the shit out of my mother at a dinner party in Tetbury after a visit to Highgrove. Well done. She has needed taking down a peg for years," she said gleefully.

This, then, had been my longest conversation with the Prince of Wales. It had been for over an hour and had started with a row. We were not to meet again for several years. Moreover, it was certainly of more consequence to me than him. However, it did allow me to observe him at close quarters. I had liked what I had seen. His children adored him, and his staff loved and respected him despite being quite aware of his frailties.

I had admired him at a distance all my life. He hadn't disappointed on that wonderful afternoon. I knew he would, one day, become an excellent king. And I have been proved to be right.

However, in 1991, the pro-Diana media campaign, designed to fantasise about a 'Saint Diana' and blacken the name of a cold, uncaring, stuffy and 'an out of touch' Charles was only in its infancy. It was not until Princess Diana realised that separation from Charles was inevitable that this campaign was really revved up to try and get the public behind her claim to her sons as she knew that constitutionally the Queen had the right under common law to take control of the boys' care and education.

From then until her untimely and awful death in 1997, Diana was to wage a media war against the House of Windsor, which was usually as untrue as it was successful.

However, in 1991 that ongoing campaign was restricted mainly to winning public support for the way she was bringing up the boys.

She would tip off her favoured newspapers to which theme park she would be taking her sons on a Sunday – so they could fill pages in their Monday editions and show them all in jeans and having a Big Mac, like ordinary folk.

The campaign was hugely successful, because it showed the princes with her in complete contrast to them going to church in suits and ties when with their father and 'Granny the Queen' the next weekend.

## This Life In Death

However, the campaign was turned into all-out war in 1992 with the publication of the Andrew Morton book, 'Diana. Her True Story'. This book was not what it seemed.

Firstly, it was only typed up by Morton, it was composed by Diana herself on a small dictaphone, given to a mutual friend, a Doctor James Colthurst, who would cycle to Kensington Palace to collect the tapes and then deliver them to Morton. He would then type them up and send them back, via Colthurst, for Diana to edit – which she did. All of this was done secretly and in a giant deception to fool the people.

It was only after considerable public criticism of Diana's behaviour in passages of the book, where she had misjudged the nation's opinion, did things start to unravel slightly.

For instance, she reported a suicide attempt while pregnant with William, believing that this would bring her sympathy. On the contrary, the public opinion was that good mothers do not endanger their children's lives by such actions. She responded immediately by blaming Morton for making these events up.

However, Morton, who had become the richest typist in history by this time, bided his time and after her death, he then published 'Diana. In Her Own Words,' which made it clear that these false stories had come from Diana herself.

Secondly, the book, when published, after a poor initial start became, thanks to the efforts of Diana's other media mates like the Sunday Times to promote it, the second-best selling UK book of 1992 and gave birth to such a lie that it became known by all who knew the couple as 'Diana. Her Completely Untrue Story'.

It also prompted a letter from them to the Queen, having been denied access to the press by Wales himself, asking for permission to tell the true story as to how the Prince of Wales had been a thoughtful husband and a fine father throughout the roller-coaster ride of his marriage, due to Diana's private mood-swings and obvious mental health issues.

## This Life In Death

Nobody is perfect. We could fill pages with our own faults and those of others. The Prince and Princess of Wales were not exceptions to this fact in the 1990s.

However, he sought to protect her, knowing of her mental troubles, while she sought to destroy him and increasingly wanted to see Prince William replace him as the next King of England, so that she could become the 'Queen Mother' if not the 'Queen' upon her husband's accession to the throne.

However, I had not only come to realise this, but that in the case of the Prince not only did the good in him far outweigh the bad but that a lot of that bad was no more than malicious lies invented by his wife and then dripped out into the press to support the fabricated falsehoods in her fantasy tale 'Diana. Her True Story.'

I hadn't enjoyed hours of uninterrupted conversation with the heir to the throne that Jonathan Dimbleby was to experience a few years later. However, Prince Charles did not know when talking to me, that I one day would commit such conversations to paper; therefore, I had the benefit of talking to him in a natural and unguarded fashion. And yet I was to draw the same conclusions as Dimbleby: we were both talking to a very decent human being. And I, for one, have always found it easier to admire the truly honest endeavours of a hard worker who cares for others, than the fake charm of a superstar whose favourite word is 'me.'

Nevertheless, this second volume of my memoirs is supposed to be about me and not the King of England nor his beautiful but borderline personality disorder suffering first wife. Not least, because I have already written the 750-page book called 'Charles. The Man who will be King' about this very subject which was first published in 2007.

I took four years out of my life between 2003 and then to do this. Why did I bother? Because the mounting criticisms of the then heir to the throne were grossly unfair because they were built on falsehoods, mainly invented by Diana, and then that deception kept alive by a press, such as the Daily Mail, where Richard Kay was the major-general fantasist, keen to please their female readers, who were encouraged to keep believing in a largely mythical Diana fantasy about a woman who never existed. The real Diana was nothing like the manipulated tabloid press version that the public was fed banquets of.

I was to come across the Princess of Wales only once more before her tragic death in 1997. This was in 1996 when I was invited to attend a charity dinner hosted by Imran and Jemima Khan, the former Pakistan cricket captain, who was starting a new career in politics, and his beautiful wife, who was a friend of Diana's. Princess Diana was the star guest and due to make the main speech before Jeffrey Archer raised a lot of money while upping the bids by accepting some off the curtains at the back of the room while conducting the auction.

Her speech was vastly better than the last one I had had to endure four years earlier. Clearly some good had come from the work done with Peter Settelen, her voice coach. She spoke with more authority, diction, and conviction. Indeed, although still slightly stilted, it was altogether a better effort.

I was with Tim Rice and Michael Parkinson. 'Parky' knew of my Prince Charles sympathies, and like the true Yorkshireman that he was, was looking for the next row.

"Well, that wasn't such a bad speech was it Howard," he told me as we applauded its conclusion.

"No, it wasn't. But would you buy a second-hand car off her?" I replied.

So, despite my temptation even now, seventeen years after that book's publication, to write so much more here about the shocking injustice of it all, I will refrain from doing this, because in all honesty, King Charles III and Queen Camilla have laid to rest these Diana fantasies by their own stoic hard work and unswerving sense of duty to the entire British community and the Commonwealth nations.

I believe that, in the end, we must all hope that the truth will always prevail and triumph when actions are allowed to speak louder than words and subversive 'Soviet type' media propaganda is not employed.

Therefore, today, I do not feel the need to write more as the truth of who their Majesties are is evidenced by their own unselfish industry and dedication, which is clearly on view for us all to see.

However, as we go through the next 33 years here, we will encounter King Charles III, Queen Camilla, Prince William, Princess Anne, the Duchess of York, the Count & Countess of Wessex, the Duke of Kent and other members of the Royal Family again – as well as eight UK prime ministers.

Nevertheless, and lastly at this stage, I will just record that those months of 1991 working for and, on occasion being with, HRH Charles, Prince of Wales was a huge privilege and a very meaningful experience for me.

Therefore, and given my devotion to him, how unfortunate that, when his and my paths next cross, so do our swords for a second time as you will see.

# This Life In Death

## Chapter III

## Every Which Way I Lose

## 1992

1991 had been a very pleasant year. I had enjoyed the celebrity status still afforded me by BBC and local radio stations, most TV channels, and the press, without having the long hours and responsibility of running a fully listed London Exchange quoted company while having to constantly worry about the devious French or the 'Judas' Barber.

I took to wearing jeans and trainers and could spend more time watching my three children grow up. Howard was eighteen in the December and had been at the Lycée studying his 'A' levels until that summer. Jamieson became eight in the May and was at the Hampshire School near Hyde Park. He had grown up attached to me at the hip and hated to be separated from me – even for a few hours. Davinia was one in the June and naturally remained at home with a nanny as Marianne still went to Birmingham most weekdays to mollycoddle her Aston Villa players' wives, and other large spending clientele. Our marriage was strong and homelife was good.

In addition, I had not only enjoyed immensely my time working for the Prince's Trust but had also really enjoyed presenting a three-part series for BBC 2, hideously named 'How Euro Are You'. These 40-minute programmes were dedicated to see how Britain would fare when the single market was introduced on 1st January 1992 by the European Union.

The programmes were made all over the EU only three weeks after my discs had been removed. I drove the Jag that Prince Harry had had his first driving lesson in on the filming trip which took in Paris, Brussels, Hanover and numerous other less exotic locations such as Dover, Calais, Redditch, Amber Valley and Walsall.

David Nelson, the extremely pleasant director of the programme, travelled with me and a crew of five followed in a camper van. This number might seem excessive now but was quite usual then.

There was a very practical female assistant producer, who ensured we went to the right hotels and restaurants; a cameraman and his assistant; a sound guy, who never stopped complaining that he didn't have an assistant; and a very attractive young girl whom I was to have a sort of adolescent 1964 sexual relationship with for several months. In other words, we did everything to each other but the final act.

Initially, I was shocked how these five were typical Auntie Beeb work to rule merchants. I thought that none of them would have survived five minutes at Hodgson Holdings. However, I quickly came to like all of them and by about day three had become their shop steward and leading spokesman when we decided we needed a beer. They warmed to me too as soon as they realised that David was more likely to listen to me rather than any on them on this subject.

It was a very pleasant trip and by and large filming was achieved without a hitch. However, there were occasions when things didn't always go quite as planned.

The grumbling soundman looked like Dan Aykroyd and wore a white trench coat as associated with the actor. I spotted him going down some companionway steps on the cross-channel ferry (the tunnel was still being constructed in 1991). I could not resist bounding down after him and kicking him in the arse while singing "Ghostbusters" at the top of my voice. This faded fast as the recipient of my flying kick turned round to reveal that he was not our soundman but a very surprised and angry Frenchman.

Then in Paris, I had a piece to camera to be shot high up in public gardens on one side of the River Seine so that we had the Eiffel Tower in the background on the other.

My dialogue began, "This is Paris. It is closer to London than is Newcastle..." as I raised my arm to point to the Tower behind me. I did it perfectly. However, the cameraman said that we needed to do it again as the moment I had raised my arm a fountain had started up between me and the Tower and that the effect was that it appeared that gushing water was cascading out of my armpit.

## This Life In Death

Clint Eastwood is a popular director with actors because if he gets what he wants on one take he moves on. Nobody likes retakes and that includes me.

Nevertheless, I looked at what the camera had captured with David and could see that we needed to do it again.

Take two and roll, "This is Paris..."

"Cut". A little boy was pulling faces behind me.

Now crowds started to gather as some people thought Robert Redford was filming in Paris and quite soon, we had several hundred spectators. This made me even more nervous. The pressure was mounting.

Take three and roll, "This is Paris..."

"Cut". A ball bounced in front of me followed by a little boy trying to retrieve it. Now the camera crew are turning away a few Redford autograph hunters. The pressure is growing and I'm starting to go from nervous to frantic.

Take four and roll, "This is Paris..."

"Cut". A plane flew overhead and drowned out my dialogue. Shit. The pressure is enormous. The need to get the next take right in front of the camera as well as now hundreds of non-English speaking Robert Redford fans, who were wasting their day by not watching Robert Redford but me, had me shivering inside.

Take five and roll, "This is Newcastle..."

"Cut". David walked up to me and said very quietly, in the same manner that Eric Morecambe had to Andre Previn in that wonderful sketch in the Morecambe & Wise Christmas Special of the 80s, "No Howard, this is Paris."

That was it. It took another ten plus takes to get it right. Eventually, I did. I felt two foot small as we wrapped up and found our hotel for the night, after most of the adoring Redford fans had also gone too.

I had kept everyone on set for at least an extra hour because of my amateurism. However, everyone was very kind and understanding.

At dinner, I apologised to them all. They all told me that none of them would have wanted to be in my position.

Then in an act of complete kindness, one of the two females present ran her hand over 'William' under the table at dinner and told me to concentrate on that and put the whole episode out of my mind. That did the trick, and I did.

Later, when no longer in Paris, but in the less famous and salubrious surroundings of some extensive railway sidings in Walsall, near my native Birmingham, and close to the M6 motorway, came the third and final incident.

David wanted to shoot so he could see the goods trains working beneath the bridge that we were standing on. It was the obvious shot. However, this did not please me as the wind was blowing my swept fringe the wrong way and into my eyes, and I didn't think, therefore, I looked as sexy as usual.

I wanted the shot to go from the other direction to correct this. However, we would not have seen the trains. David, rightly, put his foot down. So, I had an Elton John type tantrum. Unbeknown to me the camera was rolling throughout.

In those days, and perhaps still, BBC and ITV swapped out-takes as presents to each other at Christmas time. My tantrum was number two on the BBC's gift tape, following on after Sue Lawley's similar fit about pigeons while filming in St Mark's Square, Venice.

When the actual series was screened, it was well reviewed by the TV critics. I was compared to Sir John Harvey Jones as an entrepreneurial presenter but one that looked more like Robert Redford than the rather rotund Jones. Even various Radio 1 and 2 DJs advised listeners to not miss episode 2. I was happy.

However, during this year of good works for Prince Charles, TV presenting, and spending time with my children, I had also been laying the foundations for an 'annus horribilis' of my own in 1992. For it was the poorly thought out investment decisions that I made in 1991 as well as giving in again to my sex addiction that came to back to bite me in the arse in 1992.

## This Life In Death

First, I allowed myself to be seduced by David Nelson's wife. She was also a BBC programme director – and a good one. The fact that we ended up on the drawing room floor of my mother's Birmingham apartment, moments before she and my stepfather Baker arrived there from Poole was even more exciting. How childish, how disloyal to David, whom I really thought was a good guy, but how typical of me not to be able to resist the pleasures of the flesh.

Worse, this re-ignited by desire for extra-marital sex. The need for it had nothing to do with my wife's sexuality or my love of her, but instead, that I was addicted to dangerous sex in every sense of the word. This desire was to finally destroy an otherwise perfect marriage where Marianne and I had been through so much and had achieved so much together – not least the family that I had craved so very much twenty years earlier and which we had created. Shame on me.

Second, while I had batted away most people beating a path to my door and wanting me to invest in them, since my highly publicised sale of PHKI stock, I did make investment decisions which turned out to be disastrously bad.

This was in the main because, while I was prepared to invest in start-ups with people that I liked and trusted, I did not intend to run them and so apply that HH discipline that had made Hodgson & Sons Ltd so successful from 1975 onwards.

This was both a naïve and costly mistake. Somehow, I now believed in my own publicity that everything I touched would turn to gold without me ever bothering to take any interest in it. Only a fool does this, and I was, at that moment, a fool.

John Gunn wanted me to start a business called Hodgson & Partners along with him and my childhood friend Ricky Cressman, where we would source seed-corn capital to decent business concepts. I duly agreed.

However, our first investment was not along these lines but to save Colin Webb's Pavilion Books. All three of us invested £50,000 each. It didn't save Pavilion Books, nor Colin from a nervous breakdown. We all lost our money. However, both Parky and Tim Rice were delighted as we had managed to get them off the hook in the process and both remained grateful friends – whom we will hear more about over the coming years. Nevertheless, it was an atrocious start.

Moreover, things didn't improve either as we then took an expensive suite of offices in Bishopsgate, despite the fact that we only boasted penniless imbecilic clients whom we had about as much chance of raising funds for as Charles Hawtree had of becoming Mr. Universe.

Next, my old pal from NWM in 1971, whom I had employed to good effect in PHKI to run Dignity in Destiny, David Meakin, wanted to leave the firm, since I had, and wanted to set up two companies. The first was a company which would sell franchises to people who would then supply monthly management accounts to their clients. It was to be called Prontac. The concept was sound and did have every chance of success.

However, the second was to be an updated re-run of NWM as it would sell financial services. I should have remembered how easily blown off course NWM had been in the early '70s, but I can't recall giving the matter any attention as my mind was elsewhere.

Worse, I also then agreed to sign cross guarantees which meant that if one company failed it would bring the other down with it.

I simply was not thinking like the man who had struggled out of the gutter to become 'Entrepreneur of the Year.' I was more concerned about the Prince's Trust work, finishing the book 'How to Become Dead Rich' and making 'How Euro Are You.' Bad mistake? No. A very bad mistake.

It had taken me twenty years of fanatical discipline and very hard work to go from a penniless boy to the author of 'How to Become Dead Rich' with a wonderful family that lived a very comfortable life. I now seemed determined to throw it all away in 20 months.

Not only was I risking my money, but by using my name in two cases, I was risking my reputation and potentially giving a golden opportunity to my old enemy, Jason Nisse, to have a field day in the press.

## This Life In Death

So, the seeds for disaster were set in 1991 and would explode into serious problems in 1992, but only even then with a lot of extra help from me.

In early February, a chance event was to blow up my life, as I knew it, and chuck it all over the national press.

Marianne and I were due to have a dinner party at home in Wilton Place, London, just before I was to start filming the second series of 'How Euro Are You'. The guests were to be Michael Hackney, who had left Grindley Brandts in Milan and returned to London to start his own storage business; Anthony Ashe, our doctor; Richard Oldsworth, my long-suffering PR consultant, and his wife; and our friends Charlie and Isa Brocket.

Marianne and I had appeared with Lord and Lady Brocket on an ITV morning chat show sometime in 1991 and had become friendly while waiting in the green room to appear on the programme.

However, the Brockets too had some nasty issues appearing on their horizon and these would be far worse than mine. Charlie was to become embroiled in an insurance swindle over Ferraris he had stolen from himself to raise £4.5 million from General Accident so that he could save the family stately home, which he had built into a successful conference centre in the '80s, only to see it destroyed by the '87 crash and following recession, where corporate redundancies were likely and executive conferences considered a luxury. Demand had plummeted and left his entire inheritance exposed.

Then, worse news, General Accident refused to pay out and so Charlie was forced to sue them. He was now struggling with both financial and domestic problems.

This was because Isa had developed a serious cocaine problem and was finding it hard to look after their three children.

Eventually, she got caught forging prescriptions to feed her drug habit and when interviewed by the police spilled the beans about her husband's insurance fraud.

Charlie was arrested but before the trial we had lunch together in Verbanella's in Beauchamp Place, London. Charlie assured me he was innocent. He was a genial guy, and I liked him, but I didn't believe a word.

Nor did the judge and he got five years. He was sent to a normal prison, from where he wrote to me a heart breaking six-page letter saying how he was being bullied and terrorised by thugs who were threatening to shove a bog brush loaded with razor blades up his arse. Could I help?

I got a message to the then Prime Minister, John Major, explaining Charlie's plight. He was immediately moved to an open prison. Charlie never thanked me and when he was released our paths never crossed again. It was not until I came to write this that I suddenly realised that perhaps he never thanked me because he never knew it was me that asked the PM to get him moved. So perhaps, I have done him an injustice in my mind for the last twenty-five years.

However, this was all to happen in the future, but in the early evening of the said dinner party day, Charlie telephoned me and confided in me that Isa (or Issy as he referred to her) was 'off her head' thanks to cocaine and that with great regret they would be unable to attend.

I told Marianne. She wanted to find late substitutes. She called Anthony and told him to bring his girlfriend. He said she was away but that he could bring his sister Caroline. This was a 'Sliding Doors' moment.

Caroline duly came. She didn't sit next to me, and I spent much more time talking to Richard, his wife who was attractive and I had an eye for, and Marianne. Therefore, Anthony, his sister and Michael, who were at the other end of the table, spent more time together.

At some point during the dinner, the nanny reported that Dink had a temperature. Anthony, as our doctor, duly left the table to see how she was, only to be met by an eight-year-old critical J, who claimed that he had had too much to drink to be of any use.

Marianne was very pleased when it was over as the dinner party had been a great success and had only finished in the early hours of the next morning. The Oldworths had already gone when Anthony,

Michael, Caroline and I ventured outside as they were leaving now too.

We saw some poor sod on his way to work on a bicycle. Encouraged by Michael, we threw the fruit that we had carried from the dinner table, and in a typical, but horrible, privileged English public schoolboy fashion, we laughed as he was pelted and could only offer 'V' signs in return.

Caroline tripped and I caught her before she smashed her head on the pavement. I had stopped her fall by placing both hands on her ample but pert breasts. She wasn't wearing a bra. Suddenly I noticed her.

A few weeks later, Marianne and I were invited to Anthony's birthday party at Random Dock, on the South Bank. We went and Anthony and Caroline met us at the top of the stairs. Marianne was led away by Anthony to be introduced to other guests. Caroline slipped her arm round my waist and said she would do the same.

She didn't. Instead, we talked. I admitted when being questioned, without too much prosecution, that I had a sex addiction. She gave me her number. I called her and asked if she would like to have dinner. We did. She invited me back to her flat in Earls Court for a night cap. I readily agreed. Once there, we kissed in the dining area of a split-level apartment.

My fingers slipped inside her blouse and were about to enter her bra (this time she was wearing one) when she stopped me there and then in my tracks.

"I don't see why it is always the girl that ends up naked. I want you to strip for me."

She sat down and watched with her eyes staring at my every move as I duly obliged. When I was naked, she smiled and stood up, walked round me once as I stood still and then she led me to her bedroom. This was fantasy sex beyond my wildest dreams and once under 'Miss Whiplash's' power it only got better.

So now I was having adolescent sex with a BBC young assistant, marital sex with Marianne and dominatrix sex with Caroline, while still having occasional sexual encounters elsewhere. I should have sought psychological help. But I didn't realise that I was ill. I just thought that I was a Hodgson and, like my ancestors before me, it was only natural to want and get as much as I needed to satisfy me. I actually thought that the problem was with others who did not understand this.

At half-term we went on our usual family skiing holiday to Lech in Austria for once, and not France. I was proof-reading 'How to Become Dead Rich' when not skiing and I stopped smoking – which I had been trying to cut back on for a decade but couldn't get below ten-a-day.

J had said to me just before we left for the trip, "Daddy, if you really loved me, you wouldn't smoke. I don't want you to die."

Well, if I couldn't do it for myself, I should do it for my wonderful children was my conclusion and I stopped there and then thirty-three years ago and have never smoked a cigarette since. This was to prove to be a miracle given what was to happen next.

Prontac was becoming a success and well on the way to selling over 80 franchises. The actual software had some teething problems but none that David's 'boffin' Tom Madely believed that he couldn't resolve.

Indeed, I pointed out an advert for franchisees in the Daily Mail, while having yet another expensive lunch, to our ski guide, who seemed to have a high-frequency antenna for eye-wateringly costly restaurants.

However, as well as Meakin was doing at Prontac, Integrity was losing twice as much money as David was making at Prontac. It had low sales, low acceptance rates, high lapse rates - especially by someone called Peter O'Brien, poor administration and a total misuse of company expense credit cards.

I had been paying scant attention to any of this but that all changed when I suddenly realised that my investment capital had all gone, the overdraft for Integrity was at its limit and so I had nothing to show for my initial investment but shares in a very unprofitable company that was bound to cost me more money for no reward unless I did something. I woke up and started to worry.

However, while starting to grapple with these issues far too late in the day, events on the domestic front exploded into a frenzy of excited media reporting as Marianne and my marriage started to unravel to the intrigue of the public. It had become a press addiction for celebrity marital bust up stories to take the front pages, especially with the tabloid press.

Reading celebrity tittle tattle had become a national pastime and personal marital pain, due to the reported troubles regarding the crumbling marriages of the Wales' and Yorks', was a very popular subject. Moreover, as there were no new current stories on that front, Mr. Death's would have to do instead. Bad luck me, Marianne and our children.

However, I could hardly complain because like Diana I had courted the press, and if you lie down with dogs, you will get fleas.

We had all enjoyed a very happy skiing holiday together during that winter half-term. However, in the 2nd half of the winter term, my sexual addiction to Caroline's version of dangerous sex, by the introduction of handcuffs, riding crops and vibrators etc. increased and Marianne, somehow, I can't recall the details, found out about it.

Just before the end of term, I was due to fly out to Germany to complete filming the 2nd series of 'How Euro are You.' I took Lynn, my PA, and J with me. Howie was by now working with David Meakin at Prontac and was in Manchester. Dink stayed in Wilton Place with her nanny and Marianne went on a week's off-piste skiing trip to Courchevel in the French Alps with an instructor from Tigne.

When she returned, she refused to travel by car with the boys and me to Port Grimaud for Easter, so we took Betty, our longstanding housekeeper, and went without her. Was this the end of the line? I don't think either of us really thought it was. But we were wrong because once the press got hold of the story battle lines were drawn.

I have never known who informed the now defunct 'Today' newspaper. I have always suspected it was Pavilion Books as they were in financial trouble and really needed 'How to Become Dead Rich' to be a success – so this was a godsend for them given the public's need for these juicy intrusions into private lives and the resulting free publicity for the book. I have no evidence of this. But they had a motive.

Once, 'Today' got hold of the story, they went hot-foot round to Caroline's office, she was a PR executive in a Saatchi & Saatchi subsidiary, with an army of journalists and photographers. They caused so much disruption that her boss had to mediate and eventually a deal was reached where she agreed to walk down the street to be photographed saying, "No comment."

Marianne refused to answer her phone, and I was in France. However, the coverage of the story by 'Today' the next day somehow favoured Caroline and this understandably enraged Marianne. Never known for being slow off the mark the 'Daily Mail' saw an opportunity, got hold of Marianne and said they would like to tell her side of the story.

Consequently, the Femail part of the newspaper took her to the extraordinarily expensive Mosimann's restaurant in West Halkin Street, London SW1.

They lavished her with champagne, told her she was much better looking than Caroline and asked for her version of events. This resulted in a four-page article where Marianne began by explaining that her doctor's sister came to dinner with him but then stole her husband. The rest of it was mostly our life-story but once the death of Charles was mentioned, I was damned. So, neither Caroline nor I came out of it well. I don't suppose for a minute that we should have, but the result was only to pour petrol on the fire and now the whole of the national press was covering the story and taking sides.

By this time my mother was in the South of France with her husband Alan Baker ('Baker' as we affectionately called him). She brought her ubiquitous Daily Mail, which was 2 days old, and, like most women of a certain class and age, she believed every word in it was the gospel according to Paul Dacre. Then, over coffee with Baker, she glanced at the banner headline letting readers know what was inside that addition.

“God, Ivana Trump looks like Marianne” she said casually.

She opened the paper and then exclaimed to her horror, “It is Marianne!”

Some weeks previously, Pavilion Books had sent a photographer and his daughter assistant round to Wilton Place to capture a photograph worthy of being the cover shot of ‘How to Become Dead Rich’. He had taken many pictures in various locations including outside the London Stock Exchange, the Bank of England, the steps of Barings Bank and lastly some at home in Wilton Place.

The idea was that Pavilion would select one after consulting me, for the cover. As his daughter was packing away the lighting gear, he suddenly said, “Let’s try a more unusual and wacky shot – like you in a bubble bath with a glass of champagne. I saw one of George Best doing that,” he enthused.

“Yeah, so did I, but this is a serious business book. I have put a lot of effort into giving people simple business advice. I’m not sure,” I responded uncharacteristically sensibly given my current short supply of common sense.

“Well, let’s just do one and you can discuss which photograph is selected with Colin” he replied logically.

So, I prepared a pleasantly warm bubble bath but vetoed the champagne as being just too like the George Best photo. I also kept my knickers on as I got in – as his daughter was present. This turned out to be another sensible decision as we shall see.

In the end, a smartly dressed but not particularly good shot of me sitting on the steps of Barings Bank was chosen and I forgot about any of the others.

However, now that the Howard and Marianne break-up was hot news, the Sun, not used to being left out of such grubby tittle tattle and horrified that the Daily Mail seemed to be grabbing all the juicy headlines, decided to enter the scene from stage left.

Nina Myskow, a particularly unpleasant woman who seemed determined to allow poison to drip from her pen every time she wrote anything, had her own column in the Sun. Most people tended to agree that her negative and vindictive attitude stemmed from a loss of self-esteem caused by her own inability to lose weight.

Naturally, to have such a viper on the payroll suited the Sun, who could rely on her to stamp on any 'not invented here' stories that they had missed.

In a crushing dismissal of me as a vain, arrogant and attention-seeking man, who thought he was God's gift to women, she was able to dignify her opinion by writing it next to me pictured – yes you guessed – topless in a bubble bath.

The photographer had seen his chance of earning some extra cash, and the Sun had bought his picture. I complained bitterly to Pavilion, but they assured me of their innocence by telling me they had only bought the photograph to be used on the cover and that consequently, the others remained his property.

Naturally, the Sun article did nothing to dampen down the media fever, and people I had known since the flotation of Hodgson Holdings six years before were contacting me now to give them interviews. I turned these down in the main to try and deprive this media fire of oxygen.

However, I did agree to appear on Kay Burley's Sky News programme as we had been friends for 6 years and I believed that she liked me. She also promised to allow me to tell the story and be pleasant about everyone. I believed that this might not make matters worse and could even start peace and reconciliation talks with Marianne.

For I still loved her, and whatever the outcome, knew that we must not let our lives descend into the chaos that my parents had, as witnessed in Volume I, in the early 1970s.

Moreover, while I realised that I was a terrible man as a sexually unfaithful husband, that did not detract one iota from the fact that I wanted to defend her and the children from this media tornado that I, and no one else, had brought upon our family.

I duly appeared on her show, and Kay was as good as her word.

Now comes the book launch at the Savoy Hotel in London. There were more journalists and photographers in the private function room than guests. I had to push my way past them to get into the room.

I was horrified by the number of people there who had professed to be my friend over the glorious 'Mr Death' years to get an exclusive, who were now there to witness and describe my family's pain without any compassion or thought for my children.

I had banned Caroline from attending the occasion and let Marianne's invitation stand. The latter duly turned up looking most beautiful. My mother was also there and most supportive of her son as she was photographed several times being kissed by me with a copy of the 'book' in her hand.

However, for most of the rest of the time, I sat at a desk in the corner of the room, accompanied by my ever-present stoic supporter, the nine-year-old Jamieson, as I signed books bought by invited guests.

John Gunn was there too and was excited for Hodgson & Partners, as he thought that he had never seen such a media circus since the Beatles. He was not that far off the mark, when a comment by a journalist made Marianne cry and the room exploded as the flash guns of the heartless paparazzi popped to ensure that they captured the moment so that the UK public could see her distress while eating their boiled eggs at breakfast the next morning.

These moments ensured that I finally understood that being a slave to publicity was not worth it, and that I would banish any such intrusion in future.

Of course, I could not deny that I had had a great ride with the UK media, and like most others, I had really enjoyed the ego trip and thigh-stroking acclaim, but as I had told a journalist earlier, I knew that you had to get off the media train before it crashed. I hadn't and was now paying the price.

## This Life In Death

The next day Marianne's tears featured everywhere in the press. I had tried to pour oil on these troubled waters by agreeing to give an interview to the 'supportive' Today to try and draw a line under the whole matter before the launch.

Today duly produced a largely supportive and conciliatory article under the headline, 'I May be Dead Wealthy, but My Dream Marriage is Over.' However, it still didn't quite hit the right note with quotes like, 'The forty-two-year-old suntanned blond with rock star good looks makes a very unlikely undertaker.' This was bound to be disliked by a lot of men, infuriate most funeral directors and horrify sections of the female community, especially the feminists who were starting to see me as a typical misogynist who thought women were only good for one thing.

On the other hand, it did state that my children were the most important thing in my life and that my greatest achievement was having married Marianne and having them.

Now I was starting to function more like Mr. Death again while killing off this irresponsible 'rock star' who was approaching middle-age but behaving like an eighteen-year-old spoilt child.

Nonetheless, the damage to my marriage and my family savings had already been done and it would take a lot of work to restore stability in both cases. However, before I could set about putting both right, I was to be hit by another broadside. I had paid the capital gains tax on the sale of my PHKI shares and invested the balance in an offshore assurance bond held in trust for my children. It had been taken out with Hafnia Life by Richard Jennings, my financial services advisor. Now Hafnia hit the news as being in financial trouble. I got the news on a Friday night and spent the weekend trying to understand how all that I had worked for since 1971 was now at risk and how everything that had been so good had gone so sour so quickly.

Hafnia was saved by Canada Life. Phew! Next, I persuaded John Gunn and Ricky Cressman to close Hodgson & Partners and even got the lease surrendered on our London Offices. Then, I refused to fund Hodgson Integrity any further. This brought it down but unfortunately, due to the cross guarantee with the bank, took Prontac with it. I bought the rights to the software and gave it to the franchisees so that they could continue in business. The hard-working successful ones were grateful; the useless ones were not. All this cost me close to £1million and I became the Times's quote of the week when I announced in an interview that, 'I was jolly cross' about it all.

There had been a lot of shit hitting the fan all at once. I knew that it was all my own fault, and I had to act fast and with my old determination. I was not sleeping; I was very homesick and felt very stressed. However, I had started the fight back and I was going to see it through – now older and wiser than the man who thought that he could organise the Prince's Trust better than anyone else.

A few weeks later, I took the two boys to our Dorset home in preparation for a short sailing holiday on Fat Girl to the Isle of Wight so we could watch Cowes Week. We went without Caroline, who remained at work in London. On board would be them, a friend of Howard's, and his nineteen-year-old sister who would be the 'galley girl.'

We went to an up-market Tesco in Westbourne on the first afternoon and bought provisions to take on board the following day. We all got on well and I felt relaxed for the first time in months. I had missed family life with my children terribly and was delighted to have Howie and J with me.

We then had dinner and while I helped do the washing up the three boys went off to the cinema. I retired for the night as we were to make an early start the next morning. I ran the water in the large circular bath and got in. I looked up and to my surprise saw "the galley girl" dressed in a white towelling gown standing in the doorway to the ensuite bathroom. She smiled, slipped the gown over her shoulders and as it fell to the floor to reveal the perfect figure that only nineteen-year-olds, and then only some nineteen-year-olds, have. She smiled.

"Can I join you?" she enquired politely, as she bent one knee slightly to go on tip toe with that foot as she placed her hands on her hips.

For once, I had not invited this latest potential dance with trouble, but nor was I going to turn her away. I nodded and made way for her to get in next to me.

Later that night, once the three lads were safely asleep, J in my bed as usual, I even crept downstairs to her room for a dessert course. My desire for older women had clearly changed now in favour of younger models.

Next, we were off to France for the main summer holiday. Marianne and I decided to take the children together. We slept in separate bedrooms but made a good fist of getting on well for the children's sake – and for her wonderful parents. There was also the bonus that I got to spend time with Dinky as she obviously lived with her mother due to her age. Caroline flew out to spend a week with me on Red Rose Speedway. The sex was exciting but when not engaged in that I was increasingly homesick for my children and the family life that I had been seeking when it had been ripped from my bosom by my own parents' divorce and finally had ended a blissful childhood.

September saw me back in London and the ravages of 1992 were really taking their hold on my mental health. I visited Anthony. He prescribed a drug called imipramine. Now I was becoming a junky, my sex drive even dried up, and my speech became slow. I met Colin Webb in October to discuss 'The Walrus was Paul' book. He took one look at me and was shocked. I was sat in Langan's Brasserie, by the Ritz in London, with a baggy flat cap on my head, dark glasses hiding my eyes and doing a good impression of John Lennon with one-word flat answers.

He said, "What the fuck are you on Howard? Whatever it is throw it down the toilet." He went on to tell me that if he couldn't be with his family on his last evening in this earth, he would spend it with me and Seb Coe, whom I had met with Colin as he published both of us. "So come on Howard. You have got to change all of this, before you sink any further."

Unlike me, I hardly even replied as I hid under my cap and behind my dark glasses on a rainy Friday lunchtime in late October. However, when I got back to Caroline's Earls Court apartment, I tipped the tablets down the toilet. I had decided on a plan on the way there in the taxi.

I was due to fly to Egypt to cruise the Nile that evening. I would go and have a final week's orgy of very dominated sex but leave her on my return. This was premeditated and most unfair on her but the only way out that I could see of saving myself from a nervous breakdown caused by my own stupidity as I had descended from the determined and creative heights of Hodgson Holdings through the stress of PHKI, and fun of making TV shows to this drug induced state and having lost a £1million on the way.

Amazingly, I took comfort from this plan and was able to enjoy the pleasures of the late October sunshine on the Nile, the wonders of ancient civilisation on the banks, riding an Egyptian stallion for fifteen miles across the desert, and, with no drugs to hinder my sexual appetite, the joys of being handcuffed to a bedhead by Miss Whiplash.

I returned to London, refreshed, renewed and with the 'old' Howard head back on my shoulders. I left Caroline's apartment, but she didn't leave my life altogether for another two years. Our affair had done her a lot of damage too over those torrid six months.

Now she wouldn't believe that it was over. I knew that I must have some compassion and sympathy with her as the affair had been very intense and I had been a very willing participant in those wild games.

However, the real me was back in charge and a purposeful fightback had begun to restore order and recover wealth. Therefore, I now felt able to put the disastrous 1992 behind me – with lessons hopefully learnt for the future.

## This Life In Death

Chapter IV

Back to Basics

1993 – 1995

In late 1990 'The blessed Margaret' had been ousted in a nasty coup d'etat by unlikely bedfellows from both the left and right wings of the Conservative Party. As a result, John Major had become both leader of the Tory Party and Prime Minister.

I had met Mrs Thatcher just once, which was after I had infuriated her by mildly criticising her economic policy in an article in the 'Director' magazine and just before her resignation as Prime Minister. I considered her then, and still do, to be only second to Winston Spencer Churchill as Britain's greatest political leader. However, as a person to meet she wasn't immensely likeable. Major, on the other hand, will not be recorded by historians as one of Britain's greatest ever leaders, but was an extremely decent and likeable man.

Indeed, out of the eight Prime Ministers I have met he ranks first as a pleasant human being, whereas Mrs Thatcher only comes fifth as a likeable individual to chat to. Eighth is Edward Heath. I found him to be pompous and distant. Seventh is Tony Blair. He was an intelligent young shadow minister when I first met him, but he had had his moral compass removed by the time I met him again as Prime Minister. Sixth, Gordon Brown. I suspected he had more moral fibre than Blair, but like Heath, he was awkward, and his fingernails were filthy. Fifth, Thatcher, who didn't talk to you but over your head to the rest of the room as if she was giving a speech. Fourth, Boris Johnson. He was immensely entertaining, but like Blair, you would think twice about buying a second-hand car from him. Third, James Callaghan. He was warm hearted and pleasant – like everyone's favourite uncle or grandfather. Second, David Cameron, a genial man, good father and Aston Villa supporter. Like me, he is left-handed and that ticks another box. First, John Major. He talks to you, never at you, and we always talked about cricket.

## This Life In Death

In 1992, I sent a copy of 'How to Become Dead Rich' to both Thatcher and Major. John Major immediately sent me a letter from 10 Downing Street, to thank me and promised to read it while on holiday. I doubt he did but it was a nice thought. Thatcher had not responded after a month. I wondered if she had received it. I telephoned her office to find out. I was told that they had it and were reading it to see if I had written anything about the former Prime Minister that they might wish to sue me over. I put the phone down completely amazed that she was still smarting over my 'Director Magazine' article from two years earlier.

Then in 1992 against the odds and all pollsters' predictions the 'galloping Major' won the Tories a fourth consecutive term in government. He promised his government would get 'back to basics'. This was exactly what I needed to do too.

xxxxxxx

In the summer of that year, and before I had determined to leave Caroline and sort myself out, I got a call from a BBC radio journalist, who worked at Radio 4. His name was Nigel Cassidy. He asked me if I would like to become a permanent member of a new panel game about business to be aired that autumn. He didn't mention then, but I later discovered, that I hadn't been their first choice. Richard Branson had been and had accepted but then changed his mind. On learning this, a senior executive at the 'Beeb' had then ordered, "Get the other long haired one – you know the funeral bloke." I accepted and went into the BBC to discuss the show, which we did, but only after a long whinge by the production team about staff parking places. How typically 'Beeb' I thought as I waited patiently.

The new programme, named 'The Board Game', was to run for a decade. It was recorded in front of a live audience and was wonderful fun to make.

Nigel Cassidy was the droll quiz master, another BBC business journalist, Peter Day, who was also very funny, was a panel member, as were the clever Chairman of the investment fund Hermes, Alastair Ross Goobey, the pretty Jeanette Rutherford, and me.

Initially, I was partnered with Alastair, but because we poked fun at each other, the production team decided this was an entertaining feature and the teams were changed so that Peter was my new partner and Jeanette teamed up with Alastair.

Occasionally and after several successful series, if Peter was on an assignment or holiday, Adrian Chiles would be my partner. The first time he appeared on the show he asked me if I had a funny story to tell that week. I had become the outspoken comedian of the programme. Indeed, a chap once stopped me on the King's Rd one day and told me how much he enjoyed my outrageous comments and asked me if I minded never winning the game week after week. I was amazed by this as I had won as many as I had lost. He obviously thought of me as being on the show as just the 'court jester.'

However, on this occasion, I told my joke to Adrian as the audience were taking their seats. He roared with laughter and then repeated it as he was introduced by Nigel on air. Not a nice thing to do – but then he was a West Bromwich Albion fan and so I should have expected him to behave like a cad. I never got caught out like that again.

Over the years, I gave Alastair as good as I got. However, I can't recall anything I said which got as big a laugh from the audience as his, "If you want a really rare copy of Howard's book get one that isn't signed."

However, in the first series, I did get a burst of applause from the audience for an answer to a question.

"What has been in the news this week, which is fat, rubbery and tasteless?" was the question on the card read by Nigel. I immediately buzzed.

"Howard Hodgson", said Nigel so that the folks listening on their radios knew who would be answering.

"Nina Myskow."

The audience roared and burst into applause. I was delighted. I had paid her back for her bitchy Sun article about me. In fact, I was so delighted that I was to answer any question about anything that didn't sound pleasant over the next decade with "Nina Myskow" and it became a long-standing joke. Years later I went to Debbie Moore's birthday party and Ms. Myskow was there too. We didn't speak.

On the first programme of the last series in 2002, I was shocked by Alastair's appearance. He had terminal cancer. I was very sad because I really liked and admired him. I just felt choked and couldn't take the 'mickey' out of him. Neil Koenig, the programme's producer, called me after the show and asked me why I hadn't responded to Alastair's taunts with my usual barbs. I explained that I couldn't take piss out of a very sick man that I was so fond of. Neil explained that Alastair wanted everything to be as normal. In the second show we returned to our usual format and last series finished on a high. It had run a decade, would air mid-week at 18:30, immediately after the national and international news and just before the world's oldest soap, The Archers at 19:00, when people were driving home from work, and listening to their car radio.

It became one of the station's most popular shows with up to 500,000 listeners. Thank you Nigel et al for asking me, and thank you Richard for turning the BBC down. I have very happy memories of every series – even when Adrian Chiles appeared.

xxxxxxx

If, as 1992 became 1993, my 'back to basics' phase was to be a success, I needed to sort out my domestic and business affairs with as much ruthless drive and determination as I had applied to saving Hodgson & Sons Ltd in 1975. Of course, the mountain I had faced then was harder to climb. However, it had been my father's mess that I was clearing up then and now it was my own, which, as I had once told Alan Sugar, was the hardest mess of any mess to clean up.

I told Marianne we should try very hard to become friends as we had to run a company together called, 'Bringing up the Children plc.' To her eternal credit, as I had caused her so much pain and anguish, she agreed. We decided that it was a bad idea to give our marriage a fourth or even fifth chance as we would doubtless end up back where we had got to. She accepted that I loved her and couldn't live without the children. I accepted that I was unlikely to be faithful and there lay the fault.

So, I rented a flat round the corner from Wilton Place in Lowndes Square and J often stayed the night there and I would pop home to take Dinky to nursery school most mornings.

We decided not to divorce but that I would give her a financial settlement in lieu of a divorce. I signed over the Wilton Place and Port Grimaud homes to her and agreed to give her £3,000-a-month to look after the children. In addition, I would also pay for all school fees. This was a generous settlement. However, it came at a price. Howard, now over eighteen, could do as he pleased, but I wanted my two younger children with me every weekend. This was tough on Marianne, because it meant that I got all the quality time. However, I had given her everything she had asked for and so it was agreed. Moreover, I knew that, if I wasn't going to slip back into that awful malaise of 1992, I needed to have my children with me.

So, Marianne and I made peace and became friends. She has remained a wonderful and loyal friend ever since. Not long after this, she and Michael got back together, and he moved into Wilton Place with my blessing. We have spent almost every Christmas, and most family birthdays together since and usually have at least one holiday together every year.

With stability restored on the home front I now turned to my financial affairs. I had already taken steps to stop the damaging outflow of cash caused by Hodgson Partners and Hodgson Integrity. However, I knew if I wasn't going to slip back into a life of 'wine, women and song' I needed to do something. We already know about the 'women' but, since giving up smoking, 'wine' was also becoming an issue. Therefore, I needed other goals to distract me and that meant working.

## This Life In Death

I contacted my old friend Chris Callaway. He had by now moved from Capel Cure Myers to Coopers & Lybrand. We had lunch together in Beauchamp Place at the famous San Lorenzo restaurant run by my friends Lorenzo and Mara.

I told him that I wanted him to find me a quoted vehicle so that I could build another empire. We decided that this would have to be a conglomerate as I still had restricted covenants re funeral directing following my sale of PHKI shares. I didn't mind this as I still felt exhausted by the awful PHKI experience.

He agreed to put Coopers' fees on the 'clock' which meant I would not be charged until we got the vehicle. This was a great act of faith, especially as I had been so undisciplined during the last year. It was to raise a lot of eyebrows at Coopers, but he never told me that. He was a true friend and has remained one ever since.

Chris and a senior manager called Simon Hawes started to look for businesses, and preferably quoted companies, which were for sale. We would then go to visit them. It was an exacting task, and we were to spend hours on trains going all over the UK.

We worked hard and we played hard when we were off duty. We had a purpose, and we had fun. Moreover, with my marital problems sorted out, I no longer had this shocking conflict going on in my head when it came to women. My plan was to have many but get involved with none. This worked and I had peace of mind on this front for the first time in years.

One trip we made was to Manchester to visit Coopers' corporate finance department, where a pretty northern lass called Joanne Hartley had a list of companies for sale which she wanted to discuss with us. We went up the night before and stayed in the Britannia Hotel. After dinner, we went to the bar for a drink and met a group of girls. Chris soon left and went to bed. Simon and I stayed chatting. To my amazement, I heard him tell a girl, whom we knew as Mavis 'with the watery eye' (because this is what she had), that he was a forty-two-year-old funeral director. In fact, he was a thirty-something-year-old corporate finance advisor. He explained to me, at breakfast the next day, that if the Mr. Death tag had worked for me, he thought that he would also give it a go. It hadn't done him much good apparently.

I had entertained her buxom Mancunian girlfriend, who was married but enjoying a girls' night out with Mavis and co, in my bedroom where she delighted in the fact that I was the first man she had ever seen naked without a beer belly. She just kept staring at it and saying "Eee, that's fine."

According to her, all Manchester men had beer bellies from twenty onwards.

While this was going on Mavis had insisted on sitting on the floor outside my room, in the hotel corridor, waiting for her friend, and demanded that Simon kept his distance.

Simon was a very likeable guy; I was a bachelor once more and he was in the throes of a nasty divorce. We started to hang out together. One night Chris, Simon, another Cooper's client and I had dinner in Belgravia. After dinner the client wanted to go to the very up market club called 'Miranda's' in Carnaby Street near Soho. Chris went home and the three of us went on there without him.

Once there, the client ordered buckets of champagne, and we were joined by three hostesses. After at least three or perhaps four bottles had been drunk, Simon disappeared for a few minutes and returned with a slightly drunken smile to announce that Coopers had paid the bill. We all thanked him.

About twenty minutes later he disappeared again but this time he didn't return. I volunteered to find him. I did in the gent's toilet where he was crawling over the sinks and shouting, "Sacked. Sacked, I'll be sacked in the morning."

"What on earth are you talking about?" I asked.

"I didn't have permission to pay that bill" he said with a look of desperation in his eyes. I calmed him down and said that I would plead on his behalf with Chris tomorrow.

Eventually, Simon and I left with our escorts in tow to go to the Eden Hotel on the Cromwell Rd. My companion, who looked like Linda

McCartney, and I retired and were soon in bed. However, before the fun had started, there was a knock on the door. It was Linda's mate. Apparently, Simon had gone off the whole idea as he was too worried about what was going to happen tomorrow when he had to report having spent more than £500 in Miranda's. I told her to come in and join us instead. She did.

Simon got off with a reprimand and was told to repay the exact amount to Coopers by his boss Tony Bartlett. "If you want to go out playing with the big boys Simon, you do so with your own money," he had lectured.

I talked to Simon about sharing a small mews house together. He declined saying that he would die if he lived at my pace in the fast lane and warned that I could be dead before I saw fifty if I didn't slow down.

However, the idea of a house share became irrelevant as he was soon promoted to being a partner of Coopers and moved to Milton Keynes. This gave Chris a problem as he certainly didn't want to do all the leg work himself and so he needed an assistant.

He told me that I was entitled to have a senior manager as his assistant, but he had selected only a manager. Did I mind? I said no, having no idea how this was to affect my life. So, enter Christine Mary Pickles stage left in the spring of 1993. We will hear a lot more about her on all fronts later.

However, for now my 'back to basics' plan was working. Marianne and I were living in friendly harmony, the children were happy, I was working hard and drinking less than half what I had consumed in 1992 as I tried to fight my depression.

Moreover, as a bachelor, I could have a harem of around ten women that I could have dinner and casual sex with by seeing each only circa once a fortnight. This suited me very well and so I developed this routine in the week and would then invite one girl down to Dorset each weekend.

The children would sleep with me, and they would sleep in one of the spare rooms – usually the 'Chinese' room, where I would visit them, because it was next to mine and I would hear the children if they woke up.

Davinia never thought any of these girls were as good looking as her mother and would tell them so. Jamieson liked them if they played cricket with him and didn't if they didn't. Therefore, he didn't like Debbie Moore but loved her secretary.

In early March, a London stockbroker called Clive McGuire brought Chris Callaway a USM listed company that sold duty free products. The largest shareholder and CEO was his brother Bruce. The company was called, after the Gatwick call sign, LGW.

An offer of £9 million was accepted and Coopers threw a celebration lunch for their corporate finance team in Champagne Charlie's, which was a local wine bar near their offices overlooking the Thames and not far from Trafalgar Square. It was situated underground, with low arches and was dimly lit.

I sat next to Chris and Simon, who was just about to leave for Milton Keynes. We could hardly see the people at the other end of the table. Over coffee, I made a speech to thank everyone and especially Chris and Simon. Chris then asked me what I intended to do besides build LGW. This took me by surprise and without really thinking, I blurted out that I might consider finding a new wife and settling down to have a couple of children.

"Don't you think you are a bit old for that?" came a female voice from the far end of the table. I smiled but was not amused as I was only just forty-three and had never been accused of being too old for anything before – except by Joe Jordan and that had resulted in the birth of Davinia.

"You won't have to see her again" whispered Chris.

"No. She's entitled to her opinion. It's fine," I whispered back calmly as I peered into the mirky light to see who had made the comment. It was Christine Mary Pickles, and I marked her card there and then.

However, the celebration was premature, because within a week the SFO announced that it had received a complaint from a group of franchisees and was to investigate the closure of Prontac. This could lead to the directors being struck off and I was included in the investigation as a 'shadow' director because I owned all the shares.

The publicity was bad and all over the national press. But nothing was half as bad as my old enemy Jason Nisse's article in the 'Independent.' This was just the opportunity he had been waiting for. He was to remain a thorn in my side until I bumped into him at a cocktail party in 1997, when I quietly informed him that if he ever wrote another nasty article about me, I would let it be known that he was persecuting me because I had turned down his sexual advances when we had had dinner together in Rules Restaurant years earlier. We had had dinner, but he had not made any such advances. However, I suspected he was gay, and I was desperate to get him off my back. Either way, it did the trick.

However, then in March 1993, this was a severe set-back and it seemed to me that my idiot abandon of 1991 and 1992 was going to haunt me forever – and it did on and off for several years. Hardly surprisingly, Bruce McGuire changed his mind and called the deal off.

So now Chris and I had to start all over again but this time with a new team member – Christine Mary Pickles.

It was to be a set-back but thanks to Chris and his faith in me that was all that it was. Amazingly, he managed to convince Coopers to let him and CMP work on my case full time and with fees still going on the clock. This saved me and allowed my recovery to continue despite the terrible publicity.

Lots of people wrote to me lovely supportive letters, including one from my old chum Dennis Amiss in which he wrote, 'You can't keep a good man down.'

I took Marianne out to dinner at Langan's. Kay Burley was there and sympathised with me on her way to the ladies. As we were leaving a party of four asked us if we would join them for a drink. Marianne didn't but I stayed. They were all nice people. They had recognised me and wanted me to know that they had made a lot of money on Hodgson shares and that I should not let Jason Nisse get me down.

# This Life In Death

They were up in London to see a show, lived in The Cotswolds and invited me to a party there that weekend.

Marianne had the children on Saturday night, and I caught a train. It was a splendid house; they were lovely people; and they introduced me to a remarkably pretty and smart young lady. She was a twenty-three year old head-hunter, she drove a Porsche, and she liked me.

In the early hours, as people were either leaving or going to bed, she asked the hostess if she could make up a bed for us on the floor, in front of the fire in the drawing room.

It was very easy to make love to her as she was very attractive, very gentle and very attentive. Eventually we fell asleep. However, I woke up to her gently licking 'William.' Well, that was until I opened my eyes to see her fast asleep on the pillow next to me. What! I raised the covers and looked down. The family's labrador was the culprit.

When I awoke a second time, it was breakfast time. I had a black coffee, called a cab, made my apologies and made a dash for London. Didn't I like the girl? I did very much, and I was to see her again. Didn't I like the family? I thought they were wonderful. Well, why then? I had woken up stricken with a severe attack of homesickness for the children.

As the publicity died down, Chris, Christine and I re-started the search for a listed vehicle. My goodness we had fun travelling the length and breadth of the land looking for companies. Indeed, Christine was later to comment that she could not believe that she was being paid to have such fun.

One such trip took us to the Potteries to look at a dinner service manufacturer. We had a meeting with the management in their board room before embarking on a trip round the factory. I had to take a call on my mobile before we had finished and left the group. When the call finished, I couldn't see them so went back to the boardroom, but no one was there. I set off to find them, couldn't and so returned to the boardroom again. Now they were there. We thanked them and said our farewells before leaving to catch the train back to London.

Once on the train, Christine opened her briefcase to find items belonging to Chris inside. This prompted Chris to do the same. To his horror he found items belonging to her in his case. Both were appalled that the pottery folk had been riffling through their private documents while they had been inspecting the factory. The more they talked about it the angrier they became. In the end Chris decided that Coopers should make a formal complaint. He was about to call Tony Bartlett on his mobile when I let on that I had returned to the boardroom on my own and swapped the contents of their bags!

One lady friend that I always found to be intelligent as well as very attractive was Debbie Moore. We had known each other since the heady days of the 1980s, when she was famous for being the first woman to float a business on the floor of the Stock Exchange and I became the last man to.

One day we met for lunch in San Lorenzo and as Mara was showing us to our table a voice called out, “Hi Debs.” We turned round and saw the celebrated actor Terence Stamp waving. He was sat at a table at the bottom of the stairs, where Mara put all her star guests so they could be seen. This was good for them as well as the restaurant. As a result, there was always a group of paparazzi outside and Lorenzo’s was really a place to see and be seen.

At the table with Mr. Stamp were an array of other diners. These included Jacqueline Bisset, Gloria Hunniford, whom I had met previously, her famous photographer friend, Terry O’Neill, and at the head of the table Roger Moore.

As we approached, Gloria’s man leapt to his feet, “Hi Debs. Didn’t know you were dating Kenny Dalglish.”

Terence and co laughed and I bristled. Sir Roger smiled at me and beckoned for me to take a seat next to him.

“I know you are not Kenny Dalglish. You are that funeral chappie,” he said in that rich and charming voice which he had put to such good effect in the ‘Saint’ and ‘Bond’ parts which had made him recognisable anywhere in the world.

We chatted and then he asked me, since I was no longer a funeral director, but an entrepreneur, if I did any public speaking. I replied that I did.

"Might I give you some advice?"

"Please do, sir," I replied with genuine respect.

"When you get up to speak, make the audience laugh within the first ten seconds and make them laugh at you. That way, those who want to take the piss out of you can't, because you have already taken it out of yourself, and those that didn't, think you are the nicest guy on the planet."

This was excellent advice, gratefully accepted by me and put to good effect over the next years, as I derived a decent income from public speaking.

Many years later, in the same restaurant, one rainy and cold winter's day, I walked in and there was Sir Roger, having lunch with his third wife and her daughter.

I went up and announced, "You won't remember me."

"I do. You're the funeral chappie" replied the distinctive voice.

"I just wanted to thank you for the speech making advice. I put it to good effect," I said in gratitude.

"Where's my commission then?"

"I gave it to UNICEF."

"Good answer, young man," he smiled.

When he died of cancer about a decade later, the world really did lose a James Bond superstar personality, who was just as impressive in person as he was on the screen.

It was also at San Lorenzo that Mara introduced me to Eric Clapton. We were both there dining alone. She asked me to talk to Eric, who had lost a son, like I had a decade earlier. She thought it might help him.

Eric was understandably seriously suffering. We chatted and as I drank more red wine I seemed to lose all inhibitions and announced that Macca was a better blues singer than him.

He looked up and said, "Perhaps, but I'm a better fucking guitarist than he will ever be."

Eric Clapton recovered, and having managed to keep off the drink and drugs, became an even more likeable bloke, who we will hear more about later.

Normally, weekends meant a trip to my house in Canford Cliffs, Dorset. However, on one weekend I stayed in London as Simon Draycott had asked me to attend a banquet at the Temple in the city opposite the law courts. I took Debbie as my partner. Marianne and Michael were also invited, along with other guests to make up a table of ten.

Marianne and Michael were on the opposite side of this large round table to Debbie and me. However, this did not stop Marianne from sniping at Debbie from the moment she sat down. Debbie was restrained and did not get provoked. Eventually, another guest said to Marianne, "Look love, I've come out to have a nice time. Put a sock in it."

I whispered to Debbie, "Look I'm really sorry about this."

She replied, "That's OK. I'm going to fuck you tonight and she isn't."

So, despite this little episode, the summer of '93 was a very pleasant one. Chris, Christine and I had an enjoyable working week, which was then followed by weekends in Dorset with two or three of my children, a different woman each weekend to have fun with and sometimes other house guests.

Simon Draycott, who had left his wife, was ever present and his eldest daughter, Natasha, would often come too. We sailed in the day and partied at night. I didn't feel guilty any more and I was happy.

Then the SFO decided that I didn't have a case to answer after all, which was a load off my mind, and that made me even happier. I was on the road to recovery and there was nothing Jason Nisse could do about it.

xxxxxxx

After the Prontac closure I had sent Howard to work in Aix-en-Provence with his Uncle Alex. If I was England's 'Mr. Death,' Alex was France's 'Mr. Rent-a-Car.' His business, which he had opened in the early 1980s was now starting to take off and would, in time, be sold for an absolute fortune. But even by then he had already come a long way from the lad who had driven on funerals with me in the '70s.

Alex worked Howard hard six days-a-week washing and delivering cars. This did him no harm. He lived with his grandparents in Pertuis and after a wonderful dinner cooked by Raymonde would go to bed early to listen to the new McCartney album 'Off the Ground', which he still knows every track of by heart today over thirty years later.

Marianne and I took him, with the two younger children, to France for a brief holiday before leaving him there. I was very sad to say goodbye to him at Nice airport, as I would love to spend every day of my life with my children, but at least I knew that he was in safe hands.

Meanwhile, once back in Lowndes Square, I was surprised to discover that I had collected a new secret admirer. One Friday afternoon, I was preparing my toiletries for a weekend in Dorset, when my doorbell rang. I answered it to see a large lady in a pale blue summer dress. She announced, in a strong Swedish accent, that she was my neighbour. I invited her in and made her a cup of coffee. She sat down and while drinking it explained that she knew me better than I imagined.

"How come?" I enquired.

"Because you do your exercises every morning at 7:00 in your bedroom stark naked and I can see you from my bed."

I had no idea and taken by surprise only managed "Gosh."

"So, I thought I would come round, introduce myself and ask if I could take a closer look."

Naturally, being me and a psychiatrist's dream, I obliged. However, I quickly realised that this would only lead me back to another Caroline Ashe relationship of dominated sex and so this should not be repeated, whatever the temptation.

As a result of this and the fact that Caroline would arrive at midnight occasionally, uninvited, and ring the bell and bang on the door for over an hour which would wake J, if he was staying, meant that I determined not to renew the lease and moved out when it ended in August.

In the meantime, the search for a listed company continued at full speed ahead. Nothing had been found as August approached and with it the holiday season and I was due to go with J to France, collect Howard in Aix, before departing on Red Rose Speedway on a trip to Cannes and beyond to meet up with Simon and his two daughters, Natasha and Charlie, to spend long days swimming, having a little food at lunch and dinner but a lot of rosé wine at both.

Before, they caught up with us, we stopped the first night in Cannes. It was unbelievably hot and Red Rose had no air-conditioning. We had a torrid night sweating while attempting to sleep on deck.

Caroline was staying at her brother's girlfriend's air-conditioned apartment in Juan Les Pins. The boys begged me to contact her and see if we could stay there. I said I thought this was a bad idea in view of the stalking and that it was unfair on her too and so declined. The next night was worse, none of us slept. The following morning, I gave in and picked up my mobile to call her. I was prostituting myself for the boys.

Once with Simon we left for Cannes, anchored between the islands, and as already reported, I burst an ear drum recovering Natasha's gym shoe. After a visit to a doctor and a prescription for lots of completely useless drugs, we moved on to Cap Ferrat.

I had been receiving calls from Chris Callaway for three or four days; Clive McGuire and his partner Dennis Bailey had found a USM quoted brewery that was 'hot to trot.' It looked likely a deal could be struck immediately.

We were having lunch in the port at Cap Ferrat, when my mobile went. It was Chris, I wandered away from the table and up on to the flat roof above the restaurant.

"Congratulations, Mr. CEO." he said.

I thanked and thanked and thanked him. I put the phone down and standing alone on that roof burst into tears. I was on my way back.

I was to fly home in two day's time, a Sunday, to have dinner with Chris, his lovely wife Jacqui, my lawyer David Mandell and his pretty girlfriend Jo on Sunday evening, before officially signing the deal on the Monday or Tuesday and doing all the press interviews before flying back to France.

This meant I would have to billet Howard and Jamieson with Sami and Raymonde. Howard didn't mind. J did and cried solidly for the whole time I was away.

I had to buy a business class seat on the flight out of Nice on that Sunday afternoon as all tourist class seats were sold. It was 1D. There was no one in 1C. The usual queue for the 'loo' formed after the hostesses had cleared away the meal. I noticed a very pretty and petite girl in the queue. I invited her to sit down in 1C while she was waiting. She did. She was French but worked for the British Coal Board.

She was wearing a nice little red camisole top with a white bra underneath. When she came out of the toilet the bra had gone. I invited her to take a lift in my taxi from Heathrow back into London and took her to tea at the Ritz, where I had decided to book a room. I didn't think it was right to invite her to this dinner with Callaway and Mandell. Moreover, I had intended to invite Christine, as she had worked very hard on the case since March, but she was on holiday in Portugal with her boyfriend.

I asked the young lady to excuse me while I went to see if the Ritz had a room. She asked me if I would like to stay at her place instead. I accepted and after the dinner took a cab there. She was pretty, funny and very delicate. It was a beautiful finish to a memorable night.

The next morning, I dropped her off at the Coal Board offices near Victoria, before visiting my new doctor, Peter Wheeler, in Sloane Street, about my ear drum. He stood over his wastepaper bin and having read each packet of French drugs one at a time dispatched them into the bin with the word, "Rubbish." He then gave me a course of antibiotics which had me feeling much better within the hour.

Next, I was off to the offices of Coopers & Lybrand in Charing Cross. I was determined to look after those who had supported me, believed in me and stood up for me over my poor performance in 1992.

I had already leaked the story to my old friend John Jay so that his Sunday Times article could forecast the news in advance of the release. This was to infuriate his rival, Jeff Randall, later to become the Sky News business editor and that was to cause me a problem in the future, when John had retired, and I needed Jeff's help.

The company I was becoming CEO of was Hoskins Brewery PLC, a small brewer in Leicester which boasted a decent micro-brewery but only a small estate of four pubs, one at the brewery itself; one in Loughborough, which did very well when the elite athletic students were there, but not when they went home; one opposite the Trent Bridge cricket and Notts Forest football grounds in Nottingham, which did do extremely well but was very small; and lastly, a complete stinker. This was an old-fashioned long bar saloon, as if out of 'Peaky Blinders' in Coventry, which was completely 'out of time and touch' with the 1990s.

However, the important thing was that Hoskins was quoted and that is all we were really interested in – although I immediately determined to get to grips with the brewing business as I was not going to allow another 1992 to happen to me now that I had been granted a second chance by God and Chris Callaway.

The Brewery was founded in 1875. It had survived despite a chequered career but in 1991 the business reported a sizeable loss of £167,000 and the share price fell to 40p from 120p. As a result, they were unable to buy 18 pubs from Bass.

## This Life In Death

A new business, T Hoskins was formed in 1992 by Barrie Hoare and his brother Robert, who together controlled nearly 30% of the stock. The resident brewer was a decent one called Nigel Burdett, who brewed an excellent 5.5% proof winter warmer called 'Old Nigel'.

Many combinations of hostile take-overs or recommended mergers were either fought off or considered over the next year, but all failed to be realised. Hence the Hoar brothers were happy to be offered this 'Howard Hodgson' lifeline and a deal was struck very quickly.

When the news broke, it seemed as if Mr. Death hadn't been away from the financial pages for nearly three years, as all the articles were positive, kind and seemed genuinely pleased to see me back on their pages, even those who were a little miffed that John Jay had, as usual, got the story days in advance of anyone else.

Amazingly, the Independent was also factual and fair, probably because the story was not reported by Jason Nisse:

'HOWARD Hodgson, a well-known City figure in the 1980s, has staged a management buy-in at Hoskins Brewery, the pub and brewery company beset by boardroom rows and shareholder unrest.

The deal took just a week to piece together and was brokered by an un-named City institution aware of his plans to buy into a quoted company.

'I had to come off holiday in France to do the deal,' said Mr Hodgson, who bowed out of the PFG Hodgson Kenyon International funeral business in 1991, with over £6m in his pocket.

For £715,000, the new management is gaining control of a company sitting on £850,000 of cash and a stated asset value of £3.2m.

Mr Hodgson's management team includes James Roe, deputy chairman of Kleeneze, Shaun Dowling, former director of Guinness, and Bill Caldwell, a former partner at Price Waterhouse.

A finance director, who will also have to oversee the operations of future acquisitions, is being sought.

Meanwhile, Robert and Barrie Hoar, the brothers whom shareholders wanted to oust, have sold most of their 26 per cent stake and resigned their executive directorships.

The brothers will each receive £50,000 compensation, and Barrie Hoar will remain a non-executive director 'for the time being', the company said.'

I insisted that I was photographed by the press with a pint of beer in my hand in front of the large 'Coopers & Lybrand' sign outside their London HQ. This was to pay back their faith in Chris Callaway, who had risked all to support me. That night he and I walked up the hill together towards Charing Cross and Trafalgar Square – he to get a train home and me to catch a cab. We were both silent. I touched his hand and said, "Thank you." We parted without looking each other in the eye. I couldn't because I was crying.

The next day, I left for France, this time with Marianne and Davinia in tow. Once seated and waiting on the tarmac, my mobile rang out. It was Christine. She wanted to congratulate me. She sounded very excited and enthusiastic.

"Who was that?" Marianne asked.

"Christine Pickles. She works for Chris Callaway."

"Well, she sounded very keen."

"Of course. We have succeeded. We have won."

"That's not what it sounded like to me." said Marianne in a knowing tone.

We collected Howie and J from Pertuis and had a very pleasant few days as a family together before returning to London and work.

Howard returned with us and was engaged by Hoskins to sell our beers into pubs as a 'guest beer.' He took to it like a duck to water and was an immediate success, making a significant contribution to increasing sales, and quite soon Hoskins 'Old Nigel' or 'Churchill's Pride' could be seen all over the Midlands and increasingly further afield.

I would go up to Stratton Audley Hall, in Stratton Audley village, near Bicester in Oxfordshire every Wednesday. This is a quasi-stately home Marianne had bought with the proceeds of the sale of Wilton Place in Belgravia. I went there to take Howard and Jamieson out for dinner on what we came to call, 'boy's night out.' I would then stay the night. This meant that J got to spend 3 or 4 nights-a-week with me and that kept him happy as he had moved school to Brackley and still missed Daddy badly.

On these evenings we would always have dinner in pubs that sold Hoskins' beers. Howard would do the driving – so I could sample the beer. They were very happy evenings and made the week a bit more bearable for J.

Back in London, I moved my apartment to Lowndes Court, which was also in Lowndes Square. It was a fantastic two-bedroom apartment with a beautiful drawing room and a unique conservatory, which served as a dining room, and I doubled it up to be my office as well.

Not long after I moved in, I was approached by an attractive woman, whose name I can't remember, because she became known as 'flat 22', that was her apartment number. She was beautifully built and had an enormous sexual appetite. Lying in her bed and feeling quite exhausted after a lengthy session of us both showing off, she announced that her apartment was paid for by Barry Hearn.

She then told me that she was his mistress, and I had better be careful or I could be in deep trouble. I had wandered by mistake, on this occasion, once more into potential trouble just as I had almost twenty years before with Eddie Fewtrel back in Birmingham. And now I didn't have my father to save my life as I had then.

Of course, I knew who Barry Hearn was. He was a major boxing and snooker promoter, and owner of Brentford Football Club. He was a London boy who had come from the hard side of the tracks. However, nothing happened, and we continued to see each for a few weeks –

purely as a sexual relationship. I can't remember meeting her anywhere but in bed.

In the meantime, I began to build my team. I needed to engage a finance director to help me plan our growth by acquisition, and a professional to run the brewery as I had no plans to build Hoskins by buying more breweries or pubs as this part of the leisure industry was going through a period of change and uncertainty and I was a funeral director by trade and certainly not a brewery expert.

Moreover, it was just the quoted company that I had wanted and had now got. Nevertheless, I needed to protect Hoskins trading performance while we decided what to do with it.

James Roe, whose wife was Marion Roe, a Tory MP who had also served as a junior environment minister under Margaret Thatcher, was the new Hoskins Chairman. He had been a senior executive at Rothschild Bank, was very intelligent, kind and highly likeable. Callaway and I were very pleased to get him. He was keen to sign up two further non-executive directors, Bill Caldwell and Shaun Dowling, whom he both knew. I agreed.

However, he wanted to also have a veto over executive appointments. I didn't agree to that and vetoed his non-approval of David Moffatt as my choice as finance director. David had read all the publicity about me getting Hoskins and had written to me to ask for an interview. He was Lord Hanson trained. We intended Hoskins to be a conglomerate like that built by Lords Hanson and White. He must be worth seeing.

I invited David to come and see me. I immediately liked him and knew we would make a good team. I took him to meet James. He wasn't so sure. However, I put my foot down and David was appointed. David and I then found a former Scottish & Newcastle director, Philip Thistlewaite, to run Hoskins Brewery.

Now we had to start looking for acquisitions to get our conglomerate moving and Coopers sent Miss Pickles to help us on secondment. Unbeknown to them Miss Pickles and I had become a little better acquainted recently.

## This Life In Death

During the summer of '93, as already declared, Chris, Christine and I had had great fun looking for a suitable listed vehicle for me to become CEO of. We had spent hours together. Occasionally, she and I were left on our own to do research together when Chris had to do something else or just catch the train home. On one occasion, this meant that she scribbled over sales particulars as she got slightly smashed in Motcombs Wine bar, much to James Roe's surprise, as he had a very high regard for her. On another, we ended up having a play fight – spraying each other with whiteboard cream in Coopers' HQ.

She was 28-years-of-age, very pretty and highly thought of by the partners of Coopers in every sense possible. They thought she was very intelligent, reliable and highly desirable. My deduction? No fact – Chris, as a partner, had told me that at a partners' 'boy's night out' she had won the vote of the most desirable female manager. Goodness, how things have changed now over 30 years later. But back then men ran businesses and women helped them occasionally if they were exceptionally talented or just pretty.

When Hoskins had been found and I installed as CEO, Christine had called me, as already recorded. I had told her that when I got back from France, we would have dinner together to celebrate as she had missed the Callaway/Mandell celebration.

I knew this could be dangerous as I realised that she was falling, or perhaps had already fallen, in love with me; that we had a professional working relationship; and that I was very attracted to her as a partner and not just a 'wham bam, thank you ma'am' one night stand or even to add her to the harem.

On the other hand, I had now established a very settled life. Marianne and the children were happy. I wasn't frightened of letting anyone down, or the strain of a one-woman relationship that I had always found so hard to cope with.

Instead, I had a ten strong harem of women, all of whom I liked and looked forward to seeing once a fortnight for the different sexual pleasures they offered. Nevertheless, I was very drawn towards Christine Mary Pickles – as a rabbit is drawn into the headlights.

# This Life In Death

Earlier in the year, I had bought tickets for a Paul McCartney concert for Christine, Chris and Jacqui, David and Jo, and a potential institutional investor and his wife. They did not cost me the £20,000 or so as they would today, but they were not cheap. I had also organised drinks in the Ritz before the concert, and a supper in Beccofino's restaurant just off the Fulham Road afterwards.

I had asked a very attractive twenty-five-year-old to accompany me. Marianne and I knew both her mother and father. Indeed, her father owned a beautiful men's boutique in Birmingham, and it was he who had sold me my now famous double-breasted overcoat and fedora. We had also bought Marianne's boutique 'Just Imagine' off him in Streetly, near Sutton Coldfield in 1986.

All the other men could not take their eyes off the appealing young girl and were probably envious that she was going to sleep with me in the Ritz when supper ended.

However, as the taxi sped away as we left, I looked back at the rest of the party waving goodbye and knew that I really wished it was Christine coming to the Ritz to share my bed.

So, now I was faced with a heart vs. head decision yet again. I argued with myself.

"For Christ and Christine's sake, Howard, this is why you are a psychiatrist's dream?

For God's sake you have just sorted your life out. Surely, you are not going to get back into a single woman relationship. They have caused you, and all the women, so much anguish for the last twenty years."

Then I had reasoned, "You know you are a good businessman; a very capable motivational leader; a disciplined man when it comes to anything but women; perhaps the most loving father ever; you also love animals; and you want to be kind to everyone. So why get yourself back into a relationship which is bound to cause you and her so much pain?"

My head told me not to invite her. Good advice. Did I take it? No. My heart had won.

We went out to dinner. This was the start of a relationship which immediately led us into bed together, for a sort of adolescent sex but not into a full-blown sexual relationship initially. I think this was because, Miss Pickles thought that if she could make me wait, as Ann Boleyn had Henry VIII, it would make me faithful. Ann Boleyn's plan failed, and she lost her head as a result. Moreover, history and my story show that I was much more like King Charles II than Henry VIII in any case.

Now autumn 1993, the acquisition express was leaving a London station several times a week to seek new targets. On board was Chris, Christine, me and now Moffatt too.

Nobody knew that Miss Pickles and I were becoming an item and never realised as we all said goodnight at any hotel we were staying in, that I would be creeping along the corridor to her room, in a few minutes time.

It didn't take long to identify two acquisitions which were complimentary to each other and of great interest to us.

The first was LGW. They had come back to us and wanted to deal now that my name had been cleared of any wrongdoing, and we had secured the Hoskins quotation on the USM. The second was the world-famous Ronson lighters brand.

Ronson was the still the 7th best recognised brand name in the world and the generic name in Chinese for lighter. However, it had endured a very chequered history of late.

Originally, it been founded not in the UK, as most people thought, but in New York, USA in 1896 by the Aronson family. It moved to Britain sometime later and was made famous the world over as more than a million British soldiers, who patrolled the then massive Empire, were all smokers and had Ronson lighters in their pockets. This caused a local demand the world over and an international network of Ronson distributors was set up to meet that.

Such demand was so strong that at one time in the 1950s, the Leatherhead factory in the UK had over 3,000 workers and boasted several amateur football teams. The 'Premier Varaflame' became the world's most iconic lighter and a major symbol of the '60s, perhaps only third to the Beatles and Carnaby Street.

Moreover, the Ronson Queen Anne table lighter sat on every drawing room in middle class Britain next to the silver cigarette boxes that everyone had and offered a cigarette to their guests from.

Since then, as firstly disposable lighters had replaced 'gift' lighters as tools to light one's cigarettes with; secondly, health warnings about smoking and its association with cancer had reduced demand; and thirdly, as a result of the decline of the company's fortunes because of those two reasons, it had fallen into the hands of less scrupulous men, seeking to make a fast buck without providing either a sensible long-term plan or the necessary investment. Nor did it manufacture its gift lighters anymore. These were tooled and then made in Japan or South Korea and not much effort was put into selling them.

However, Ronson still had good butane gas and petrol sales for all lighters; sold a lot of disposable lighters of a questionable quality; and also enjoyed a decent export business, mainly in the Middle East, for its 'Chirton' brand of household cleaning products and a hairspray, which were all made with butane gas and then distributed via local Ronson agents out there.

The household products had a good following, but the hairspray had received a mixed reception in Doha where Ronson had sold two containers to the distributor, who was soon receiving complaints as when women sprayed it on their hair it showered them in white specks which made them appear that they had dreadful dandruff.

Understandably, the distributor wanted to return the containers and have a refund. Instead, Geoffrey Richmond, who owned Ronson, offered him another container free of charge and had been miffed when the guy had exploded at that suggestion.

Nevertheless, the company had great potential because, despite this hotch-potch of sales, it could still pay Richmond £100,000-a-month and with him gone, this saving would allow the company time and space to reintroduce Ronson as a male grooming brand offering pens, watches, cufflinks, ties, after-shave, hairdryers and sunglasses as well as lighters. A more affordable version of Dunhill or Dupont.

Moreover, by acquiring LGW too, we could provide Ronson with both sales and a lot of exposure by having it listed in duty free airline brochures or placed in airside duty free shops.

Due to the power of the brand recognition that Ronson still possessed, we had to see off some competition for its acquisition, while LGW was a done deal straight away. Then while Richmond negotiated as if his life depended on it to get more money, Bruce McGuire seemed very happy with the deal that he had agreed.

This was probably because he knew that our due diligence, carried out by Coopers, would miss a few sharp accountancy sleights of hand which inflated the LGW profitability considerably. In my book this was being dishonest, but in Bruce's it was no more than a fair way that 'Del Boy' and other market traders behaved.

Eventually, both deals were agreed and could be announced right in the middle of the corporate Christmas party season.

The press was largely impressed and again the 'Independent' was more or less accurate and fair when it reported:

'HOSKINS Brewery, where Howard Hodgson recently took the helm, has mapped out a course to becoming a manufacturer and distributor.

Ronson, the maker of cigarette lighters and other smokers' requisites, is being bought for £10m. And LGW, a duty-free goods business based at Gatwick Airport, Sussex, is being bought for £9.5m.

Hoskins is raising £17m by placing 16 million shares, and via a one-for-one rights issue. Ronson's vendors are buying 3 million Hoskins shares. All three issues are at 68p.

Share dealings in Hoskins, suspended at 78p on 8 December, will resume on the USM on Monday until 11 January - the eve of a shareholder;s meeting.

Hoskins, which is being re-named Halkin Holdings, also announced a dive from profits of £50,000 to losses of £830,000 in the half-year to 30 September.

Actually, things hadn't gone as smoothly in reality behind the scenes as they seemed to the outside world. Our broker at Peel Hunt, Geoff Bowman, seemed to be struggling to find buyers for the stock and took David and me on a buying trip to see my old loyal lady buyers, from Hodgson Holdings days, in Edinburgh. The three of us were in the hotel, Geoff was on the phone to an institution, when I wandered off to consider what my future would hold if he failed to fund these two acquisitions.

Suddenly, David came running up.

"Come quickly. Geoff has got Queen Anne's Gate on the phone. They want to buy everything. He said they can't and is only allowing them 50%," panted a breathless Moffatt.

"That's because he wants them to buy more in the market when the shares resume trading," I replied. but followed David back to Geoff nonetheless. In the end, the consummate professional Bowman came home comfortably and indeed, Queen Anne's Gate pushed the price up when trading resumed.

Moreover, trading had not really slumped from a profit of £50k to a loss of £830k. This was Master Moffatt doing the job he had been taught at the Hanson school of creative accounting. He had taken lots of provisions on the books to create such a loss, knowing that they could be laid at the door of the 'old guard' and not us, and then he could release them in future years to bolster our profits.

1993 had proved to be an extremely important year and had seen me recover from a life of depression behind dark glasses and under a floppy flat cap to find a quoted company and transform it into Halkin Holdings plc which now owned the famous Ronson brand. None of this would have happened without Christopher Callaway's faith in me and his dedication to getting the job, which many had thought of as 'mission impossible', over the line.

Bruce McGuire stayed on to run LGW sales, which was very important as he counted so many airline duty-free buyers as his friends and was a skilled buyer of product. The warehouse operation also continued to be run by a truly great guy called Ken Archer, who had joined Bruce from Houbigant Fragrances. Ken was to be a stalwart over the next few years. Increasingly, I was to realise how talented this self-educated man was. When he eventually died of cancer, a decade later, I was extremely sad and often still think of him with a little smile on my face.

Richmond had retired on the sale of Ronson and used some of the proceeds to add cash towards a swap deal of Scarborough FC for Bradford City FC. Therefore, we needed a new managing director at Ronson. David and I selected a decent marketing brand manager, named Arthur Till, and John Graham remained as the operations director at the Ronson North Shields factory, where the butane gas and petrol products were produced.

We also had moved by now out of my flat and into a very pleasant suite of offices in Grosvenor Place, around the corner from Halkin Street, hence the title Halkin Holdings plc, which were opposite the Irish Embassy and at the bottom of Buckingham Palace's substantial gardens. Lord Tebbit was our next-door neighbour and would often chat to me about how disappointed he was in John Major's pro-EU attitude and would warn me that he would be speaking out against the government over it. Moreover, he made no secret of his complete dislike of Michael Heseltine. So, I could see the storm clouds gathering over the Brexit issue over thirty years ago. There would be much 'bloodletting' that would seriously harm the Conservative Party over the coming years because of it.

The shares resumed trading in January 1994, the price moved up and the acquisition express started to roll out of various London stations again in a new search for acquisitions that would either complement our existing product lines or open new markets for existing ones. On board was the usual team and by now Coopers' faith in Chris's support for me in the previous year was being handsomely repaid with both corporate finance and audit fees.

When not aboard the acquisition express, I could be found on long-haul flights to Hong Kong with Bruce where we would station ourselves at the Royal Garden Hotel to visit suppliers in Hong Kong or the neighbouring 'New Territories.'

The whole of the Far East was growing fast as a low-cost manufacturer of luxury goods, toys, clothes and other low-tech products. Due to the low wages paid in that region, it became increasingly hard for manufacturers of these goods in Europe or the US to compete on price.

Moreover, as living standards had risen in places like Japan and Hong Kong from a very low starting point at the end of the Second World War, so production had moved to newer and cheaper wage areas such as South Korea and eventually China.

However, these trips were strictly about sourcing product and agreeing prices. Sales were never considered in this area other than Japan, because the vast majority of people did not possess disposable income to buy such products as they have now over thirty years later.

These trips were also strictly about having a good time at night. Bruce and I got on well and would go to the 'Club de Hong Kong' after dinner every evening, sing Karaoke with many girls in a private room, before leaving in the early hours. He was newly married and left alone. I would always leave with two or even three girls in tow, usually of varying nationalities. My addiction to little naughty boy sex was well catered for on these trips.

## This Life In Death

The next acquisition was made in spring 1995. It was Home Shopping Ltd. A Manchester based company that was owned by a pleasant Swede called Lars Rydstrom and managed by him and his partner, a Mancunian lady by the name of Sue Liberman.

In those days, before the internet's use of being a route to market, there were several companies who issued paper catalogues to potential clients so they could order products from the comfort of their TV and fire-side chair. This was a perfect channel to re-introduce the Ronson brand through. Now we could also have a meaningful presence at not only the Hong Kong, Cannes and Orlando duty-free shows, but also at the international trade fairs at Birmingham and Frankfurt.

We also bought a company called Smiths Packaging in 1995. This was a bottling and packaging company and was acquired in preparation of our launch of a Ronson after-shave product range.

Lars Rydstrom stayed on and was to be appointed my deputy. We also hired a new brand manager to replace Arthur Till as we had selected badly. Arthur was a very decent man and a competent brand strategist for large groups with huge budgets. We were neither that big and nor did we have millions to spend on advertising campaigns – hence our acquisitions of existing routes to market with LGW and Home Shopping.

The man hired as Arthur's replacement was a chap called Fred Bassnett. He was a Scouser from a humble Liverpool background. He had worked for Allders and the House of Fraser among others and was very strong on consistency of colour, language, typeface and design, which was in complete accord with me, and better still, he understood price point and brand positioning.

He was to prove to be a good appointment. However, he and Lars being appointed close together made Bruce feel insecure and his friendship with me, which I had always felt was genuine, started to diminish, which was sad for me, but it also affected the smooth running of the company. Bruce had so much to offer when he was with you but could be a negative force when he was not.

In 1995 this issue was not helped when we hired a man called Denis Hayes. He was the husband of our marketing director, Linda Bruton, and a male grooming brand expert. We wanted him to source products for three new Ronson ranges. These were Ronson Retro, Ronson Racer, and Ronson Rebel. Retro was designed to appeal to over 40-year-old men; Racer guys between 20 and 40; and Rebel teenagers.

Rebel was modelled by my son Howard and his image consequently appeared on the side and rear of London buses dressed like James Dean and sitting on a powerful motor bike. He had by now transferred from Hoskins to Ronson and oversaw European distributors.

The combination of Rydstrom, Bassnett, Bruton, Hayes and McGuire was a powerful one. It meant we had experts in product sourcing, marketing, domestic and international sales, and brand management.

Moreover, these guys were supported by experienced and well-connected people in home shopping, multiple grocer and department store listings in the UK, and a strong list of worldwide distributors and duty-free listings with most airlines and airside duty-free stores internationally.

So, everything looked good for an exciting future, but Bruce, as a self-made man, who had become wealthy by being a trader, felt increasingly insecure when surrounded by people talking about price points and brand management. And it didn't matter how much I tried to reassure him, he became increasingly isolated and negative, which was a shame as I liked him, and knew that he had a lot to offer.

However, Bruce apart, as 1995 was ending this experienced team was highly motivated and liked each other. Indeed, I bumped into

Richard Branson at a John Major cocktail party at 10 Downing Street, around Christmas time and he complimented me on Ronson's amazing comeback. I was very proud of my Ronson team and the good work done in 1993, 1994 and 1995.

So, I had saved my sanity and reputation by getting back to basics. The roller-coaster had veered up again – but was my life going to continue in the ascendency?

## This Life In Death

Chapter V

Fire, Franchisees and Frustration

1996 – 1997

Tragedies in life can be 'an act of God', someone else's fault, or just your fault. The worst tragedy to befall me was in 1982, this was the loss of my beloved son Charles. This was neither my fault nor an act of God. The financial calamities that hit me in 1992 were 100% of my making and so 100% my fault. Now we come to one that was neither 'an act of God' nor my fault.

This crisis came about, I believe, because of a deliberate act of arson made by a person or persons that I am not prepared to accuse on the grounds that it would be supposition without actual factual evidence. To do so would not only be unfair on him or them but could prove costly to make such allegations without the absolute proof needed to support such claims.

Either way, a monumental fire, that was so big that it made the 'ITN News at Ten' and the 'BBC News', the UK's most watched national television news programmes, was to occur and was to cause so much destruction to so many decent people's lives, that it still makes me very sad to revisit these events in my mind to tell you about them nearly thirty years later.

As already reported, Halkin Holdings plc was resurrecting the Ronson brand spectacularly. So much so that we decided to change the name of our quoted vehicle to Ronson plc to concentrate complete focus on our game plan.

The policy of owning duty-free, UK retail and catalogue sales teams and international distributors with very decent presences in their respective markets, plus product sourcing and brand management ability was proving to be a 'barn storming' winner. This coupled with the media's continuing fascination with Mr. Death ensured that Ronson was not only winning but also being seen to be winning.

In late 1995, as we were approaching the centenary of Ronson in 1996, I had Christine and Fred Bassnett organise a corporate conference to be held in January 1996. This would allow everyone to present their division and thus demonstrate to other Ronson executives across all activities what they were doing and how this was contributing to the Ronson revival.

Naturally, the home shopping and duty-free divisions sold many other products besides Ronson, like 'Biggles' teddy bears or Pierre Cardin jewellery for example. Moreover, Chirton, as a household products brand, made from butane gas, was also making decent profits. However, Ronson's drive away from smokers' requisites was increasingly becoming the main thrust of our business.

We were all booked into a hotel in Buckinghamshire on a Sunday night in January 1996 before going to the Latimer House Conference Centre on the Monday morning. Morale was very high that evening at dinner and the next morning over breakfast.

Fred Bassnet was bubbling with energy and expectation. Howard and the other export guys were reporting large international orders from Ronson distributors around the world for lighters, gas and petrol. Neil Wright of Chirton, was doing the same as his products were increasingly being adopted by international distributors in the Middle and Far East. Linda Bruton was buzzing with excitement about the Ronson Rebel, Racer and Retro product launch and Denis Hayes was showing product samples of pens, watches, electric shavers, hairdryers, cufflinks and lighters that he had sourced to this end.

Everyone was on a high, the like of which I had not witnessed since the glory days of Hodgson Holdings in the late '80s.

## This Life In Death

After breakfast Christine, Fred and I set off in my XJS for the short journey to the conference centre. As we drove up the drive, a pale and haunted looking Ken Archer flagged me down. I stopped and opened the window.

"Howard, John Graham just called me. In the early hours of this morning a fire started in the next factory to ours. It quickly spread to ours. Within minutes, and before the fire brigade could get there, our factory exploded. Everything, gas stocks, petrol stocks, all the lighters and pens have gone. There is nothing left."

Christine and Freddie were speechless as I parked the car. I could understand why. I asked Freddie to assemble Lars Rydstrom, Ken Archer and David Moffatt in the hallway. I asked Christine to ensure that all the executive attendees were seated in the conference room and that none were told about what had happened until I made an announcement.

Then I took myself off to the gentlemen's restroom. Once there, I looked at myself in the mirror. I looked as if I had seen a ghost. I was almost paralysed with shock. I stood up straight, poked a finger at my image in the mirror and talked out loud to myself:

"There are hundreds of folks here or up in North Shields, Newcastle, who will be looking to you for calm leadership at this moment. You are going to do as your father would have expected you to. You are going to provide it."

I straightened my tie and went into the hallway. I explained that I had decided that Lars and Freddie, as they were highly involved in sales would remain here with me and that the conference would go ahead as planned; whereas David and Ken, as the finance director and head of production should catch a plane straight away to Newcastle, book into a hotel and remain up there until further notice. I would fly up the following day to talk to the factory employees.

That plan was put into immediate action and as David and Ken left; Lars, Freddie and I went into the conference, where I gave my best impression of a Winston Spencer Churchill wartime address. I didn't attempt to disguise how serious this fire was – after all, we now had a huge staff in the north with nothing to make and a huge staff in the south with nothing to sell. Worse, I knew that we would be dropped by the multiple grocers, department stores, shops, airlines, duty-free shops, home-shopping catalogues, and even some international distributors as they couldn't afford to have empty shelves and would have to replace our products with those of competitors, however sympathetic they were to our plight.

I also knew, but did not share with the conference, that around 85% of companies that suffered such total disruption did not survive.

Instead I told them, having explained that this disruption was serious; they should remember that we were not planning to make any of the new Rebel, Racer and Retro products ourselves; that we could immediately place orders for more Ronson gift lighters; we had many other product lines in our Gatwick warehouse to sell in the duty-free and home-shopping markets, and that we could get Ronson gas and petrol, and Chirton household product sprays filled by a contract filler. In addition, we had had a new £7 million bank loan agreed with the Bank of Scotland.

The conference then started, and everyone seemed to have taken my speech in their stride and made their presentations splendidly.

The next day, I flew up to a bitterly cold North Shields, where our staff were re-packing a new delivery of disposable lighters in a freezing cold large garage that David and Ken had hired. I addressed them, thanked them and told them we could be back in business as soon as possible. They received this news politely, but I'm not sure they were convinced.

## This Life In Death

The day before a waiter had knocked on David's door in his hotel and handed him a five-pound note. This had been given to the waiter by a loss assessor and had not been intended for David but for the waiter himself so that the waiter would introduce the assessor to David.

Eventually, the introduction was made and from there the assessor's boss, a man that I have remained friendly with since, Nicky Balcombe, called me and his firm was appointed.

Nicky wasted no time in telling me that while there should not be a problem with assessing the loss, there could be a problem getting the Lloyd's syndicate to pay up quickly. This was because several Lloyd's syndicates had been called on to shell out shed loads of cash in recent years and some had adopted a tactic of refusing to pay in the hope that the company would go bust before they were forced to cough up. If the company could survive until the court case opened, then the syndicate would hand over a cheque for the claimed amount on the steps of the courthouse.

Therefore, the problem would not be if we would get the insurance money but if we could survive until we got the cash as syndicates had wriggled out of going to court for two or more years. This news made my blood run cold because life would become very difficult if the Bank of Scotland got jittery about the insurance cash not arriving and thus their funding being used to support losses rather than funding expansion as intended.

Nicky was not wrong. Almost immediately, the syndicate queried if a roller-shutter door at the factory had been down and asked many other less relevant questions which gave me the impression that he was going to be proved right.

However, while David and Ken dealt with a lot of such problems, the rest of us had to press on with the recovery plan and the centenary events planned to promote the Ronson brand in the UK and abroad.

These included a 'a celebrity centenary party' to be held at the Bibendum on the Fulham Road, which was held for our biggest clients in the catalogue, duty-free and UK retail markets. Here they could get to meet people like Graham Taylor, the England football manager of that time; Ted Dexter the England cricket coach and famous international cricketer; Julian Lennon, son of John and a popstar in his own right; Richard Branson of Virgin, who had several of his staff there due to the duty-free connection; Debbie Moore of Pineapple Dance Studios and others including some professional footballers.

Then there was to be a 'Ronson Road Show' with Eric Knowles of BBC's 'Antiques Road Show' fame, holding road show events in the large cities throughout the UK, where people were invited to bring in their Ronson lighters for him to value and place them in an auction if that was their wish.

Lastly, we were to hold a large 'black tie' banquet in Frankfurt during the International Trades Fair, for Ronson worldwide distributors, where they could win 'Oscars' for the best performance in several categories.

The 'Ronson Centenary Party' which had been organised by Simon Preston's daughter Emma, was a roaring success, and the press featured many pictures of Branson, Lennon and others. Personally, and although I enjoyed chatting to Richard, Graham, Ted, Debbie et al very much, the conversation I had with Julian Lennon was the most fascinating.

We talked about the current remastered Beatles' hit 'Free as a Bird.' It had been written and left in a very early basic state by his father after the Beatles had separated, discovered by Yoko Ono, given to Paul McCartney, who had finished the song, which was then produced by Jeff Lynne, of ELO fame, and recorded by the three surviving Beatles, featuring solo lyrics by both Paul and George.

The song had become a major hit worldwide and had helped promote 'The Beatles Anthology', which was a multi-part TV series to be shown across the globe, and this meant, amazingly, that the Beatles were to make more money in 1996-7 than they had in those years of 'Beatlemania' in the 1960s.

Julian told me that he couldn't really hear much of his father's voice on the song. Moreover, as we chatted, he went on to explain that while he loved his father dearly, his father really had never been able to cope with Julian because he had found it hard to cope with his own life and, as an only child, who had been brought up by his Auntie Mimi, his father didn't really understand how to relate to children.

"Paul was more like a dad to me. He would build sandcastles with me or play pirate games. Paul grew up in a large family and understood children. My favourite Beatle song is Paul's 'Hey Jude' because it was written for me."

Indeed, it was, and the original version was entitled 'Hey Jules' and John Lennon loved this Paul McCartney song and wanted to keep the title. However, McCartney thought that that would be unfair on Julian and so changed it to 'Hey Jude'. Julian and Paul remain close today – fifty-five years after the Beatles separated.

Nearly thirty years after my conversation with Julian, I went to look at a house that I was interested in buying in the South of France. It turned out to be owned by Julian Lennon. On the walls were many photographs of John and Julian's mum Cynthia Lennon. But there were also lots of Beatle Paul, around the Sergeant Pepper period of 1967, when Julian was a baby, and guess what, one is of Paul building a sandcastle with him.

The 'Ronson Road Show' was also a great success with hundreds, and at some locations, thousands of people bringing in their Ronson lighters for Eric Knowles to value. Eric is a delightful man and would make everyone roar with laughter with one-liners like, "Don't worry Madam, you're safe with me. I tuck my shirt into my underpants."

These events were usually covered by national as well as local press. Indeed, even the anti-Howard 'Independent' wrote about the resulting auction:

'The first dedicated sale of collectable Ronson lighters on Wednesday (5pm) will be a market-maker. The 60 lots were collected during countrywide Ronson memorabilia roadshows led by Eric Knowles. Ronson is celebrating its centenary following its acquisition by Howard Hodgson, the former funeral parlour whizzkid. He is promoting Ronson collectables to emphasise the firm's tradition.

'Estimates are cautious. They range from £10-£15 for a 1950 Standard petrol-flint chromed brass pocket lighter, profusely engraved with a flowering urn and scrolls, to £700- £1,000 for a deco-style cigarette-box touch-tip table lighter in the form of a bar with black bartender shaking a cocktail. Missing from the sale (at the Imagination Gallery, 25 Store Street, South Crescent, London WC1): the famous Ronson Charlie Chaplin lighter of 1920. Only three are known. They are thought to be worth over £10,000 each. Auctioneers: Special Auction Services (01734-712949)."

Lastly, the 'Distributors Awards Dinner' was also a huge success with every table taken by distributors from all over the world. They applauded loudly whoever won an 'Oscar' and gave my speech a rousing reception too. If you had sat in that room on that night, you would have found it hard to believe that Ronson had suffered such a devastating fire just six weeks earlier.

Indeed, these centenary celebrations were going so well and gaining so much publicity that Ronson's great rival, Colibri of London, tried to have them stopped by claiming that it wasn't our centenary at all. However, we were able to produce an 1896 lighter, complete with the original packet to prove them wrong. The lighter was mine and had been bought as a gift for me by Christine.

It seemed to me that everybody was holding the line really well under the circumstances. Indeed, I was confident that we were on the right track when I went on a trip to Holland, with Howard, and GA, who was a Dutch trader that worked for LGW, but I had converted to Ronson European international sales.

We went to open a new cigar smoking area in Amsterdam's biggest department store. Amazingly, this event made the front pages of their national press. Ronson was still a force to be reckoned with.

Afterwards, we had dinner with our distributor, the Hart family, and at the end of which, Howard stayed loyally with them, while GA and I could not wait to escape to the delights of Amsterdam, which we did.

He and I raced across the wide main road outside the restaurant, but I caught my foot in the tram lines badly and had to hobble into the fantastic bar he had selected.

I could hardly walk but perched on a bar stool with a large vodka in my hand, I knew I was alive. Then a very pretty, very tall and very slender girl appeared on the next bar stool. We chatted as GA did to another woman on his side.

She asked me about my foot. She was a medical student. She invited me to her home because she said it needed ice packs and then bandaging.

We went to her place where she administered both. Then she took me to her bed. She was for a student of such a young age, a very gentle and genuine lover.

The next morning, I asked her what her father did for a living and whether he paid for her university fees.

"No, I pay for them by being in that bar," she said sheepishly.

Oh shit! I thought you silly vain and arrogant man. You owe her.

"Gosh, sorry. How much do I owe you?" I enquired happy to pay but sad that her love was on the meter when it had seemed so genuine.

"You owe me nothing. Is that a book of yours?" she was pointing to a copy of 'How to Become Dead Rich' sticking out of my briefcase.

"Yep. Not very good I'm afraid."

"Sign it to me and we are all square."

I did and left to meet Howard and GA at the airport. I had her number but never contacted her again once I was home.

xxxxxxx

But then the Bank of Scotland, who had been so supportive immediately after the fire, suddenly had a change of heart. They took away our two friendly bankers and replaced them with a man called David Moxon, who immediately demanded that we use 'our best endeavours' to repay their £7 million unsecured cash-flow loan.

This was devasting news, because I knew this would only encourage the insurance syndicate to delay paying out even more, and that we couldn't replace this debt with other bank debt for obvious reasons.

Therefore, the only course of action open to us would be a rights issue and this would be very difficult to achieve given the uncertainty that the fire had caused and that now the 'double whammy' of having to find £7 million while not having received a penny from our insurers, was also being applied.

## This Life In Death

I held an emergency meeting with our brokers Williams de Broe and Chris Callaway. I took Lars and Christine with me – as David was still up in Newcastle. Everyone agreed that the company was very much a going concern but that a rights issue in such circumstances was to prove very difficult without bank lending and no insurance pay-out on the horizon.

We agreed that in order to get the issue away, we would need to do three things: we would need to make it deeply discounted to the current price; we would need to be open about why we were having it and call it 'a rescue rights issue'; and we would need to find a cornerstone investor to take perhaps as much as 50% of the issue.

Our brokers set about that last task immediately and quite quickly I was introduced to a small gentleman from the Middle East who said he represented a syndicate of high net worth individuals, who were either British or American, and who would like to back my rescue plans. His name was Farzad Rastegar.

I then spent a lot of time with Farzad explaining our strategy and showing him round our LGW warehouse operation at Gatwick. He was impressed and told me that he was going to recommend the syndicate to invest £5 million in Ronson.

He came back and said that they were willing to do this if they could have someone on the board. They wanted that man to be Alan Kilkenny. He seemed a strange choice to me because he was a PR consultant who had no knowledge of the gift industry. However, we were so delighted to be making such positive progress that I didn't give the matter a second thought. Accordingly, I met Alan for dinner at Verbanella's in Beauchamp Place and liked him.

Now, with the cornerstone investor in place, the rights issue could go ahead, and our brokers started to raise the rest of the cash. One day, around this time, non-executive director Shaun Dowling visited the Halkin Street offices, after a decent liquid lunch nearby. Lars then told him that he had decided to underwrite some of the issue to take the 2% fee which was worth some £200k. Shaun said he wanted some of that and offered to underwrite it too.

The rights issue proceeded but Williams de Broe couldn't sell it all despite the cornerstone investor's presence. Not exactly surprising given all the banking and insurance uncertainties. This meant that Lars and Shaun, while getting their fees, had to buy 'the stick.' Lars duly obliged. Dowling declined.

I was making a speech in Warwick at a local chamber of commerce dinner. The fee was £3,000 and so I felt it was worth the effort to go, despite my current exhaustion for 18-hour working days. Just before I was due to get up to speak, I got a call from the head of Williams de Broe on my mobile to report that Dowling was refusing to buy his allocation of the Ronson shares which they now had on their books. He said that this was completely unacceptable, and he asked me to return to London immediately after my speech so I could attend an emergency meeting at their offices at 8:00 in the morning.

After I had made folk laugh at me, as suggested by Roger Moore, I called Chairman James Roe. I thought, as a decent man and old friend of Shaun Dowling, that he could make Dowling see sense.

To my amazement Roe put friendship ahead of doing the right thing. He blamed our brokers.

"For doing what?" I responded.

"Well, they should not have encouraged him," James replied.

"They didn't. I was there when he made that decision, and they weren't. It was his personal greed that dictated his mind at that moment. He has got left with 'the stick' as part of the deal. It was a gamble, and he has lost. Now he will have to pick up the shares."

James was keen not to fall out with me, but neither was he going to tell Dowling to do the right thing. So, I called Dowling myself and told him, in no uncertain terms, that he had to buy his share of the stick from Williams de Broe. I then drove back to London.

Next morning the whole Ronson and Williams de Broe Boards were gathered in their boardroom. Tensions were high because Lars, Christine and I agreed with our brokers, and I was furious that Dowling was pouring petrol on to a hardly under control fire at this critical time. So, this meant the Ronson executive members were siding with our brokers against our three non-executive directors.

Despite James' protestations, I spoke out against this greedy act of self-indulgence by Shaun which had backfired. At that moment Dowling chucked a share certificate for highly valuable Guinness shares on the table and petulantly said, "Sell these." The crisis was averted but I had made an enemy of Shaun which was to cost me a year later.

The successful rights issue, against all odds was due to be announced now. However, and despite being asked to name his investors on several occasions, Farzad had failed to. This had made Chris Callaway very nervous. How did we know that they were not the Mafia was his point.

Callaway and I demanded that we meet the syndicate investors. We were invited to Claridge's Hotel in London for afternoon tea just the day before the announcement. There was just one investor sat with Farzad when we arrived. He was the sole investor. Farzad explained that there were no others. His name was Jack Lyons, ex Sir Jack Lyons, who had lost his knighthood for his part in the Distillers scandal of 1987. He should have been in prison, like all the others convicted, but was allowed to remain free due to his claim, supported by his doctor, that he was dying from terminal cancer. However, and quite miraculously, here he was, looking remarkably well and unbelievably fat for a man with terminal cancer.

Once we had concluded our meeting with Lyons, who was charming and polite throughout, we left together and asked each other what this meant.

"Well, he is a free man and allowed to invest," said Chris.

"But he was convicted for insider dealing. He is not on our board but is a major investor, who has a man on the board whom we don't really know", I replied with concern as all I could see was just another problem to add to the lack of insurance payment and the Bank of Scotland's demands for repayment – never mind trying to keep all customers supplied to prevent them from delisting us as well.

"We will have to keep a very close eye on his activity and what questions he asks of us – especially in 'closed periods'", was Chris's sensible advice.

However, as it turned out, we had no time to worry about Jack Lyons. This was because the Bank of Scotland raised its increasingly unwelcome and ugly head again. We had collected the rights issue money and paid them back. Surely, this was the end of the matter.

No, it wasn't. They were apparently not satisfied with this. I got a call from David Moxon asking for a meeting. I agreed. He arrived in our Grosvenor Place offices with an assistant. I had Lars, Christine and David present with me. We met in the boardroom. Moxon explained that the bank had bought the money at a price which had been lent to us and now they owed cash on its early redemption. Therefore, Ronson must also pay out on the early redemption penalty clause in the contract. The cost of which was some £270,000.

I stared at him in total disbelief.

"David, we didn't want to redeem the loan early. It has given us a lot of extra work and heartache to do what you wanted. But you gave us no choice. You demanded we redeemed it immediately. The decision was yours and not ours. Therefore, any early redemption penalties to be paid are to be paid by you because of your commercial decision to demand that we repaid the loan. Therefore, it is your responsibility and not ours because we did not redeem the loan of our own accord but on your instruction. Subsequently, such a redemption was your decision, your cost and you must face up to it."

Mr. Moxon did not agree with me and said as much. I had been under tremendous pressure and fighting fires all over the place for months since the 'real' fire. Enough was enough. I exploded. I told him and his sidekick to leave before I physically threw them out. My parting words were that they should instruct their lawyers as we would do.

Indeed, this is what came to pass. We instructed Herbert Smith on James Roe's recommendation. The senior partner there, Edward Walker Arnott, had been a friend of James since the latter's Rothschild days and was a brilliant lawyer according to James, who also thought Ronson's lawyer, David Mandell, was not up to this task. We agreed.

As a result, a meeting was fixed up for two in-house Bank of Scotland lawyers to meet Edward, Christine and me at the Herbert Smith offices in the city. Christine and I arrived early for a conference with Edward.

We sat in a small conference room which nevertheless had fantastic views over the open plan interior of Herbert Smith's large premises.

After some time Edward entered. Christine and I were shocked. He had had a stroke and walked with a little difficulty but spoke with a lot. However, it was too late to do anything now, so I briefed him on our case.

He listened thoughtfully. When I had finished, he managed to stammer, "You know the case and I see that you like to be heard. However, please say nothing this morning. Leave everything to me." I agreed but probably thought at the time, that we were in store for yet another bad day.

I could not have been more wrong. I don't think I have ever seen my enemies beaten up so well and so quickly. I was never tempted to interrupt. I just sat back and enjoyed every orgasmic second and even had to restrain myself from bursting into applause.

He repeated the case that I had put regarding who had demanded the early redemption. He then added that the Bank of Scotland had put Ronson under 'best endeavours' to repay the loan rather than 'reasonable endeavours' which had forced our hands legally to redeem as soon as possible. Lastly, he asked them if they had any worthwhile counter argument. These guys were by now, due to this most commanding of commanding performances, too frightened to speak and just shook their heads. He showed them the door and the dispute finished, and we had won. I was never more impressed by the force of a ten-minute speech before or since.

I called him the next day to thank him. I did so profusely. He had been brilliant, and we hadn't had too many victories of late. I asked him to send his fee note and promised to settle the same immediately. He enquired if £2,000 would be OK. I nearly dropped the phone. I would have paid him £25,000 for such an achievement. What a man!

xxxxxxx

Thanks to Edward Walker Arnott getting the Bank of Scotland out of our hair, we now had a little respite from the financial pressures and could concentrate on the launch of the new Ronson Rebel, Racer and Retro products. They were launched in the summer of 1996 at the Imagination Gallery in London and were very well received by buyers and the press alike.

Christine and I invited every Ronson executive and their partners for a sailing weekend during the '96 summer, and we had 3 separate sailing days – one for international distributors, one for UK clients and one for duty-free clients, where they were all given Ronson polo shirts and caps.

The Cannes Duty-Free show went well in the autumn too, despite Bruce being in a truculent mood. During that 'Cannes Week' we threw a cocktail party in honour of Pierre Cardin. Cardin, continuing to allow our duty-free business the licence to sell exclusively Pierre Cardin earring sets on airlines all over the world, was essential to our survival.

He came. He had already decided he liked me as we had met before. Indeed, he pinched my bottom as he was leaving and invited me to have lunch with him in Paris. The thought of this gave me sleepless nights. Pierre Cardin ran his empire through a succession of boyfriends. If the one that looked after your account was in favour, so were you. The opposite was also true. It was very stressful as your fortunes could go soaring up or crash down on his loving or discarding of a boyfriend and had little to do with the licence fee that you were paying.

I already knew Cardin liked me because he had seated me on one side of him, with Christine on the other, at his London Christmas dinner. He had on that occasion, stroked my hair throughout the meal much to Christine's horror. I wasn't too thrilled either – but to upset Pierre now while our survival balanced on a knife edge, would have been fatal as the loss of the Pierre Cardin licence would have sent Ronson into administration.

In early 1997 I flew to Paris at Pierre's invitation. He took me to lunch in Maxim's, which he owned, and explained that when Bruce McGuire had taken out the licence it specifically stated that it was for the UK only. Whereas Pierre had now discovered that Bruce had been supplying Pierre Cardin jewellery sets to airlines across the world for years and therefore into territories that he wasn't allowed to be selling in and hadn't paid for.

"Oh my God. This is the end. We are going to lose the licence and face a claim for damages, perhaps going back years," I said to myself as I doubted if Pierre really did like me at all.

However, Cardin changed the subject and invited me upstairs to his new 'cigar bar' which were all the rage in 1997. We were now alone. He offered me a cigar. I hadn't smoked either a cigarette or a cigar for over five years, but I couldn't afford to upset him. And besides I would rather suck on a cigar than something else I was terrified he might offer.

He ordered coffee and asked me if I thought that Ronson could survive following the devastation the fire had caused a year ago.

I told him it would be difficult, but I believed that we could. He asked me where I had learnt my French. I explained about my schooling and first marriage. He told me that Italian was his first language. Then, he told me that he would allow us to continue to sell on airlines worldwide. I couldn't believe that this had only cost me half a cigar's smoke going into my mouth.

He took me downstairs to a waiting taxi, kissed me on both cheeks and I was off to the airport in a daze.

xxxxxxx

Towards the end of 1996, we had vacated our offices in London, made the final redundancies in North Shields and moved into new offices in Crawley not only to reduce cost but also to have everyone under one roof.

Sales in all markets were going well but we were having to live on a knife edge of having no real bank facilities and so debtors had to be collected quickly and creditors paid slowly. Whereas, since everyone knew we still had not received the insurance money, debtors tried not to pay, claiming they were able to get better terms from our competitors, while creditors wanted paying immediately out of concern that we might be unable to.

In a further cost cutting exercise David Moffatt, Denis Hayes and Ken Archer left. All were very capable, loyal and decent men and I was extremely sad to lose all three of them. Christine became acting finance director as a result and John Graham took over from Ken Archer.

The Birmingham and Frankfurt Trade Fairs went well. The second 'International Distributors Awards Dinner' was even better than the first and Lars, Freddie and I had a successful month-long trip to several Far East countries including Singapore, Hong Kong, South Korea, Taiwan and Japan to reduce the cost of product and to sign up new distributors as retail markets were now picking up in Singapore, South Korea and Hong Kong. In the process we had fascinating meetings with David Tang, Dickson Poon, and Jardine Matheson.

The Singapore Duty-Free Show went well while we were there, as did the US Orlando Duty-Free Show in the late spring. I took J with me to that as it was held during his Easter holidays, and he had missed me during the previous month when I had been in the Far East.

From the Orlando Show, Fred, J and I flew at the invitation of Jack Lyons, to visit him in his apartment on Fisher Island, just off Miami. J, who was now approaching his fourteen birthday was delighted to be offered the use of a buggy to drive round in while Fred and I briefed Mr. Lyons on the progress we were making. All Jack's staff referred to him as 'Sir Jack' and so did Freddie. I didn't. He had lost his knighthood and, in my opinion, was lucky to be soaking up the Miami sunshine while his fellow felons were soaking up prison atmosphere.

When J returned from his buggy trip, he joined us. Later as we left for Miami Airport, having bid our farewells to 'Sir Jack,' J said, "I don't think that man likes you Daddy." He was right.

It hadn't always been that way. Earlier that year when 'Sir Jack' was still trying to get me on side to be perhaps a 'second Farzad', he had asked me to go to the start of the London to Jordan Car Rally and present the Duke of Kent with a gold Ronson Queen Anne table lighter to give as a gift to the King of Jordan.

For reasons that I can't remember, it was also decided around that time, that we really must upgrade our computer software. So, while I was away on these trips through the winter and spring of 1997, this project proceeded under the control of acting finance director Christine. It was a disaster as the new software didn't work and we were suddenly finding it hard to follow orders, deliveries, debtors, creditors, stock levels or anything else. This was really frightening and totally added to the excessive pressure we were already under.

Once back in England, I received a message from Farzad. 'Sir Jack' would like me to show him round the LGW warehouse and have a private meeting with me afterwards in the board room there. A date was set.

I arrived and showed 'Sir Jack' round the duty-free warehouse, which also now housed Ronson stock. He didn't seem anything like as interested as Farzad had appeared on his visit a year ago. In fact, the tour only took about ten minutes before we were upstairs to the board room and to drink coffee.

'Sir Jack,' who had been most courteous on our tour, started the conversation:

"I want you to tell me the exact state of play now. Moreover, going forward, you will take your orders from me and only me" he said in a different tone than before.

I was polite but at pains to point out two important points:

“Firstly, you are not a board member, we are in a closed period and as a result, if I was to tell you what I know today, we would both be breaking the law, which I do not intend to do.

“Secondly, I acknowledge that you are a major investor. However, you are not on the board, hold no official position as a result, and this is a fully listed London quoted company, which is owned by all its shareholders. The company has an appointed board to look after their interests and I, as CEO, cannot therefore, give you either special treatment or break the law.”

“So, you are accusing me of wanting to break the law and are bringing up Distillers?”

“I have not mentioned Distillers. All I am saying is that I can’t give you insider information, or we both could be in trouble.”

“I have invested £5 million in this company, and you have invested only a few thousand and you have the cheek to lecture me.”

With that ‘Sir Jack’ stormed out. He thought that having invested £5 million he had a right of control, and I knew that while that might work in a private firm, it couldn’t in a public company. Moreover, while ‘Sir Jack’ had invested his money, I had invested my life to the point of not being far off a nervous breakdown and, unlike 1992, on this occasion it was not my fault.

That weekend, I went to our Dorset home and bust an Achilles tendon, racing Bobby, our family poodle, round the outside of the house. I was to be in plaster for 14 weeks but kept working.

The June board meeting approached. ‘Sir Jack’ took the original three non-executives out to a restaurant with him, Kilkenny and Farzad one night beforehand.

Over dinner, he told them that unless they backed Kilkenny's motion to fire me, he would be suing them for misleading him into making the investment in the first place. James Roe initially resisted saying that I had the staff dedicated and motivated and my removal, in these very difficult times, would make matters a lot worse.

However, lovable and decent James quickly gave in when Farzad pointed out that they all might lose their homes if they backed me, and Shaun Dowling added that he agreed with 'Sir Jack' in any case.

So, unbeknown to me, the dye was cast. However, now the plot thickens. It was decided to ensure Lars Rydstrom and Laurie Todd, the new finance director, were also on side. Laurie was told that his job was safe. It wasn't. Lars was told he could become the new CEO. He didn't. However, they were not to know this at the time and Lars was also under the threat of being sued too. They agreed.

The plan would be to pretend that the directors had only just found out that Christine and I co-habited and would insist on our resignations as a result. Then they would declare that due to the computer issues, which they intended to blame Christine for, they did not believe that certain debtors were recoverable and throw the kitchen sink at the P&L. This way they could take provisions now, with Christine and me getting the blame and then hopefully release them in future years to bolster profits.

The board meeting was set to be in Kilkenny's office. I suspected by the change of venue that something was afoot. It seemed just like PHKI in 1991 all over again, but worse because of the lying and the subterfuge.

On arrival, I was shown to a different room and told that James Roe would be joining me shortly. He didn't. As I sat there, I knew what was happening, and knew that it was 'Sir Jack's' doing, but did not realise that they would absurdly claim that Christine and I were being shown the door due to our domestic arrangements.

This was a preposterous lie as everyone from 1994 onwards, who was associated with Ronson, knew that we were living together. Everyone knew that in the week I lived in Christine's apartment overlooking the Thames and all Ronson executives and some directors, including James and his wife had stayed as our guests in Dorset, where we openly slept together and clearly Christine knew her way around the kitchen there too.

Moreover, the invention of an additional £1m loss due to bad debt provisions was also wholly unfounded and caused the share price collapse that followed my resignation to be much worse and cost other shareholders losses which need not have happened.

I agreed a press release that said that Christine and I were resigning. Christine worried that inferences would be drawn. James assured her that her departure would be but a byline. Kilkenny said he wasn't so sure. What James and I didn't realise was that in addition to the press release, Kilkenny would be briefing pet journalists with these juicy extra titbits.

I had fought too long and hard, had cared too much about my wonderful lieutenants and their staff, and knew none of us could have tried harder, to want it to end this way. However, I was exhausted and so a part of me was happy to walk away from the stress.

There was a Ronson party that night in London to promote the Ronson Rebel, Racer and Retro products. Outside the venue, there was a bus with Howard as Ronson Rebel down the side and on the rear. I now felt very sad that all this wonderful camaraderie and belief in each other was to be fried not on the fire in North Shields but on the fire of 'Sir Jack's' paranoia and greed. I knew not only had I lost the battle but, on this day, Ronson had lost the war. And so, it proved to be.

During the party a famous paparazzi photographer, that I was friendly with, appeared. He had been tipped off to get a shot of Christine and me. He said, "I can hide and get it anyway or you can agree to let me," he said decently.

"Follow me" I said and led him outside to where the bus was. He photographed Christine and me at the rear of the Ronson bus. I had disliked 'Sir Jack' a lot, but I could never ever dislike Ronson staff and having to write this now twenty-seven years later has deeply upset me.

The next morning, I went into the BBC television studios at Shepherds Bush to give an interview on breakfast TV. The interviewer was Paul Burden. He had interviewed me several times before. We agreed to talk about the results, the trading prospects and my resignation without bringing up any personal issues.

I liked Paul and trusted him. However, I suspect as part of 'Sir Jack's' plan, he had clearly been got at and brought up personal relationships despite promising not to. I was furious but kept my cool. Then, he told the audience at home, that what they could not see was that my leg was in plaster and then jokingly asked me if I had fallen off my Cuban heel boots.

"No, I fell off a big fat woman," I replied in a flat John Lennon voice. The camera and soundmen roared with laughter as the interview closed.

Now it was Paul who was furious. He told me that he did the jokes and not the interviewee. I told him that he should keep his promises if he didn't want me to upstage him. The clip was later shown, among others, on a BBC programme named 'The Interviewee Fights Back' which was presented by Angus Deayton.

The next day the press coverage was huge, with massive column inches given over in all the broadsheets as well as the tabloids. This was also because, unfortunately, there was not much else going on at that time. The Daily Telegraph even dedicated the whole of their page 3 to a giant photograph of the two of us. Moreover, these stories were to run every day for the next 10 days with even Nigel Dempster, the famous Daily Mail gossip columnist, getting in on the act.

However, the tone was not as bad as I had feared it might be. Yes, one or two tabloid papers majored on the 'bedroom and board room' aspect and a few had noted that 'women were my downfall', but by and large the coverage was sympathetic given the trauma Ronson had suffered since the fire and the brave fight it had put up to recover from it.

This is not what 'Sir Jack' had intended or expected. Therefore, if the 'free' press were not going to write what he wanted, he would force the issue. I believe that his motive was not purely vindictive but that he was also motivated by a desire to ensure that I could not recapture the moral high ground by suggesting that he had wanted to have illegal conversations with me and that I had refused and so I would demand an EGM to be re-appointed CEO.

As a result, I got a call from Alan Kilkenny saying that the 'Independent' wanted to do an interview. I said I didn't want to give one because that publication, and in particular, if Jason Nisse was writing the article, would do a hatchet job on both Christine and me.

Kilkenny assured me that this was not the case, that the journalist was a woman, an admirer and had asked him to introduce her to me. I had been very slow to realise what was going on so far and had failed to piece it altogether – but then I didn't have 20/20 hindsight as I do now after lengthy conversations with James Roe in the years that followed. So, stupidly, I agreed.

The female admirer was one Deborah Ross. She arrived at our Dorset home looking pretty, was vivacious and seemed to be a genuine sympathiser with what had happened to us. She was alluring and I was lured into a chatty unguarded discourse.

In fact, she was no fan but a smiling assassin, determined to get 'Sir Jack's' idea of what the coverage should be across to her readers.

Her article was entitled 'Bed & Board – Howard's Way' and it was advertised on the front page above the publication's name. It began:

'Howard Hodgson - the man who, in spite of a Lesley Judd meets Kenny Dalglish hairdo, managed to make undertaking quite a bit sexy - was booted out as chief executive of Ronson last week. Actually, he resigned.

But if he hadn't resigned, he would have been booted out, so it amounts to much the same thing. And, yes, he is jolly cross. Not so much with what happened, but more with the coverage.

As the tabloids had it, Mr Hodgson was asked to stand down because Christine Pickles, the company's corporate development manager, had become his mistress and the other directors did not take kindly to this swashbuckling juxtaposition of boardroom and bedroom. Miss Pickles, it was reported, was even promoted to finance director at one point.'

Actually, I hadn't been 'jolly cross' about the cover, but 'Sir Jack' had been.

The rest of the article didn't get any more accurate or kinder by making Christine 'the 32-year-old' out to be 'very pretty', 'devoted to Howard', but kept in the kitchen; while I was likeable but incredibly vain. But it had clearly achieved what 'Sir Jack' wanted, and I had walked straight into the trap and so only had myself to blame.

As a result of all this media attention, the BBC beat a hasty path to my door to ask if they could make a programme about Christine and me in their series 'Blood on the Boardroom Carpet.' We sensibly declined. Earlier, we had agreed to meet a journalist from the Daily Mail. However, having read the Deborah Ross story, Christine and I interviewed with such boring 'straight bat' answers that the Mail decided the interview was not worth printing.

Ronson then appointed Shaun Dowling as acting CEO. Subsequently, he delighted in refusing to pay up my contract as an act of sweet revenge for me forcing him to honour his underwriting liabilities. However, he didn't last long in that position, and a nice chap, by the name of Richard Furze, replaced him. Richard realised that a lawsuit from me could cause Ronson serious problems and so he settled the matter by paying the full notice period of £100,000. However, and unfairly, Christine only received £12,000.

xxxxxxx

Just when I thought that we had seen the back of these disasters, a much worse family disaster struck us and made me put Ronson and the unfairness of it all into perspective. I immediately stopped feeling sorry for myself.

My sister's eldest son, a handsome and very likeable boy called Alex, died unexpectedly from a cocktail of cannabis and Prozac – which he had been prescribed for depression. This was understandably crushingly devastating for both her, his father Chris and younger brother Simon.

I gave the eulogy at Alex's funeral. He had been working at Ronson only a few weeks before for 'work experience.' There I had come face to face with him as I descended the main LGW stairs with a party of executives and he was running up. He had his Ronson tie in his hand.

"Hi Uncle Howard, just going to the loo to put my tie on to impress that Iranian geezer."

That 'Iranian geezer' was Farzad, and he was standing next to me.

I loved Alex very much but, more importantly, I realised that Denny, Chris and Simon's devastation was every bit as bad, no, it was worse, as that that Marianne, Howard and I had been through fifteen years before. Indeed, within a few years Denny suffered from breast cancer and Chris became increasingly withdrawn from the death of Alex onwards. They did survive but at a shocking price. They were older than Marianne and I had been when Charles had died, and, as Alex was older than Charles, they had loved him longer.

After the funeral, as I hobbled to the village hall on my crutches for the wake, my Auntie June, elder sister of my father, berated me for bringing the family name into disrepute.

"Every time I pick up a newspaper, there seems to be another sex scandal involving you and a different woman. You should be ashamed of yourself."

Before I could answer, my wonderful cousin Clarissa replied, "Well, it was Mandy and I who got him started."

This was true. Mandy was her younger sister and she, Clarissa and I used to frolic as a naughty three-some when I was a nine-year-old. Auntie June was appalled.

Alex was a cheeky, fun loving but very decent lad. What happened to him was an accident – but an avoidable accident. Do not mess with drugs.

xxxxxxx

Next, I got a phone call from an American called Ed Guinan. I needed to get back to work as I wanted to avoid a repeat of 1992's frivolity and had answered his advert for a CEO. He presumed, having read the newspapers, that I was available and wanted to hire me. He invited me to meet him in London. He owned a company called

'Countdown' which sold 'affinity cards' that guaranteed the holder discounts on numerous goods or services.

Ed hired me on the spot and offered me £20,000 a month, this meant £240,000 per annum and was £90,000-a-year more than Ronson had paid me. However, there was a problem. He didn't pay me and after six weeks I left and took him to court. He paid £30,000 plus legal fees on the morning he was due to appear.

Life seemed to be very harsh. I had been unfairly dismissed by the cunning plan of a convicted felon; Christine had not only lost her job but could have had her reputation ruined because of the need to drag her into 'Sir Jack's' plot; I had had to threaten to sue Ronson to collect the £100,000 due to me; I had been appointed CEO of Countdown, but they hadn't paid me until they were due in court. How very frustrating. Gunpowder, treason and plot. And we had lost Alex. Surely, it couldn't get any worse? Oh yes it could.

xxxxxxx

Jason Nisse was now to re-enter my saga, once more as the pantomime villain. Without any warning or verification from me, he ran a long piece under the headline, 'How to Become Dead Unpopular.' It was all about Prontac from back in 1992. It appeared out of the blue and came as a complete surprise.

You will recall that Prontac had been a successful operation built by a man called David Meakin. He had sold 80 franchises for franchisees to supply monthly management accounts, and when the company got dragged down by a cross-guarantee with its sister company Integrity, it had gone into receivership. Subsequently, I bought the rights to operate the software and gifted them to the franchisees. The successful ones were grateful and that had appeared to be the end of the matter.

However, this article by our version of Boy George, claimed that eleven disgruntled franchisees planned to form an action group over five years on with the intention of coming after the man with deep pockets – me. As already mentioned, this was the last 'nasty' article Nisse was ever to pen about me.

Immediately, I called my lawyers from that time, Edge & Ellison, and asked to see them at their Birmingham offices. Graham Hodson, whom you will remember was with me at Hodgson & Sons Ltd, Hodgson Holdings plc, PHKI and Prontac, and had been introduced to venture capitalists by Chris Callaway and me to form a quasi-mark 2 Hodgson Holdings, was also there. He now was CEO of a private equity firm called Laurel and so was as worried as me by the article.

We went through their possible case and therefore our possible defence. I left and drove back to Dorset. However, upon my return, I had a fax waiting for me from James Retallack, the partner dealing with the case. In it he made it clear that, as Graham was their current client, they would act for him and, as there might be a conflict of interest in any ensuing case, they could not act for me.

I was astounded. I had engaged Edge & Ellison in 1985 and had paid them over £3 million in fees in the glory Hodgson Holdings days of the late '80s. Now they were casting me aside because they were currently acting for Graham when he bought a funeral director. Surely, this couldn't be right as they had acted for me when Prontac had gone into administration and therefore had confidential information which might be helpful to Graham and not available to me? I determined if they weren't going to act for one of us then they weren't going to act for either of us.

Nevertheless, at that moment it seemed as if even God had turned against me. However, enter stage left, a knight in shining armour by the name of Barry Samuels.

Barry had worked for Edge & Ellison and defended me against the potential charge of being a shadow director of Prontac's holding company in 1993. It was his ten-page letter that finished with the magnificent sentence 'The above facts clearly prove that the idea that my client is guilty of any wrong-doing at all is completely preposterous.'

Now four long years later, he had moved to the London and Queen's solicitor Kingsley Napley. Barry, on reading 'Boy George's' article, wrote to me and offered his services again. I asked him if he would also accept Fox and Meakin. He agreed. I was delighted.

The first thing he did was blow James Retallack out of the water by telling him that his firm could not possibly act for Graham, because they had acted for me in this matter previously. He threatened to report Edge & Ellison to the Law Society. They immediately relented and sent Graham packing to some minor other Birmingham firm.

Then we just had to wait. However, soon enough, one Saturday morning just after Christine, J, Dink and I returned from a wonderful autumn half-term break in Jamacia, a writ was served. This was to become a feature over the next year – nasty things were always being delivered on a Saturday morning.

The eleven franchisees were suing Meakin, Fox, Hodson and Hodgson for millions of pounds. Meakin, Fox and Hodgson gathered at Barry's London office, where we were sent off to look through all our papers. David and Steve did most of this work as I hadn't ever worked in the company.

Barry is a very fine and thorough lawyer. He is, like 'Sir Jack' was (Lyons died in 2008), Jewish. A high proportion of good British lawyers are Jewish. Barry is just as wonderful an advert for the

Jewish faith as 'Sir Jack' wasn't. Barry then appointed a fellow Jew by the name of Gerald as QC.

Months passed and the case weighed heavily on my mind. You saw how hard I had worked in Volume I to recreate the Hodgson family wealth. Now aged 47 I was wealthier than ever before. I had recovered the relatively small loss caused by Prontac, and while Ronson might have damaged my health and reputation, it hadn't dented my bank balance, as I held only a small number of shares, and cautious investments had paid off and raised Marianne and my joint wealth to over £10 million. This was still a relatively large sum in 1997. However, I realised that if I lost this case, I could seriously diminish that figure.

My mother, seeing me looking pensive one Sunday afternoon, asked why I didn't offer these franchisees £250,000.

"Because I have done nothing wrong. Because paying them off would only encourage the other 69 to come after us. Because 'the eleven' would only smell blood and not accept" I replied wearily.

In this frame of mind, I took Marianne out to lunch and advised her that we should divorce in case, and against all the evidence, I lost. This was necessary as, if we were to remain married, I had been advised that they could come after the settlement I had given her. We instructed a lawyer together straight away.

The franchisees' lawyers came from Preston and had been appointed by their apparent leader, a man named Chris McSpirit, who came from that area of Lancashire – and Christine even knew him. Then their solicitors advertised for more lawyers to work on a large forthcoming case by a group of franchisees against the owners of the franchisor.

Eventually, a date was set for the case, and Gerald wanted some proof of evidence to support our claim that there was no case to answer anyway as it was out of time. However, we did not have the paperwork to hand to give him that.

Our point was that the claimants were saying that their case should be allowed to be heard on the grounds that they were unaware of the administration until sometime after it had occurred and therefore the clock of time limitation should only start from when they knew and not the actual date of administration. Meakin, Fox and Hodgson claimed that they did know but we had no supporting documentation.

So, it was decided to send David and Steve to the receiver's offices in Manchester and ask for the boxes of Prontac documents that were held there for anyone to read. They went and sat under 'library conditions' reading a mountain of information.

Just before noon an excited David called me on his mobile and whispered down the phone that they had found a letter from the claimants to their lawyers clearly instructing them a year earlier than they were now claiming. They were lying and had known everything at the time of the letter being sent. And as it was dated a year before they were now claiming that they knew about the administration, they were out of time.

David asked me what he should do as he couldn't just steal the letter.

"It is in the public domain. Anyone can read it. Put it in your pocket. Go to lunch and photocopy it several times. After lunch return the original letter to the box" was what I asked him to do. But he asked me to check with Barry and Gerald first, saying that it was better to be safe rather than sorry. Of course, he was right.

So, I explained the position to Barry and Gerald. Barry was delighted to proceed, but Gerald didn't want to use it saying we had an excellent defence and had nothing to fear, and we had never received the letter from a franchisee, but we were 'borrowing' a copy from the receiver's library.

I was also certain we had an excellent defence. However, I saw no reason not to have the judge throw the case out and be therefore 100% certain of winning. The franchisees were out of time and had lied to the court and we had every right to read a letter which was in the public domain.

However, Gerald stood firm. Then it occurred to me that there was another way. There were a few franchisees who had started in 'The Franchisee Action Group' but had had second thoughts and had continued to operate their accountancy firms with the software instead. I called one and asked if he still had a copy of the original letter. He had and he sent it to me.

We went to court. We submitted the evidence and the judge, rightly, found for us immediately and awarded us costs. Game, set and match and much relief.

Soon afterwards one of the claimants wrote to me to remind me how I had helped the franchisees in 1992. He went on the say that the burden of £500,000 legal fees payable by just eleven poor individuals was crippling as it was over £45,000 each and that they had only paid £10,000 each for their franchise in the first place.

I replied:

'Dear Sir,

I am not inclined to help you given the outrageously dishonest and unfair case you brought. It has put my family and me under a great deal of unnecessary stress as a result.

Therefore, and for the avoidance of doubt, if you were on fire on the other side of the street from me, I would not bother to cross the road to piss on you to put the fire out.

I trust I make myself clear.

Yours faithfully,

Howard Hodgson'.

I did not receive a reply.

Don't fuck with the Peaky Blinders! And 'my God' I had been fucked with. But I had won through and beaten Ronson, Countdown and now this miserable claim.

Life had been enormously stressful in 1996 and 1997 and I had felt as traumatised as I had in 1992. However, there was a distinct difference. 1992 was 100% my fault. The events of 1996 and 1997 were 100% not my fault and I could take some comfort from that.

But what lay ahead?

# This Life In Death

December1959, Birmingham.

When Russell died, the unpleasant image I had of him during the latter years of his life in my head immediately disappeared and the sweet memories of our idyllic childhood replaced them 'in the twinkling of an eye'.

Circa 1967, UK.

Beatle Paul building sandcastles with a very young Julian Lennon – just as Julian explained to me in 1996.

June 1989, Birmingham.

J and me leaving for work.

December 1989, The NEC Birmingham – PKHI Annual Conference.

Father Christmas reveals himself to be a semi-naked herself. I am shocked and immediately know that the 'red tops' will have a field day.

1990, London.

The late great Sir Harry Secombe and I launch the PHKI Bereavement Support Programme in London on a cold day.

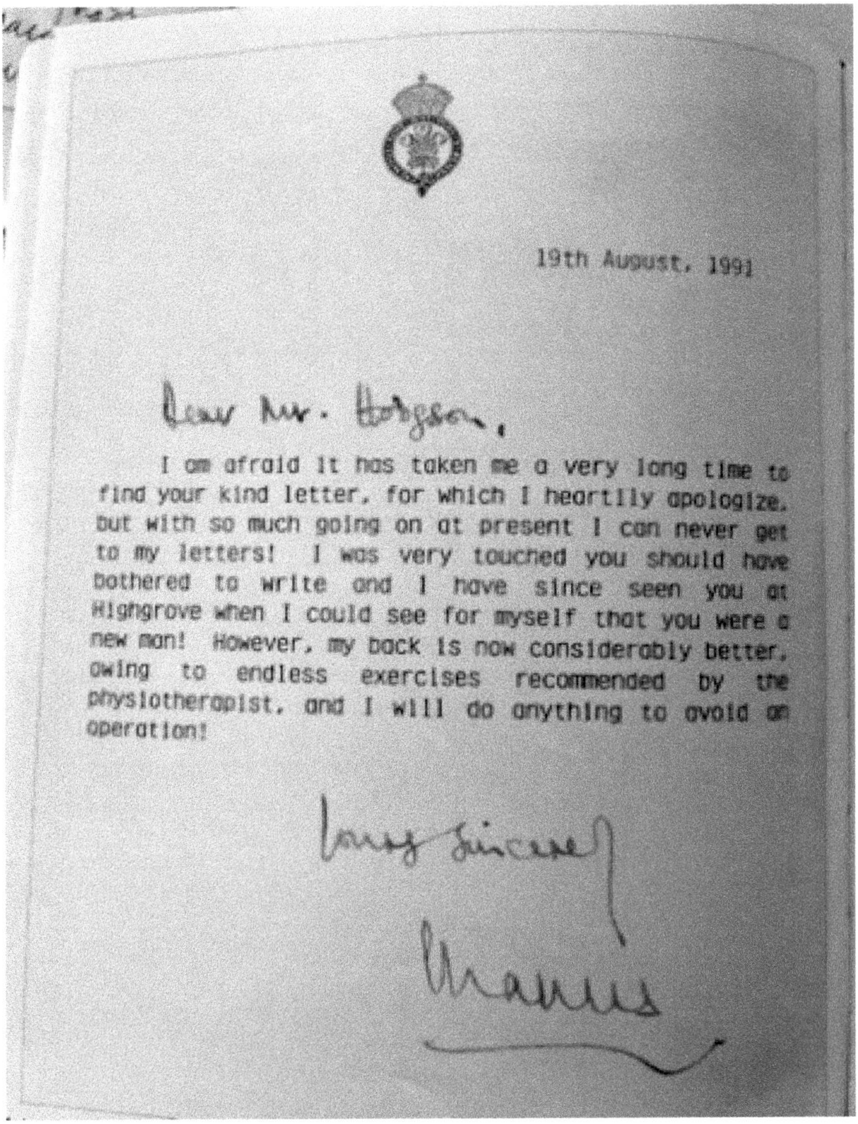

19th August, 1991

Dear Mr. Hodgson,

I am afraid it has taken me a very long time to find your kind letter, for which I heartily apologize, but with so much going on at present I can never get to my letters! I was very touched you should have bothered to write and I have since seen you at Highgrove when I could see for myself that you were a new man! However, my back is now considerably better, owing to endless exercises recommended by the physiotherapist, and I will do anything to avoid an operation!

Yours sincerely

Charles

August 1991, Highgrove.

The letter received from HRH Prince of Wales following my advice to him to consider having a back operation. It had been a 'spikey moment' but this letter, received within days, shows the true humanity and grace of the King.

1991, Belgravia, London.

Davinia smiles at her mother. She was so small when she was born that we called her 'Dinky'. And she has remained so named for 35 years.

1991, London.

John Gunn and I launch Hodgson & Partners at the Berkeley Hotel in London. It was to be a complete failure.

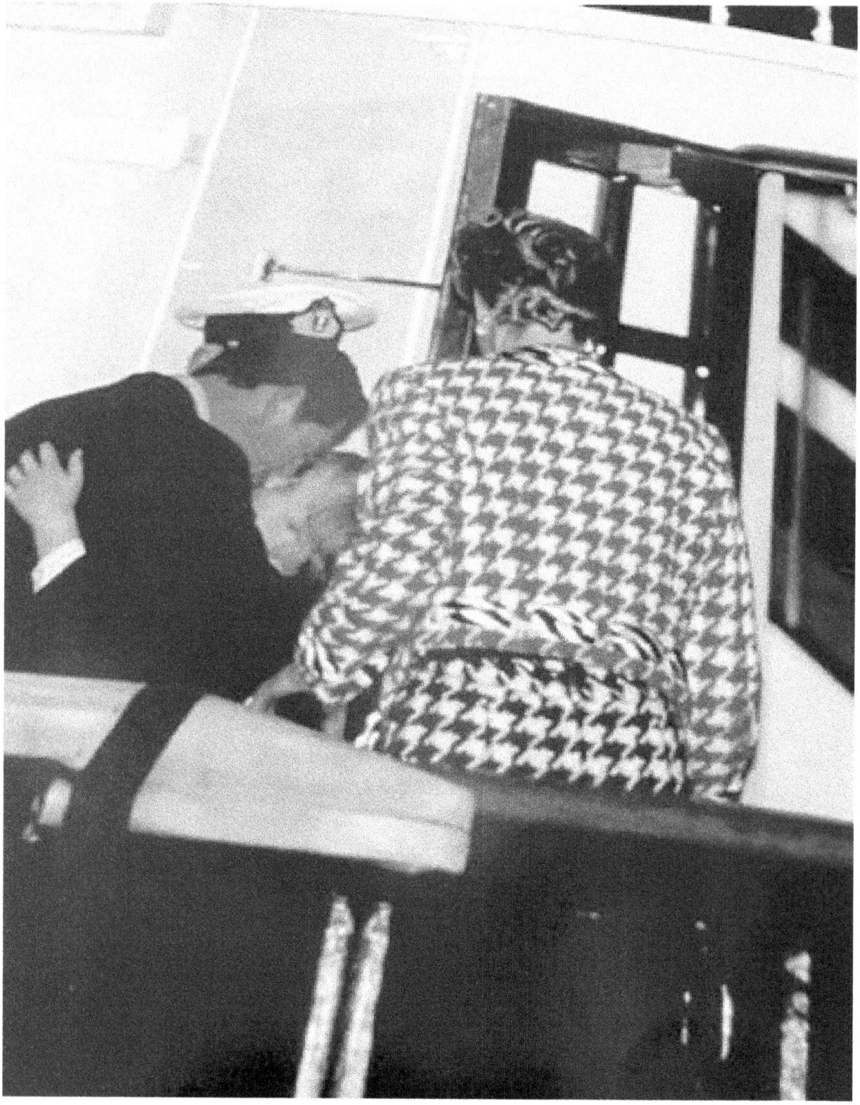

1991, Canada.

Aboard Britannia in Canada. This shot tells no lies. King Charles was a doting father to his sons. The 'Diana propaganda' that he wasn't made me determined to write his biography.

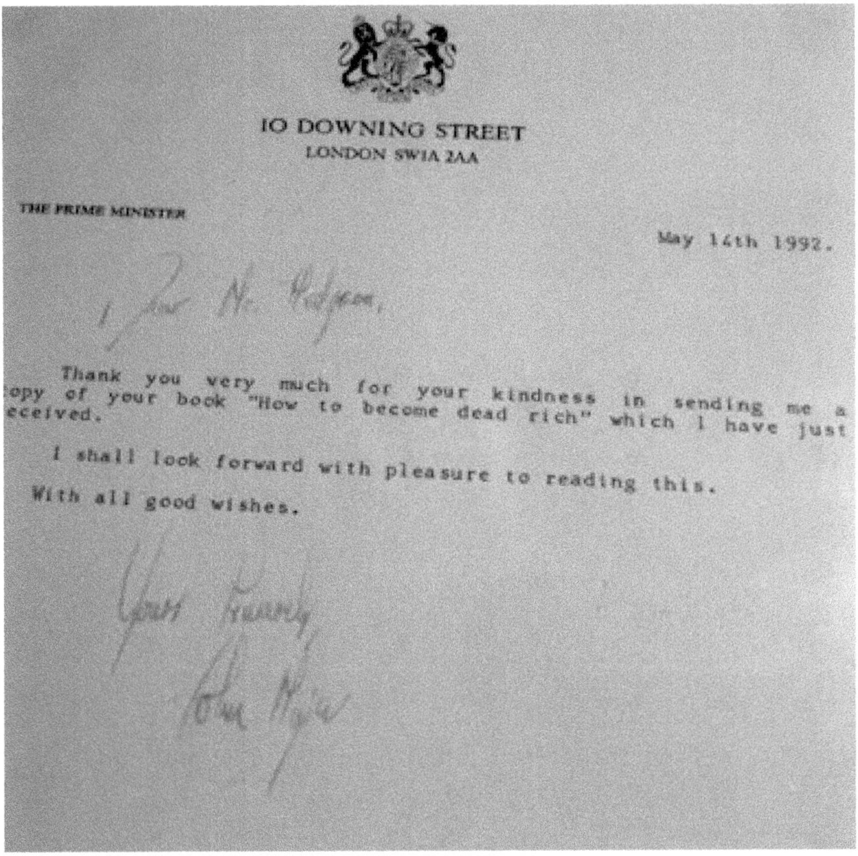

10 DOWNING STREET
LONDON SW1A 2AA

THE PRIME MINISTER

May 14th 1992.

Thank you very much for your kindness in sending me a copy of your book "How to become dead rich" which I have just received.

I shall look forward with pleasure to reading this.

With all good wishes.

May 1992, London.

The amiable John Major writes to me to thank me for his copy of 'How to Become Dead Rich'. I'm not too sure he ever did read it.

January 1993, Wilton Place, London.

A Peaky Blinder dancing with his daughter.

August 1993, London.

The Daily Telegraph reported on 23rd August, 'Howard Hodgson, new CEO of Hoskins Brewery plc, outside Coopers & Lybrand on the Embankment today'. I was back and you can see the delight in my face.

1996, Poole.

Christine and I sailing ‘Quantum Dink’. Chris Callaway took the photo.

Cyprus, October 1996.

J & me fishing.

1997 Pall Mall, London.

HRH Duke of Kent with me at the start of the London to Jordan car rally.

Chewton Glen Hampshire, 3rd September 1999.

'The day war broke out'. Christine has been a very forgiving and loving wife.

Spring 2004, London.

Marianne and I present a cheque from the Charles Hodgson Foundation for Children for £35,000 to Sir Tom Shebbeare, at the Prince's Trust HQ. Tom was devoted to the then Prince of Wales.

2004, Gloucestershire.

Christine being introduced by Dame Julia Cleverdon to HRH at Highgrove.

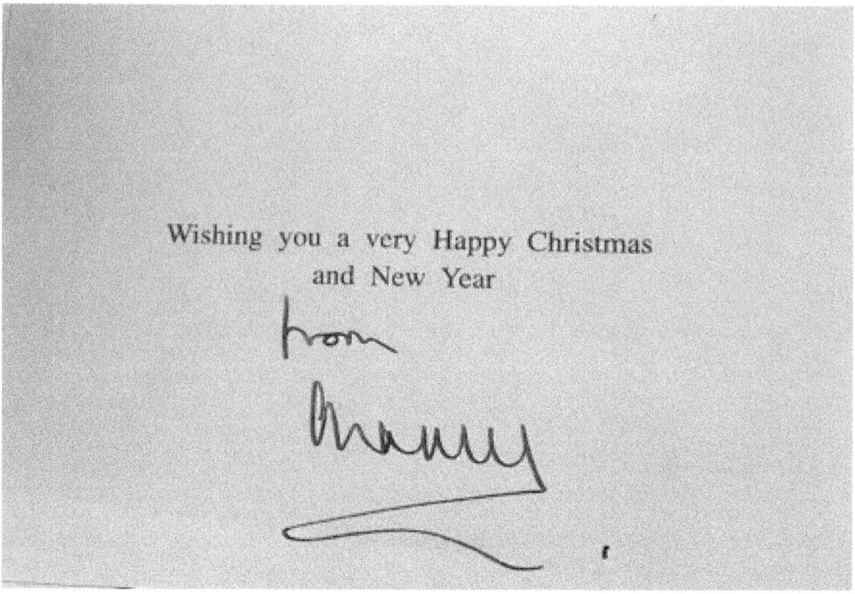
Wishing you a very Happy Christmas
and New Year
from

December, 2005

Our Christmas card from HRH Prince of Wales.

24th November 2006, London.

Davinia meets George Paul Anthony Howard Hodgson for the first time.

January 2009, Malta.

George and me in a boat yard in St Julians.

## This Life In Death

October 2012, Malta.

I am 62 and while my friends are retiring and looking after grandchildren, I am starting out to build Memoria and have these two incredible sons to keep me young.

Xmas 2012, Buckingham Palace.

Camilla, then the Duchess of Cornwall, tells me that I have captured Prince Charles perfectly in my biography of him. I am clearly star-struck by our future Queen.

# This Life In Death

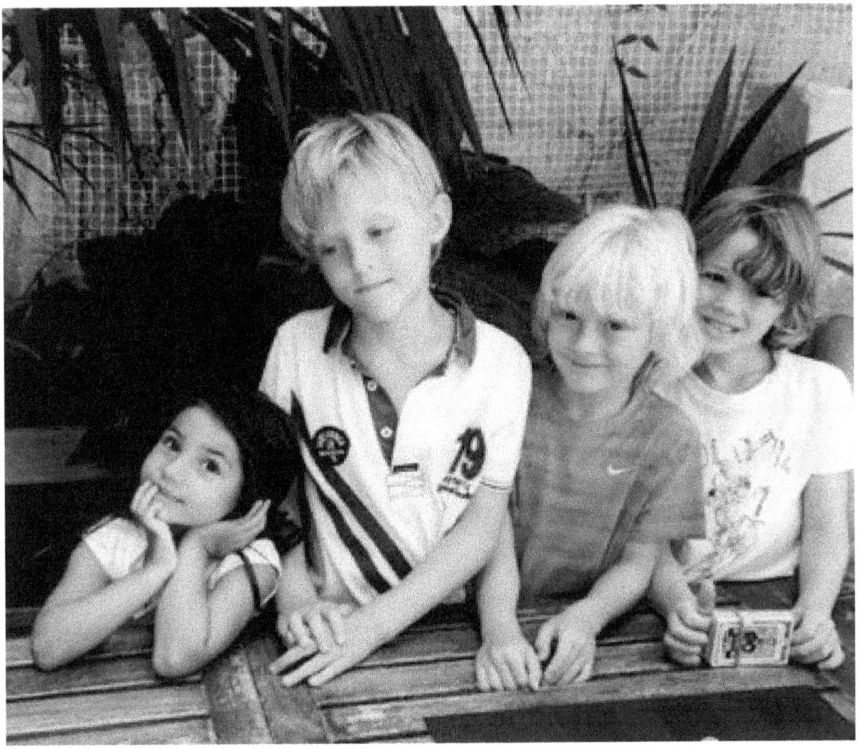

Summer 2013, Malta.

Harriet, George, Horatio and Charles at 'The Castle'.

Xmas 2014, Buckingham Palace.

"Have you read my biography of you Sir?", I asked. "No. Why would I want to read a book about myself?", replied the Prince of Wales in 2014.

Xmas 2014, Buckingham Palace

“Because you might learn something” I blurted out while inexcusably pointing my finger. The look on Christine’s face tells you that she thinks her ‘gong’ has just been flushed down the toilet as a result. She needn’t have worried. I have never admired a man more than King Charles III. This was a very strange way of showing it.

Boxing Day 2015, Villa Park.

My mother and Doug Ellis are reunited after 40 years to watch Villa draw against West Ham.

August 2017, Cannes France.

George (left) and Horatio. These boys come into the world, when my friends were having grandchildren!

January 2018, London.

Me taking Horatio back to his mum after his birthday weekend with me. The balloons are claret and blue of course.

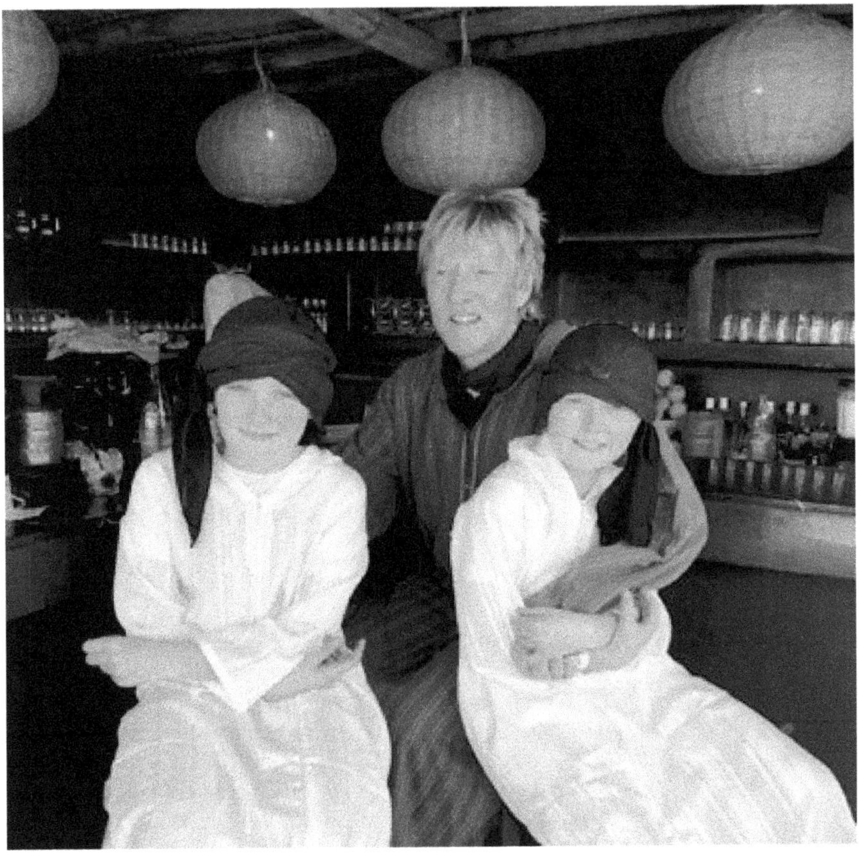

April 2018, Morocco.

George (left), Horatio and I blend in with the natives!

June 2019, Stratton Audley, Oxfordshire.

Man never had a better daughter. A very proud father arrives at church with Davinia.

# This Life In Death

June 2019, Oxford.

The last time I was to dance with my mother was on the occasion of Davinia's wedding.

June 2019, Oxfordshire.

Michael Hackney and me just before Davinia's wedding in June 2019. He has been my friend for over 40 years, in our family for over 30 and my business partner for over 20. We are great mates.

June 2019, Stratton Audley Hall.

The whole Hodgson and Steele clans together in the grand drawing room of Stratton Audley Hall.

June 2019, Stratton Audley Hall.

The boys play football the morning after Davinia's wedding at Stratton Audley Hall. Alex and most other French guys are not in Villa shirts.

July 2019, Sweden.

The Gothia World Cup. Horatio (left) represents South-East England boys. He is a genuine two-footed player and scores several goals with both at the competition.

July 2019, South of France.

Horatio, J and Emma at Anjuna Beach – a favourite watering hole in the South of France for many, not least the late and much missed Eddie Jordan.

# This Life In Death

22nd February 2020, Hampshire.

It is my birthday dinner at Chewton Glen Hotel. This was to be the last time my mother was to be photographed with me and all my surviving children and grandchildren. Within days the pandemic lockdown was announced, and the next family get together was sadly to be at her funeral.

November 2020, Dorset.

My two dogs, Oscar (left) and Ossie. Now that my six children have all grown up – I'm happy still to have them at home!

July 2022, Monaco.

His Serene Highness Prince Albert welcomes Christine and I as members of The Yacht Club, Monaco.

2023, Doncaster.

Opening Memoria's 17th crematoria in 18 years, Memoria Doncaster & South Yorkshire.

July 2023, Oxfordshire.

Davinia and I accompany a dancing ‘Lady Mary’ into a restaurant.

May 2024, Mougins France.

My godson, William, the son of my French 'brother' Alex and his wife 'Difficult Woman'. They are a wonderfully close family.

# This Life In Death

June 2024, Monaco.

Chris Callaway and me at the Yacht Club Monaco. He has been a good friend for 40 years and saved my career in 1992.

July 2024, Cannes, France.

J (left), George and me having a beer at the Carlton Beach Club. Great sunset.

August 2024, St Tropez.

I kiss an Angel. My wonderful daughter-in-law Lorraine. One of the three saints I have known.

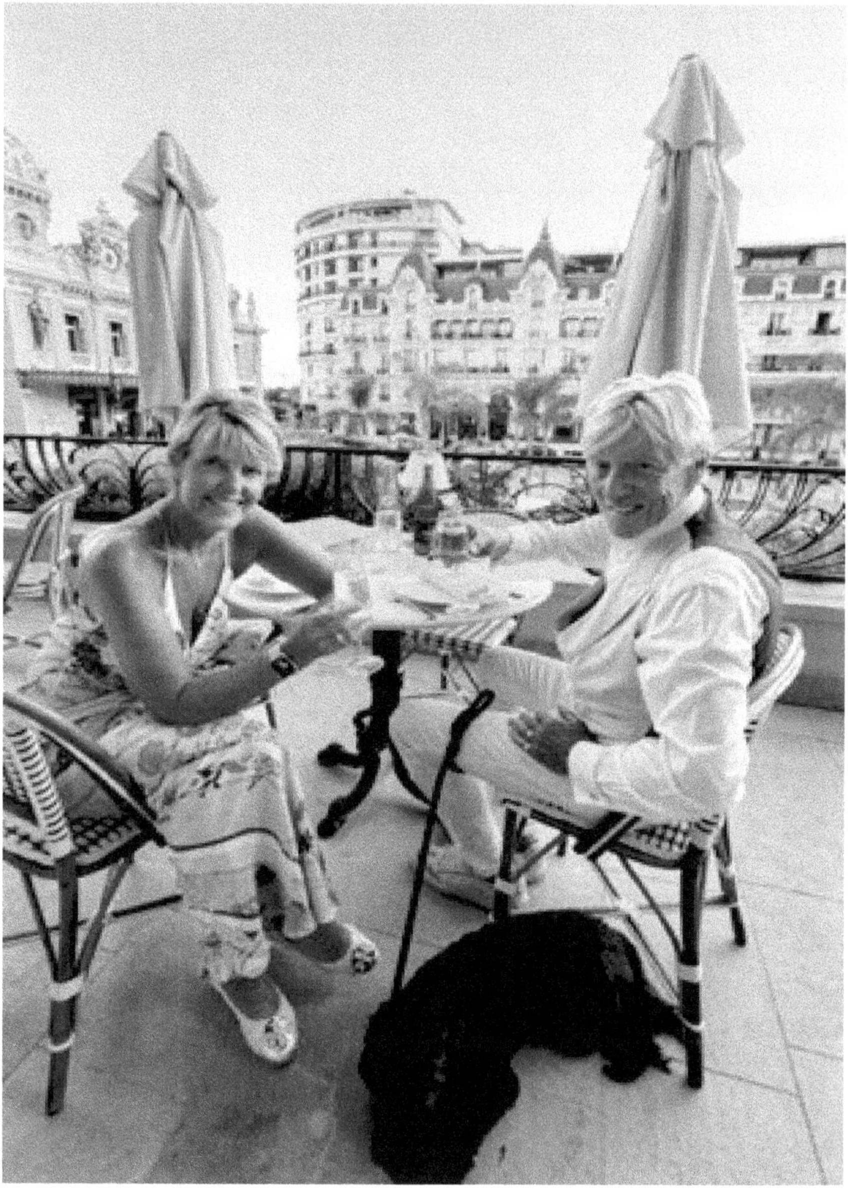

September 2024, Casino Square, Monaco.

Christine and I celebrate 25 years of marriage.

October 2024, Sardinia.

View from the top of the mast on King Charles III in the Bosun's chair.

# This Life In Death

October 2024, Stromboli.

Sailing King Charles III back from Malta to Monaco in October 2024.

# This Life In Death

October 2024, Dubai.

Howie (left) and me form 'the wall'. He is 50 and I'm 74 – but we are 'Peaky Blinders. We did win the game too.

19th December 2024, 02 London.

The whole family, Richard, George, Jamieson, Howard, Lorraine, Harriet, me, Davinia, Emma, Horatio, Charles and Christine – oh and James Paul Mozart (aka McCartney)

## This Life In Death

December 2024, 02, London.

The ever-youthful James Paul McCartney on stage. I took the whole family, and we all cried tears of joy.

Christmas Eve 2024, Stratton Audley Hall.

Marianne and me Christmas Eve 2024 at Stratton Audley Hall with the entire family.

Christmas Day, 2024, Oxford, England.

Marianne and me with our three surviving children.

Mougins, France, January 2025.

Me with my granddaughter Alexandra, known to me as ‘Lady Mary’.

## This Life In Death

Chapter VI

Back In The USSR & Into A Wilderness

1998 – 2004

Christine was offered, in the autumn of 1997, a job with Ernst & Young Southampton which looked likely to lead to a partnership. I advised her to accept it. However, instead she accepted an offer to become Company Secretary of Capgemini UK, part of the Capgemini Group, a French competitor of the likes of IBM and Accenture in the world of technology services. I was surprised because the job only paid £65,000 per annum and meant she would have to travel up to London and back from Dorset five days a week. My advice was wrong.

Within months she became the UK Finance Director and went on, via many other promotions, to end up on the Group Executive Committee and become CEO of the UK over a glittering twenty-two year Capgemini career which also led her to a second portfolio career with roles such as the senior independent non-executive director of Standard Chartered Bank and Chairman of Severn Trent Plc amongst other directorships. So, Sir Jack's plans to put her on the scrap heap utterly failed.

But what about me? I had looked at buying Ronson and saving the ship and its crew with both my friend David Tang and another Hong Kong acquaintance Wilfred Wong. However, neither effort got off the ground.

One Friday, in December 1997, Christine and I went up to London so she could attend her first Capgemini Christmas party, before we took the train to Paris for the weekend.

While she was in the party, I had room service and watched a little TV. An idea came to me. Why didn't I take all of the stories I had collected over my twenty-five-year career in funeral directing, condense them into a week, and weave them into a plot about three fictional funeral firms in Birmingham and call it 'Six Feet Under.'

One firm could be Sloane & Sons Ltd, est. 1850. Another Higgins & Co. The third, Richards & Gridley. The storyline would be that Sloane & Sons and Richards & Gridley would be rivals to buy Higgins & Co as Joyce Higgins, the firm's owner, wanted to sell. Then three big opinion formers in Birmingham society, from different religions and backgrounds, would all die at the same time and then the scramble could be on to obtain their arrangements by the rivals to increase their standing in the community and impress the smart and sexually charged middle-aged Joyce.

I retired to bed and mapped out the whole 'treatment' in my head. The hero would be a guy named Stillion Sloane and the villain named Sydney Gridley. I knew every scene perfectly because I had been to all of them thousands of times. I knew every character brilliantly because they all existed, I would just change their names. A lot of them now appear under their real names in Volume I of 'This Life in Death.'

I fell asleep and woke up with the book completely written in my head. Indeed, I never bothered to write any notes because of this but went straight to putting the chapters down instead.

I hadn't opened a copy of the book ever – as I had to read it so many times at the proof stage. However, writing this, now over twenty-five years later, I had to reach for a copy to ensure I got some of the names right. I was amazed as I flicked through the pages that what I was reading was 100% fact rather than loosely based on fact. I realised that the story completely related to real scenes with real people in my life and not vaguely imaginary ones in Stillion's imaginary life which was supposed to be loosely based on mine. The pictures in my head were of true stories that didn't all happen in the same week and, of course, they weren't all related to each other, as in the book, but they had all happened. There is a subtle difference. So much for my 'Agatha Christie' style imagination. Obviously, I had none!

After the party, Christine had a brief sleep before we caught the train and arrived in Paris to stay in the Hotel Alma very close to the tunnel where Diana, Princess of Wales, had died tragically only months before and the entrance to which was still strewn with flowers.

I told her we should go up the Eiffel Tower. She wondered why I was so determined to get through the hordes of people to get to the top. She asked me if I really wanted to queue as I had been up to the top before.

"But you haven't," was my reply.

We pressed on through the masses and eventually made it. Once there, as we looked out over the stunning views, I asked her to marry me.

She burst into tears. An old American woman, seeing this, and thinking that I had upset her, berated me for making her cry. Christine told the old woman that her tears were those of joy.

We had faced the most appalling public examination of our relationship together, thanks to 'Sir Jack' and we were now bonded to each other and therefore joined at the hip.

I had known for years that I could love more than one woman at a time, just like the rest of mankind can love more than one child at a time. I knew that in 1993, I had been happy without having a 'single partner' to report in and be faithful to. I knew all too well, that I felt very uncomfortable trying to shoehorn in my personality to conform with society's conception of how we should live our lives.

Therefore, I knew that I might fall off the 'One Woman Express' train at some point, but that would be my fault rather than hers and something we would have to deal with together.

Moreover, she wanted to marry me, and I wanted to marry her. And despite a few bad times, all caused by me, it was a brilliant decision because Christine continued to be a wonderful friend, great lover and the most reliable 'rock' in my life over the next 27 years just as Marianne had been during 20 years of marriage.

So,1998 started with Christine settling into her new job and me settling down to write 'Six Feet Under'. Then one day I got a call from Providence in the USA. It was a man called Fred Levinger. He owned Colibri USA. He told me that he intended to buy Colibri of London from a British high street retail entrepreneur, called Stephen Hinchcliffe, whom I knew, and build it into a large international company selling male grooming products. Fred went on:

"What if I tell you." Fred started nearly every sentence with 'What if I tell you.'

"What if I tell you that, I think you are a rainmaker. What if I tell you that, Ronson just shot themselves in the foot by letting you go. What if I tell you that I want you to become my new international CEO. Wouldn't you like to get Lyons back?"

I said I would certainly consider what he had to say. He told me that he was coming over to the UK with his US CEO, a very pleasant man as it turned out, called Mike Reynolds. I told Fred to contact me when the deal was done.

As you now know Ronson was an American company that became British. Whereas Colibri was a British company that had sold the US rights to Levinger and now he was going to reunite the world brand under an American company.

## This Life In Death

Fred and Mike duly arrived in London and checked into the Athenaeum Hotel. Fred called me and invited me to come up to London to see him. I duly went.

Fred explained that he wanted me to become CEO and offered me an attractive salary to take the position. I accepted but limited it to two years as I was not being offered equity and thought Fred might be quite difficult to work with. However, here was my chance to get even with 'Sir Jack.'

Fred then went through the very small Colibri team that he intended to keep. All accounting, order fulfilment, delivery and administration would be done from Providence. Therefore, he had only three that he wanted to keep in the UK. UK Colibri sales were obviously important, and he thought that the man in charge of these, Roger Morriss, was good enough. I knew of Roger and knew he had immense experience not only in UK sales, but international sales and the sourcing of product. He would certainly do. The duty-free sales were to be handled by a man called Paul Martin, who I didn't know, but turned out to be excellent. The processing of orders and passing the same over to Providence was to be undertaken by a lady called Annette Spencer. I didn't know her either, but again she turned out to be very good.

Fred then asked me what else I needed. I told him that I needed a secretary/PA and two international salesmen. One for Europe and the other for the rest of the world. This would therefore only mean a team of seven including me and Fred was delighted by that prospect as it was a lot lower than he thought.

"Have you anyone in mind?" enthused Fred.

"Yes. Vicky was my PA at Ronson and is available. My son and Robert Platt regarding international sales," I replied without hesitation.

"The PA and Platt are fine but not your son. I don't like guys from the same family working together," pronounced Levinger in a tougher tone.

"Well hire him rather than me then. He is Platt's boss and personally knows the Ronson Russian distributor and all those in Europe. He often stays at their houses. You need him more than you need me."

Fred was taken aback. He was not used to people talking straight with him.

"But you're the 'rainmaker,'" he protested.

"I cannot make rain without the contacts. Moreover, if he stays at Ronson, the distributors are likely to stay there too."

"What if I tell you, that makes sense," he said in a much sweeter voice. "Can your boy come in to meet me today?"

"I'll call him." I did and he set off from his Stratton Audley office in Oxfordshire while Fred, Mike and I had a decent lunch.

I left Fred and Mike to interview Howard without me. When I returned Fred was grinning from ear to ear.

"What if I tell you, I always wanted a son. A son like yours. He is a fine young man. You must be so proud, and he and Platt are hired."

Howard and Robert Platt were very pleased too as they had been very keen to leave Ronson as it was already steering a rudderless course, as when I left so did the motivation, the conviction and belief. Most staff were looking for other jobs.

Next Fred asked to speak to Vicky. I got her on my mobile. Now the booming voice was now purring like a pussycat to tell her that he would become like a favourite uncle to her. I doubted that would be the case and I was right as we shall see.

Nevertheless, I got on the train back to Dorset fully energised. I now had a gunboat to blow 'Sir Jack' out of the water with what I knew I could and would achieve, and, as the French say, 'revenge is a dish best served cold' and I was going to enjoy every bloody mouthful.

This desire to get 'Sir Jack' became even stronger when he suddenly appointed Victor Kiam as CEO of Ronson as things were not improving as quickly as he wanted. I knew Victor. He was an American who had become extremely famous in Britain for advertising Remington electric razors with the tag line, "I loved the razor so much that I bought the company."

He was a nice guy. However, upon his appointment, he had criticised our decision to launch Ronson Rebel, Ronson Racer and Ronson Retro. He said that we had been subligating the lighter brand as a result. This was rubbish because we had rightly wanted to get away from Ronson being a lighter brand and wanted it to become a male grooming brand. This was the last straw, and I was furious.

Nevertheless, as our appointments virtually coincided, the Financial Times put both of our photographs on their front page with a lead story about us. This was completely ridiculous. Victor Kiam and Howard Hodgson might be colourful entrepreneurs, however, Ronson plc and Colibri International had a combined value of 'Jack shit' compared to most small, quoted companies – never mind FTSE 100 companies.

xxxxxxx

The next night Fred hosted a dinner in Elizabeth Street, SW1 to introduce me to Morriss, Martin and Spencer. I liked them all. They were less dynamic than my Ronson team, but they were very experienced, sensible, and likeable. I really liked them, felt comfortable and they seemed to really like me back. We got on well.

We quickly found offices in Esher, south of London, and next to the Sandown Racecourse, which housed Roger, Annette, Paul, Vicky and me. Howard and Robert remained in their Oxford office – which was part of Stratton Audley Hall and therefore had nothing to do with Ronson. Game on.

Fred said, “What do you need to win in this market?”

“Nothing but a little ‘oil on the wheels’ entertainment figure for duty-free. Nothing at all in the UK market but reasonable credit terms, but an extended credit programme for the international market” was my precise answer.

“What the fuck is extended credit?” asked a perplexed Fred, who thought I was talking ‘double Dutch.’

“It is where you allow a distributor more time to pay your bill and therefore, he has more time to recover the cash from his wholesaler or retailer clients as a result. It is a great incentive to distributors as it allows them much more freedom to put product out in the market in the knowledge that they will get a return before they must pay us.”

“What if I tell you, that that is a ‘dating program,’” was Fred’s response before he went on, “OK, this wasn’t invented by you ‘Rainmaker’, but we have had ‘dating programs’ for years.”

“Dating programs sounds like me going to an agency to find a good fuck,” I responded somewhat bewildered by his shockingly poor use of the English language.

Nevertheless, we agreed that all distributors could have an ‘extended credit programme’ in English or ‘a dating program’ in American English.

Accordingly, I sent Fred a list of the amounts that Howard and I, or Robert and I, would give out when we visited each distributor, whether they were a very small number of existing Colibri distributors or a much larger list of Ronson ones. These amounts of credit were personally signed off by Fred.

As I previously mentioned, the cigar boom of the early 1990s was in full swing and, credit to Fred, he had a much better product line than Ronson and that was also useful.

As a result, Howard and I in Europe and Russia, or Robert and I in South America, took off on a whirlwind trip to make the Ronson distributors switch to Colibri. I took over 50 flights in 30 days and travelled the world to make this happen. I was a man on a mission and hoped 'Sir Jack' was watching.

These trips brought Howard and I 'Back in the USSR' to quote the Paul McCartney, Beatles song. Well not quite, as it was now Russia and enjoying a brief period of colourful democracy before being cast back into the dark ages of 'Putin' once more. Nevertheless, it was still a little like the wild west and dangerous to go off the beaten track anywhere in Moscow.

Valerie and his partner Igor, always looked after us well. We always had armed guards, drank the best vodka, went to an increasing number of good restaurants and were always offered an array of beautiful girls. Howard would politely decline such opportunities.

The Fred 'dating program' or the Howard 'extended credit programme' was a huge success. An already disarrayed Ronson fell like a pack of cards, their distributors were inclined to follow me rather than Ronson and, with this incentive, they came over in their droves.

We held the 'Colibri Awards Dinner' in February 1999 during the Frankfurt World Trade Fair, in the same room, in the same 5-star hotel, as we had the Ronson awards dinner in 1996 and 1997, but now with nearly all the same distributors in the Colibri family.

Strangely, I was in fact more delighted by our success than I was about Ronson's failure and 'Sir Jack's' demise. How strange but healthy for it is always better to be possessed by positive thought than negative ones.

Fred had flown over for this awards dinner as headman of Colibri, and he had a good dinner with the Colibri International executive, i.e. Roger, Paul, Howard, Robert and me, the night before the main event. He was very grateful for the huge success we had brought about at the expense of Ronson.

Indeed, his animal cunning of turning my anger against 'Sir Jack' had paid huge dividends as Ronson's international business now lay in ruins, and I had feasted on that but more on the creation of our new success.

However, he owned the fruits of my labours, so well played Fred. Nevertheless, I was happy all the same. I knew I could now look in the mirror and say to myself, "You don't fuck with the Peaky Blinders" and that was enough for me. 'Sir Jack' had tried to destroy my life. He had failed and I had paid him back by costing him his £5 million investment.

However, during this night of massive self-congratulation before the 'main event,' Fred in a party mood managed to lose both his black tie and, worse, his wallet.

J and Christine had turned up too the night before the dinner and had managed to leave J's computer in the taxi from the airport – naturally, it was never recovered. However, a not very pleased me sent them to ask the reception the next morning to see if it had been recovered. Fred was there before them. They waited their turn. Fred asked if the staff had found either his tie or his wallet. They answered that they had looked in the bar, the restaurant and all restrooms and they hadn't.

"Have you looked in my room?" was Fred's next question.

"Uh no" came back the German response with more than a little surprise at the question.

"Well why the hell not?" screamed Fred in disbelief. The idea that the staff might have considered that Fred might be capable of searching his own room certainly had not occurred to him.

On the big night, I was to give out the 'Oscars' and make the main speech before inviting Fred on to the stage to thank everyone for coming.

A month before this, Fred had told me that he thought that Roger was now expendable. Roger was a very talented guy and certainly not expendable – just like Paul, Howard or Robert. The truth was that Providence did not like the fact that he had sourced product at cheaper prices on lower Colibri of London volumes than the Providence ever had on much bigger volumes and he could not resist pointing this out to increase margins without increasing prices.

Perhaps, given the Fred 'Putin' rule of terror in Providence, instead of thinking, 'Let's get Roger to do the sourcing or at least help with it,' they thought, 'Let's silence the bastard before Fred puts him in charge of us or, worse, replaces us with him.'

Therefore, I had a wine duck engraved as a 'Lifetime Achievement' award to Roger and after all the 'Oscars' had been given out it was his turn. When I announced it there was a roar of approval from all the tables in a packed room, and spontaneously the room rose in a standing ovation amid huge applause. Both he and I had tears in our eyes, as I whispered in his ear, as I handed his 'gong' over, "Let's see if they can sack you now."

I finished the speech by introducing everyone to the man who made all of this possible; the man who had approved a $3 million credit programme.

I welcomed Fred on to the stage to a generous round of applause and returned to my seat next to Christine and J.

Fred opened with, “When I just heard I gave out $3 million of credit I nearly crapped my pants,” as he stood there in his dinner suit, white wing collar shirt, but no tie. The room roared with laughter. But Christine whispered in my ear, “I think he means it.”

“Don’t be stupid. He approved every single credit,” I whispered back and thought no more of it.

However, on Monday morning UK time, and therefore, in the very early hours of Providence time, I got a call from Fred.

“The whole thing is off.”

“What?”

“The whole damn thing is off. I can’t possibly approve $3 million worth of credit.”

“But you did.”

“Yeah, but I never added it up.”

“Well, I will resign then because my word is my bond, and these guys bought, on my say so, on the deal you offered and then approved.”

“Look, damn it, what if I tell you that no one in their right mind, would offer $500,000 credit in Russia.”

“Well, you have, and Valerie will pay you. If he doesn’t I will.”

There was a silence. Then a small soft voice said, “Oh my God. That’s some commitment. OK the whole thing is on again.”

Six months later when everyone had paid bar $2,000 in Australia, I received an email from Fred. It read, ‘You may think that I have had a lobotomy, but I just wanted to say well done Mr. Rainmaker.’

## This Life In Death

On one trip to London, Fred, Christine and I were having a drink at the bar in San Lorenzo before going down to the restaurant. Liz Hurley walked in and stood at the bar waiting to be joined by her dining companion.

"Is that who I think it is?" Fred said in a voice that could be heard down the steps in the restaurant, while pointing at her. We hurriedly made for our table before any further embarrassment occurred. Once there, I went to the gents.

Now on his own with Christine, Fred said, "What if I tell you that your husband says whatever he likes to me. He can be very disrespectful."

"That's because he cares about Colibri and you and he isn't frightened of you because he doesn't need your money. Whereas your other staff do," responded Christine tactfully.

"What if I tell you that I have never been spoken to like that by anyone ever," he then said in his 'hurt' little voice.

This wasn't true as his wife beat him up much more than I ever did – and she screamed and shouted at him which I never did.

Nevertheless, I couldn't but like Fred and be fascinated by his transparent mood and voice changes as he responded to varying circumstances.

This was never better demonstrated than when I mentioned during one of our transatlantic calls that Vicky was pregnant.

"Fire her!" screamed Fred on hearing this news.

I quickly moved out of Vicky's earshot and whispered down the phone, "I can't do that. You can't fire someone for getting pregnant."

"What if I tell you that I could fire Noonan, you know Noonan our FD, I could fire him with a week's money."

"Well, we could debate the morals of that if you want. But that isn't my point. You can't fire someone in Britain for becoming pregnant. It is against the law."

"Just God damn well do it or I will."

"Fred, you are not listening - to fire Vicky for getting pregnant could cost you a fortune."

"You would say that. Is the baby yours?"

"What?" I said in complete disbelief.

The conversation ended without resolution. So, I called Colibri's UK lawyer and explained what Fred intended to do. They were horrified and said Colibri could be sued for hundreds of thousands of pounds. I asked them to talk to Fred directly.

About an hour later my phone went again. It was Fred. He had his pussy-cat voice on. "Could I speak to Vicky please?"

I passed the phone over to her.

"Hello my dear. I just wanted to phone to congratulate you on your great news. I have sent you flowers, and I want you to know that you should take it easy and don't let that Howard push you too hard. I'm so happy for you and your husband."

I couldn't believe what I was hearing. But that was Fred, a larger-than-life character, abrupt and childlike, but altogether a preferable man to 'Sir Jack.' Moreover, I will be eternally grateful to him for the giving me the opportunity to take on and smash Jack Lyons into the ground.

On leaving, when my two years was up, Fred had commissioned a truly beautiful cut glass eagle set on a base which thanked me for making Colibri an international company. He presented it to me with genuine emotion. He didn't have to do this, but he had.

For reasons which I can't explain it meant every bit as much to me as my 'USM Entrepreneur of the Year' award and I have kept it close to me ever since, because I was that deeply touched. I suppose I should have commissioned one for him to thank him for giving me the chance to commercially kill 'Sir Jack.'

I have enjoyed writing about this part of my life and that hasn't always been the case in either volume.

Fred was to sell Colibri to a management buy-out not long after the Millennium. It soon went down without him. Recently, I looked him up on Google. At the time of writing, he is still alive, now aged eighty-seven. When I discovered this, I smiled to myself and felt warm inside. Take care Fred. I will always remember you with affection.

xxxxxxx

Victoria Worgan was a rare breed of woman. One that I utterly adored but never had a moment's intimacy with. I had had many very loyal and lovable girls look after me to that point in my life, such as Pat, Beryl, Velma, Nula, Lynn, Vivienne, Eldine, Vicky and today, Jane. I had always followed my father's advice of 'don't mess with the payroll.' Nevertheless, they and I always became very close.

Vicky was extraordinarily devoted, incredibly competent and yet wonderfully naive. For example, when Viagra first came out in 1998 or 1999. I asked if she knew what it was before the five of us started work in the Esher office one morning.

"Of course," she said with a shy smile. "It helps men do you know what."

"Do what?"

"Have sex," she said, now blushing.

"OK. So how does it work then?" was my next question.

"It's a cream which your partner rubs on for you."

The rest of us exploded into hysteria with coffee being spat out. We weren't laughing at her but with her. We all loved her.

She and I used to repeat a mantra every morning together before we started work. It went: 'I dig a pigmy by Charles Hawtree and the Deaf Aids, phase one, in which Doris gets her oats.'

It had been written by John Lennon to the introduction of the first track on Beatles Album 'Let it Be' which was 'Two of Us' by Paul McCartney. Hence the message to each other. We had started this back in the Ronson days during those terrifyingly hard times as some barmy calming message to each other and had continued it when we moved to Colibri to the amusement of the staid Roger et al.

She had originally been Fred Bassnett's secretary at Ronson. Fred and I were due to go on a trip to the Far East together. I looked at the itinerary that she had prepared for him and then at the one my PA had prepared for me. She was leaving anyway as we were about to leave the London office for Crawley.

"Fred, is Vicky a good PA?" I asked casually.

"Brilliant," he replied.

"You wouldn't want to stand in her way would you?" I then asked.

"You bastard Howard," he reacted.

She was transferred to me that day.

One evening, now at Colibri in Esher, her car wouldn't start so I ran her home in mine. When the others arrived the next morning to see her car in the car park, but she was not in the office, the nodding winks started. However, they were wrong.

On another occasion, she came to Dorset as I had a huge piece of work to type up – and in those days, bosses didn't type, they dictated, read and then signed. She arrived at 11:00 in the morning on a Friday. Christine was away but J was there, but after I had cooked the three of us supper, he went to bed as we worked through the night.

I called her a taxi on the bright summer's Saturday morning at 7:00 to take her to Bournemouth railway station. It duly arrived and, as I was an account holder, it was a driver that I knew well.

We had been up all night and probably looked the worse for wear. As we came down the ten or so front doorsteps, I kissed her on the cheek and thanked her for everything.

"Oh, that's OK. I had a great time," she replied with a smile.

The taxi driver's jaw dropped open. But for once in my life, I was innocent as charged.

In 'Six Feet Under' there are no made-up characters. Most of the cast are based on people from the 1970s or '80s in the Birmingham funeral industry or holders of religious posts there at that time. Only three come from a later period. 'Stephanie Sloane' was based on a duty-free girl called Mandy Cohen, 'Sydney Gridley' was based on Shaun Dowling and 'Vicky' was based on Victoria Worgan. Read the book and you will get the relationship I had with Vicky straight away.

XXXXXXX

## This Life In Death

In the summer of 1999, after J had pulled in truly brilliant GCSE results, Christine and I got married at the wonderfully appointed and very well run, but equally very expensive Chewton Glen Hotel on the Hampshire/Dorset border on 3rd September. Of course, this was also the 60th anniversary of 'the day war broke out.'

Earlier in the year, she and I had gone to Rome with her parents for a long weekend. They were both great folks. Lancastrian, no messing, well-educated and honest. Her mother was kind, loving, brilliant, and I genuinely loved her. However, her father was only the second saint I have ever met. The first being Raymonde, Marianne's mother.

We had a truly great weekend, and I really enjoyed their company as we, having been before, showed them round this truly wonderous city.

However, after dinner on the Saturday night, Christine's father, Tony, asked if he and I could have a drink alone. Naturally, if somewhat nervously, I agreed. We went to a bar at the top of the Eden Hotel. I ordered a vodka tonic and Tony, who loved and knew a lot about beer, also had a vodka tonic. That worried me.

"Right then," he began in a no messing and straight to the point fashion. "I know you are wealthy, and I know you might want a say in all of this. But I don't want any trouble here. Chris is my daughter, and I intend to pay for her wedding. Do you have a problem with that?" He looked me in the eye.

I looked him back in the eye and said, "The last time anyone paid anything for me was probably the last school fees bill my father paid. I am honoured to accept." He was delighted and it felt wonderful to be part of a thinking that I grew up with – that British Empire attitude of then, rather than the 'How can I get out of paying - I, me, mine' attitude of today.

My mother, who was to become great friends with Christine's parents for the last twenty years of their lives together, was so happy as she adored Christine. However, she wasn't pleased with J, who said he would boycott the wedding. However, on the day, not only did J turn up but he agreed to be my joint best man with Howard.

The night before the wedding, Tony paid for a huge Pickles gathering of over forty guests, in a smaller, but hardly cheaper hotel nearby, to enjoy a great dinner.

On the day itself, everything went like clockwork. The bride entered, with Tony, to 'Here, There, and Everywhere' off 'Give My Regards to Broad Street', rather than 'Revolver' – as Christine preferred that version. Russell, my brother read the words to Macca's 'I Will" and Christine's sister, Jacqui, read a delightful poem written by Sir Hugo Holbein. She and no one else had any idea that he was aka Howard Hodgson.

Then we had champagne in the gardens before a maximum of 80 guests in the 'Orangery.' Tony made an excellent speech as did the two best men, although most of their fond memories of the groom seemed to centre on his brawling and street fighting – a subject that I have steered away from in this book.

Dink, now aged nine, and accompanied by the string quartet hired for the wedding breakfast, sang 'Mamma Mia' brilliantly after being counted in by J. She was by now at the Tring Academy for Acting and Dance.

The evening finished with a Beatles tribute band, which was the only thing I paid for over the entire two days, rocking the night away and finished, after a two-hour trip round 'the Beatles catalogue', with a 15-minute version of 'Hey Jude' where my lasting memory will always be Dink singing the 'nah – nah – nahs' on her elder brother, Howard's, shoulders.

Christine and I only stayed a couple of hours in bed in a beautiful and totally unused suite, before leaving for Positano and our honeymoon.

Everything had been all recorded-on video but was never watched again until over twenty years later through tear filled eyes by a lot of the family not long before the death of Christine's mum. It had been a 'grand' day.

xxxxxxx

Now free of Colibri and harrowing calls from Fred, and with my mission against 'Sir Jack' accomplished, it was time to finish 'Six Feet Under.'

Two years earlier, and just before starting at Colibri, Howard, who had bought Marianne a poodle dog called 'Bobby' a year or so before, had then bought me a poodle bitch, whom I named 'Sydney.' She was a fantastic little dog, not dissimilar to Scamp and I adored her. Where I went, so did she, and if she wasn't allowed to go then neither did I.

She sat, as a puppy with her head in my armpit as I scribbled away - as I still hand wrote books then. 'Charles, the Man who Will be King' was the first book that I was to type.

When I joined Colibri, she had come with me to Colibri meetings in the UK. When abroad she stayed with Marianne. One such occasion, she came back pregnant. Bobby was the father. She only had one puppy. We called him 'Bozzie' and kept him. Syd and Boz became inseparable and Boz remained a puppy for the whole of his life because of him never being separated from his mother.

## This Life In Death

Now back in Dorset, in the autumn of 1999, I was leading a civilised life of writing mostly while riding a horse on the wonderful Shell Bay beach once or twice a week.

On one such occasion there was a gaggle of middle-aged nervous lady riders on well fed Welsh cobs, me on an old racehorse, saved from the knacker's yard by this retirement job and a young lady, on her own very expensive looking horse, complete with expensive new saddle and bridle.

The other ladies were scruffily dressed, I was smart in my white riding britches, red topped leather riding boots, hacking jacket and navy-blue riding hat. However, the pretty young lady was wonderfully immaculate in her cream jodhpurs, matching black boots, black jacket and black riding hat, white tie and blouse held together with a very smart diamond encrusted tie pin. She obviously came from a well-off family, who sensibly didn't want her to go off hacking on her own.

The stable girl leading the ride suggested that the young lady and I might prefer to ride together and pointed the Welsh cobs towards 'Old Harry's Rocks' in order that the two of us could take off towards the Sandbanks ferry without the cobs wanting to follow suit.

The young lady smiled at me and said, "Fancy a race?" But before I could answer she was gone. She rightly went into the shallow sea as the going was firmer than the dry and deep sandy beach.

It was about a mile and half to the ferry. My horse, 'Biffen' and I were losing, and we were getting soaked by their spray. I stood in the stirrups and got into his ear.

"Come on Biffen, we are not going to lose to a spoilt girl on a horse you can easily beat."

Slowly we caught up and were now neck and neck, she started to crop her horse. I didn't need to. Biffen had already got the message.

Suddenly he was, in his mind, back at Kempton Park and with a quarter of a mile to go he spurted as I guided him onto damp firm sand out of the water.

Now we were ahead, and we pebble-dashed the smart young lady with wet sand. We won easily, stopped and waited for the now bedraggled girl to arrive.

"Well, that wasn't very gentlemanly was it?" she complained.

I just smiled and thought, 'you don't fuck with a Peaky Blinder.'

XXXXXXX

Around this period, when I was writing 'Six Feet Under', J was injured while playing in a game of football at Stowe public school, which was where he was now studying. He was tackled by a master and sent flying into a fence which both dislocated his shoulder and broke his arm.

I drove up to the John Ratcliffe Hospital, near Oxford, where he seemed to be in the operating theatre for hours, much to my concern as I had never overcome the death of Charles in this regard to any injury to any of my children.

When he was allowed home, I took him back to Dorset. There he could recover in bed while Syd would go and sit on his bed. Two nurses would come to 'Belvedere House', our home, twice a week to change his dressing. One was pretty and the other was ugly.

From where I sat, I could see which one was walking up the drive. If it was the pretty one, I would open the door and escort her to J's bedroom. If it was the ugly one, I would call out to J to come down to let his nurse in.

I berated the headmaster for the considerable damage one of his staff had inflicted upon my son. He asked if I wanted him disciplined. I replied that a good talking to would do but I also settled on a free term as well as compensation for his staff wishing to imitate Vinnie Jones.

The Millennium came and went and now it was time to publish my first novel 'Six Feet Under,' which was published by 'The Book Guild Ltd.'

The inside cover gave you an insight:

'On a cold December Sunday in 1979 the City of Birmingham loses three of its most influential and respected men: a white Anglican politician; a black Baptist community leader and an Irish Roman Catholic industrialist. Thus does a city and three families in mourning turn to the matter of a dignified send-off for each lamented luminary. Each man's last rites must be observed with the proper pomp and ceremony. Only the best funeral directors will do, and the two most seriously in the running are Sloane & Sons and Richards & Gridley.

'The young Stillion Sloane has a reputation to build, a business to expand and a fledgling marriage to protect. The older Sydney Gridley has a reputation to keep, family discipline to maintain and a growing grudge to foster. Both of them see the prestigious three funerals as a means to all these ends and each is determined to arrange all three.

'An obsessive desire to win such funerals and even sabotage those lost becomes the highly irregular state of affairs. As a result, events, fuelled by suspicion, greed and professional as well as private jealousies, quickly spiral out of control, until it seems that both men are set to lose everything from their reputations to their wives, even, in Stillion's case, his life.'

It concluded:

## This Life In Death

'SIX FEET UNDER is a highly original, fast paced, sexually charged and darkly funny book. It examines the frailty of human nature in the face of temptation, whether the lures be sexual or material. The author's in-depth knowledge of business and the little-known machinations and practicalities of the funeral trade bring this dark and often obscurely motivated world to bitterly funny and revealing light.'

I can't be sure, but I think Carol Biss, the managing director of my publisher, wrote this and well done her for a brilliant precis and thank you for not commenting on my own in-depth sexual knowledge, which she did to me in private saying, "Is this actually how you like your sex?"

So, there you have it. My bloody life, conscious and sub-conscious, all there with the ruddy kitchen sink thrown in too.

On the back cover there was quoted praise for my efforts from broadcaster Michael Parkinson, singer and actor Adam Faith, film producer Philippa Braithwaite, England Football Manager Graham Taylor, United Film & Television executive Graham Stuart, who bought the film rights, and England cricketer Dennis Amiss.

Yes, you guessed correctly - I called in favours from lots of mates.

The actual launch of the book took place in the Crypt in the City of London, where His Royal Highness Prince Henry, later to become the monster His Royal Majesty, Henry VIII, had his post nuptial celebrations for the first of his six weddings, which apparently ran for three days.

I appeared by bursting the lid off a coffin on trestles, in the middle of the room, and proceeded to jump down in a shroud, which was, in reality, the long white night shirt Marianne had bought me, when I had to go into hospital some fifteen years earlier, as reported in Volume I of these memoirs.

That had been preceded by the welcome speech from the lovable national treasure Adam Faith.

Adam had sprung into the spotlight of British pop history in the late 1950s. Unlike Cliff Richard, Eden Cane, Billy Fury and others, he had a style not 100% bent on being the UK's answer to Elvis Presley. He had had several hit records before the Beatles arrived to conquer Britain in 1963, then America in 1964 and the rest of the world thereafter.

The result was that the UK's addiction to Beatlemania, which as a contagious disease, infected the planet, confined Elvis to being an expensive cabaret singer in Las Vegas, while all of his 'tribute' performers were either completely washed away or subligated to minor chart successes behind the Beatles, other Merseybeat bands, the Rolling Stones, Kinks, Small Faces, Hollies et al.

However, the enterprising Adam turned his attention to acting and in the early '70s had a huge success with a TV series called 'Budgie' where he played a forerunner to David Jason's 'Del Boy' in 'Only Fools and Horses' which burst on to UK TV screens some fifteen years later to become a national favourite.

Then, and only God knows how, Adam managed to land a job as 'The Mail on Sunday' stock market share tipster, which led to another TV interviewing role about business.

Thus, he met me on the first of several TV interviews when I was CEO of Ronson. The very first time we bumped into each other was when I went to take a pee before his interview with me and came face to face with a shirtless Adam having a wet shave with a Rolls Razor shaver, which he was very proud of as he owned the brand name of this now defunct company.

He had the largest scar, in the form of a crucifix, that I had ever seen, across his chest. He noticed that I had noticed it.

## This Life In Death

"Open heart surgery John. Got a dicky heart you see."

In London, men use the term 'John' to one another just as men in Birmingham use the term 'mate.'

We did the interview, became firm friends and started seeing each other socially, sometimes with Christine and sometimes without her. Adam always turned up with a girl, nearly always a foreign waitress from another restaurant on her night off.

My party piece was to explain to them that Adam had been as big as the Beatles before the Beatles. This was designed to impress them, and it usually did.

Once, while waiting for his latest love interest to arrive, he told me an amazing inside story about the music world.

He had invited Paul McCartney to Sunday lunch as they did not live far apart in Sussex. Paul and Linda had accepted, but on the Thursday evening before the event, Paul had telephoned and asked if he might bring a guest.

Adam had responded that he would be delighted and enquired who the guest was. Paul said he couldn't say as the person in question didn't want anyone to know that he was in Britain. Adam accepted this.

On the Sunday at 12:30, Paul, Linda and the third person turned up. The third person turned out to be Michael Jackson. He had come to Britain to record with Paul. You will recall, no doubt, that they had two huge hits together. One, 'The Girl is Mine' written by Jackson, the other, 'Say, Say, Say' written by McCartney.

Over lunch Michael had asked how he should invest his money. Paul explained that, while Yoko had opted to invest John Lennon's estate in either property or farmland, he had stayed close to what he believed that he understood and, consequently, he had bought the rights to Buddy Holly, Cage aux Folles, Rupert Bear and other literary or musical catalogues.

A few weeks later, when back in USA, Michael had phoned Paul.

“Hey Paul, I took your advice. I just bought the Lennon McCartney catalogue,” and that was the end of a beautiful friendship as Paul had been trying to buy the same off Sir Lew Grade for years but had been stalling as Yoko refused to pay for half.

Adam did me proud as a return favour for me singing his praises to waitresses with a fantastic speech at the launch. Nevertheless, he tried to ‘pull’ Christine, while I was making my speech, and on the following morning, I received numerous complaints from women there the night before that he had undone their bras or worse as the evening had gone on.

Adam’s sexual appetite made mine look like I was bulimic by comparison. Eventually, his troublesome heart was to kill him in a Stoke-on-Trent hotel while in a play on tour there. I was extremely sad when I learnt the news. He was a real friend, a comrade in spirit, a London version of a ‘Peaky Blinder’ and I loved his cheeky Cockney attitude, his desire to win and his dislike of sleeping alone.

The Book Guild was able to attract a lot of publicity for the book, it featured in more than one Sunday colour supplement, there was a lot of other press coverage and I was invited on many TV chat shows too – one was with Gloria Hunniford, where I seem to remember dropping in a swear word to the conversation to be reminded by her that her show was before the 9 o’clock watershed.

United took an option on the film rights for £80,000, which was renewed several times at £15,000-a-time, and Graham Stuart commissioned Philippa Braithwaite of ‘Sliding Doors’ fame, to make a ‘treatment’ and write a script. She in turn got her brother to write the script. When it eventually appeared, I hated it.

I had wished at the time that there had been more coverage about the book and less about me personally. Nevertheless, it sold well enough, and I embarked on a sequel called 'Exhumed Innocent.'

Unlike 'Six Feet Under', 'Exhumed Innocent' was much more fictional. However, it had, like 'Six Feet Under' a decently worked plot.

Moreover, I thought it was better written than SFU. I was starting to learn my craft, and, while it was nothing like as well written as 'Charles, the Man who will be King', it was better written than 'Six Feet Under' and I had done it without an editor for the first time.

However, the book was a lot less successful than SFU. Perhaps because the Book Guild didn't splash out on a marketing budget as they had with 'Six Feet Under' but perhaps also, because I had toned down the sex and especially that involving Stillion, as he had received quite a lot of criticism, mainly from male literary critics, who thought his sexual appetite was indecent, he was 'a serial shagger' and some had even flagged up the comparison with my own rather public history in that regard. So even on a reduced print run, I did get left with several hundred copies, which are housed today with me in Monaco.

My next book was to be 'Charles, the Man who will be King'. It was to take four years to research and write. By the time my agent Peggy Vance, whose adorable mum was an actress and well-remembered for her performance in the John Cleese and Connie Booth Fawlty Towers' episode 'The Waldorf Salad', where she plays the English wife of that ghastly American guest, was ready to place it with a publisher, my mind was once again distracted by the 'death' industry.

In 2003, I was approached by a German man who commissioned me to investigate a crematorium project that he had been offered. He didn't wish to proceed in the end, because he rightly judged that the site on offer was not quite right.

However, while looking into the project, I became 100% convinced it was time to re-enter the one thing I knew I was better than anyone else at. I was going to go back to my roots and come up with the biggest success of my business career. Which is precisely what I did, and this was to signal the end of my wilderness years – but it wasn't to be all plain sailing as we shall see.

## This Life In Death

Chapter VII

Million Dollar Babies & Pantomime Baddies

2004 – 2009

Michael Hackney, who you will recall was the corporate financier with ANZ Bank, that I met in 1985, floated Hodgson Holdings plc in 1986, and had lived with Marianne since 1992, but following the collapse of his space storage business in the early '90s had worked for Abbey National in France.

However, he then returned to the UK to start his own business, French Mortgage.com, to cater for the increasing market of British people wanting to either retire to, or perhaps buy a second home in, France.

He ran this from the converted stable block in Stratton Audley Hall and had built it into a useful success. However, he also recognised that this exodus fashion to France might be short lived and could be blown away either by an economic down-turn in Britain, an upturn in French property prices – due to increased demand, or a banking crisis, which I had been predicting for some time as the world economy seemed to be busy living at circa 6% higher spend than earnings and I believed that this was bound to come out 'in the wash' sooner or later. I was to be proved right eventually in 2008.

I had explained to Michael on one of my weekly trips to Stratton Audley Hall for 'boys' night out' that I was thinking of starting a crematoria business following my investigation into that industry as a consultant. He was very enthusiastic and wanted to be included.

A few weeks later he and I travelled to Salisbury to see our pension provider. We had lunch together, and I asked him how many shares he expected in the new company which would be set up for this purpose.

“Not as many as you, given your knowledge of the industry,” he replied.

“Well, that is where you are wrong. If we are to be true partners, we will put equal cash in and we will have equal shares,” I said. And that is what we did.

Then I got a call from a guy that was head of Dignity’s cremation division. His name was Chris Johns. I knew him. He wished to see me. We met at the White House Hotel near Regent’s Park.

He told me that he wanted to leave Dignity as they were to re-float on the London Exchange, but he had not been offered any shares or a seat on the board despite running the trouble-free and very profitable cremation division.

With Michael’s agreement I offered Johns the same terms as I had Michael – equal money in, equal shares granted. He accepted.

I mapped out the plan. I knew I needed to go offshore soon as I wanted to change my offshore trust, which had been set up thirteen years earlier following the sale of my PHKI shares to PFG, to a new one where my three surviving children would be the sole beneficiaries. I had been advised that if I was to do this then the gains made over this period would be taxable if I was still a UK resident.

I was not going to put up with that. I had paid a fortune in tax when I sold the shares to PFG. I was determined not to pay tax again on tax paid cash.

We had holidayed in Malta in 2001, and I had fallen in love with the walled city of Mdina, which had been the capital of Malta before the Knights of St John changed it to Valletta in the 15th century.

I then found and bought an extensive property with its own bastion, which was very rare, and even more rare, it had a swimming pool unlike anyone else, as now that Mdina was a world heritage site, such developments were banned.

This property, which I called 'Bastion Charles' in honour of the book I was writing about HRH Prince of Wales, became known as 'The Castle' by my family. It had been built originally during the Roman occupation of the island nearly two thousand years earlier; extended considerably in the seventeenth and eighteenth centuries but was now in need of extensive renovation.

I bought it in the autumn of 2002 and engaged Malta's top interior designer, a talented and attractive woman, called Pippa Toledo. She brought the project in 120% over budget and nearly a year late. Nevertheless, it was spectacular, and Christine and I moved in with Dink in the summer of 2004 for a holiday and entertained Alex, Beatrice and my godson William, who were then followed by the rest of the family over that summer. Everyone adored the place.

It was decided that I would start to live there permanently from 6$^{th}$ April 2005 and become a permanent Maltese resident as a result. I duly applied for and received my resident's card.

However, I had also decided that with conference calls regarding the development and by keeping a tight eye on operations, I would not repeat the mistakes of 1992. So, I believed that I could use my expertise to build this new crematorium venture in the UK, despite living in Malta for most of the year.

And so, it came to pass that I decided that we should list all possible target areas. This was vital, as even then, twenty years ago, a new build crematorium would cost somewhere in the region of £4 million to build and one needed to ensure that it would mature within five years to be conducting 1,000 adult full-service cremations per annum if was going to give a reasonable return on the investment. Moreover, suitable areas with suitable sites were becoming rarer by the year.

Therefore, an accurate analysis of local demographics was essential to ensure that those numbers could be reached and that the need to have a crematorium situated in that location could be proved – as without such proof then a planning consent would not be forthcoming.

Chris Johns was a good team addition in this regard. He had a useful and current knowledge of where there might be such areas to look for land throughout mainland Britain and so I had him list all so that we could have a conference call every Friday and discuss. He also introduced us to a dear man by the name of Tony Walker, who was engaged on a commission by future cremation numbers earn out, to work out the demographics, in a much less scientific way than we would come to use in the years to come. Nevertheless, it worked well enough for us at the time.

Thereafter, Michael would visit those areas we prioritised on the list, armed with a knowledge of what he should be looking for to provide the least problems when attempting to obtain a planning consent – and believe me getting a consent for a new crematorium in a rural or worse a semi-rural area, is extremely difficult.

I had preconceived ideas about standards of service and facility I wanted to offer, and these had to be captivated in a certain language, typeface, colour, name and logo. Chris Johns was a good cremation man, Michael was a good banker, and I was the visionary.

After all, I had accompanied over 10,000 families down the aisle in a church or crematorium chapel in my youth on their awful day and had felt their pain. I knew what they found distressing, and I knew what they wanted. Thereafter, as you now know, I had built Hodgson & Sons Ltd from 1 branch to over 500 in fifteen years. I was Mr. Death.

However, this was to be different. I was going to be low-profile. I determined that all media fuelling was to be banned as I did not want business success, fedoras, white expensive double-breasted overcoats, comments about my hair or sex life etc. to get in the way of this new company's 'do unto others as you would have done unto you' message.

Moreover, and as a result of the business being built organically, and not by acquisition, we would be able to carefully hand-pick all staff, rather than inherit loads of undedicated mercenaries as we had done at Hodgson when we had merged with Kenyon.

Therefore, internally, and with only a dedication to service to focus on, it was going to become a place where the staff couldn't wait to sleep at night because they couldn't wait to get up and continue their mission the next day. This in fact became more the successful reality in Memoria MKII than MKI, as we will see, however, the intention was there from day one.

I knew that I couldn't take away the pain of death, but I knew I could make it a much better experience. I knew what families hated, like being on site with one or more funerals at a time, and I felt certain I could build exceptional places where this didn't happen; that would be airy; would adopt all modern technology; would have wonderful peaceful and immaculately kept gardens; and all would be spotlessly clean and overseen by a dedicated small team of multi-tasking staff.

However, we needed a name for the company that encapsulated all of that. Michael came up with it, 'MEMORIA.' I loved it.

Then in early 2005 we won our first consent in Nottinghamshire, near the town of Ollerton, an old mining community, that had survived the demise of coal mining some twenty years before.

Now we had a chance to show what our new designs and ideas could do when pitted against old municipal crematoria or those bought off councils by Dignity. It was also to become the first crematorium in the UK to have a mercury abated cremator.

We named it 'Sherwood Forest Crematorium and Memorial Park' and building got under way in the spring.

However, Michael and Chris Johns were not as wealthy as me. But we needed funds to build this first crematorium to be supplied equally between the three of us to maintain the 33% each shareholding. As they had no funds whatsoever, this was easier said than done and a solution needed to be found.

Therefore, if both had nothing, we would have to fund the operation without me funding it myself – or why shouldn't I have all the shares? Moreover, I was not going to give any personal guarantees for the very same reason.

However, our in-house banker by trade, Michael, came up with an apparently perfect solution at that moment. It was to prove to be a totally imperfect concept, further down the line, but then, in 2005, it seemed very good indeed.

He had found, very close to Stratton Audley Hall, a firm called Brackley Builders. They would fund the building of any consent that we got and thereafter we would pay them a 10% return on that cost of build per annum on a thirty-year lease. Therefore, we seemed to have found a perfect partner.

XXXXXXX

In January 2005, my mother treated Christine and I to a cruise with her on the Nile. It was quite cold but, nevertheless, a wonderful experience. However, we returned to receive the awful news that my sister, Denny, had been diagnosed with a very aggressive form of breast cancer.

This was devastating for her and her husband Chris, both of whom had struggled for the last eight years to come to terms with the death of their eldest son Alex. Indeed, I remain convinced that the stress, trauma and anxiety that she experienced following this tragedy probably played a significant part in the cancerous tumour forming.

I called her and told her that whatever treatment she needed I would pay for and that we were going to beat this together – just as we had forty years before during those uncertain teenage years when our parents' marriage was falling apart and with it our world.

We spoke every day. She was very brave and, in the end, elected to stay with her NHS oncologist. The operation, followed by chemotherapy and radiotherapy worked and she fought the illness and won.

On the 6th April 2005, as planned, I flew alone to Malta and took up residence in 'Bastion Charles.'

Mdina had a small and slightly elderly British community, which was largely not British, but Maltese, with British connections through the army, when Malta had been a very important part of the British Empire.

Indeed, during the Second World War, Malta, had been crucial to Britain, for there were no allies then as France had fallen and the US was doing its very best to stay out of the war – a bit like they and Europe are doing today regarding the Russian Ukrainian war.

In fact, the Maltese were so important to Britain that they were bombed five times-a-day every day by first the Italians, who caused few problems, and then the Germans, who caused serious ones.

There were more bombs dropped on Malta, mainly on Valletta, than there were on London in the much more famous London Blitz.

## This Life In Death

At one point the Chiefs of the general staff canvassed Churchill to give the island up as they claimed that they were losing too many plans trying to defend it and too many ships trying to supply it.

Churchill refused and posed the question of how these admirals and generals proposed to supply the North African campaign against Rommel, for the control of the oil fields, without it.

"Around the continent of Africa and up the Red Sea, is the only other way. Don't you think the U-boats will have an even bigger feast on those convoys," was his valid point.

"Well, sir, if you won't agree with our view, please at least think of the Maltese people." they pleaded.

"Oh, I see," said Churchill as he puffed on his ubiquitous cigar, "You want to bomb the Maltese people."

"No, we don't," came back a horrified chorus.

"But, if you give up the island to the Nazis, who do you think is going to bomb them?" was his immediate response, followed by a forceful, "Now get out."

It was this logic that made Churchill head and shoulders the most successful war leader since Napoleon had been in his early years.

Nevertheless, the Maltese were to continue to suffer, and in 1942 were awarded, and the only collective one ever to be awarded, the George Cross.

Now, some sixty years later, I engaged with the next generation of this community, and despite being the youngest, galvanised it into a club within a week of being there, in a way chaps going out into the Empire a hundred years or so earlier would have done.

However, my club had a very non-empire name. I called it 'The Johnnie Rotten Club' and proclaimed an old and most colourful

Scotsman, called Cameron, who apparently swung 'both ways,' as 'Johnnie Rotten.'

In the club, besides Cameron, was an ex-British army officer called Michael Bonello, who was Maltese, his Australian-Maltese wife, called Kate; a pro-Italian member of the Maltese aristocracy, as one of the 'six big Maltese' families, but he was also fixated by the film 'Sink the Bismarck,' called Peter Sant Cassia; his young Maltese wife, Marie Louise, who did the cooking in the restaurant next door to the 'Castle' and so by her usual absence, made me the youngest of the group, aged 55; and a very talented English lady painter from Hertfordshire, who, while having grown up in England, was indeed Maltese by birth, called Valerie Roles.

I liked her a lot and would take her to dinner when we didn't have a 'Johnnie Rotten' night out, because, like me, her family was in England, she was chatty and very artistically minded, which appealed a lot to that part of the Piscean me.

One night, after a month there, I was due to have dinner in Pete's restaurant next door, on a less than perfect rainy evening, in early May. He apologised about not joining me for a pre-dinner drink as he was off out for dinner elsewhere. He lent me a copy of the Maltese Times to read.

Malta had two English language papers, one the Times and the other, which I was to write a whole page in every Sunday for several years, was the Malta Independent.

While perusing the paper, I failed to notice an English family of three enter and one had asked Peter, if the wonderful and brand-new Mini Cooper S, parked in the square outside was his?

"No, it's his," replied Peter pointing at me.

I caught the end of this conversation and looked up. The family was Valerie's. She had come in for dinner with her English husband Chris, and their younger daughter Natalie, who had flown out to join her parents at their Mdina holiday home. They invited me to join them for dinner. I did. This was to prove to be another important dinner party in another 'Sliding Doors' moment.

Valerie asked me if I recognised her daughter. I'm afraid that I didn't.

She announced she was an actress, she had been in 'Cold Feet', 'Men Behaving Badly', 'Doctors'; many other TV shows; and had starred in 'A Girl like You' with Rupert Graves and Hugh Bonneville; appeared in a film with Pierce Brosnan and for the last four years had starred as the 'bad girl cop' Debbie McAllister in the very popular soap-opera, 'The Bill.'

Not wanting to offend, I explained that I only watched TV in bed to put myself to sleep and that I had never seen any of those shows, which hit the air much earlier in the evening, as a result.

After dinner, which Chris insisted on paying for, we went next door to 'Bastion Charles' aka 'the Castle' and, as the weather had brightened up, we had drinks on the bastion terrace by the pool.

I invited them all to dinner the next night to pay them back for my supper. After dinner this time, we went back to their place. As I followed Natalie up the 'Gary Gore' a windy and narrow Maltese staircase to their roof, I was fatally attracted by her legs – which were ten out of ten. I could feel my resistance slipping away with every step up as a result.

We had drinks on their roof, during which time, Valerie and Chris explained that they had two tickets to see a floating opera in Portomaso the following night. Natalie would be on her own. Without a second thought, I invited her to dinner.

We went to a very pleasant restaurant called 'The Barracuda', run by friends of mine, which looked out over the sea and back to St Julian's on the other side of the bay. We had a pleasant dinner and afterwards, I drove her, in Luke, the only exciting Mini Cooper S on the island at this point, home.

All Hodgson cars had a name and were called after an Aston Villa player, my car had been allocated the name Luke – after Luke Shaw as a result.

She invited me into her Mdina home, as her parents were going to stay in St Julian's after the concert. I went.

We chatted until 4:00 in the morning and even had an arm in arm walk round the 'silent city' of Mdina during this time, where we felt sure we could hear nuns cavorting with monks in the cellar of one of the monasteries, which made Mdina this 'silent and holy city.' We both liked the idea of nuns and monks having drunken orgies.

She told me that she was 36 and that she had no boyfriend but would love to have a baby one day. I thought that I would like to be the father of that child. However, I behaved like a gentleman, and nothing further happened.

At 4:00 I left, as I had to fly home on the BA Saturday morning flight at 7:00 from Malta to Heathrow and be re-united with Christine, J and Dink by lunchtime in Dorset. It was my first return home in a month, and I was looking forward to it as I would be staying a few days in the UK with them for half-term.

Nevertheless, Natalie had given me her phone number, and I managed to resist calling her until the following Tuesday. When I did, she said that she was in a meeting with her accountants and could I call her back. I replied that I had only called to invite her to lunch. She left her meeting for a few minutes and accepted. Now the dye was cast.

XXXXXXX

## This Life In Death

Meanwhile, my new business venture, Memoria, was going according to plan. Memoria's first build was underway, and we were actively looking for more.

Then Dignity, the new name for PHKI, suddenly took the very strange decision to stop building new crematoria or selling pre-paid funeral plans and concentrate on the running of its funeral division.

I was frankly staggered by this. Firstly, they had easily the biggest crematoria group in the UK, it was very profitable and, unlike its funeral division, did not have to constantly worry about lost market share. Secondly, its pre-paid funeral plans would help, in the future, to address that lost funeral market share issue, and was also profitable.

Therefore, the Dignity directors had taken a strange decision to leave two profitable sectors of the funeral industry, to concentrate on its problem child, which by now, fourteen years after my departure, was developing into a problem teenager and would eventually become a seriously troubled adult.

In time, they were to see the stupidity of that decision, as we shall see, but just at that moment, Memoria was to benefit from it.

Chris Johns was offered two land options where they had intended to build crematoria. One of which had a consent and the other was very likely to get one. The consented site was on land overlooking the Pennines adjacent to the existing Radcliffe municipal cemetery in Bury, while the other was also in Lancashire at Charnock Richard, which is near to Chorley. Both were expected to mature at between 1,200 – 1,500 cremations per annum.

The package offered to us was worth over a £1 million. The asking price? Nothing! Chris Johns called me in Portugal, where I was staying with my mother, while researching and writing my book on

HRH, Charles, Prince of Wales, to give me the news. I couldn't believe our luck. In fact, I didn't and suspected that there must be a catch somewhere. However, there wasn't.

So quite quickly we had three sites that were at various stages of development and a growing list of other target areas, which we were keen to exploit.

Brackley Builders, who handed us the 'turnkey' developed crematoria, in exchange for a signed 30-year lease with a rent uplift of 10% per annum, were really developers as opposed to builders.

They were run by two partners Nick Owen and Matthew Roberts. These chaps had developed a business by providing new doctors' surgeries on the same basis and were now keen to form a partnership with us where we would find the site; they would obtain a planning consent and build; we would sign the lease and operate; they would get a 10% return on their capital year on year; and we could develop new crematoria, each costing some £4 or £5 million at the time, without investing a penny. We were all very happy.

Brackley decided to set up a subsidiary company just to deal with our projects. They decided it should be called 'St Peter's Gate.' I went through the roof when I learnt of this. It was named 'Mercia' instead.

Moreover, Matthew had two uncles, Robert and Peter Wakeford, who owned a large and well-run building firm called Stepnell and they built the sites for us.

xxxxxxx

Throughout the summer of 2005, Natalie and I were getting closer and closer. I think that we realised very early on that we were falling in love, mainly over the telephone, as I was obliged to spend most of my time in Malta and she was still a working actress in London, where she also had a small number of apartments with mortgages, which were naturally paid off from her earnings. She didn't like London but needed to be there all the same.

I started to write a spoof book 'The Life & Times of Robert Redbridge,' in between finishing the 'Charles' book and would send her the fruits of these labours each day.

It was a about a middle-aged James Bond type character, who had a pen pal novice nun called Scarlet Pert Breasts, who owned a Vespa scooter and vowed to save Robert from the self-destructive trouble that his letters to her detailed. These mainly centred around close scrapes with the wicked nuns of Mdina, and how insane life was in Malta, mainly due to the interbreeding of the population. The letters were littered with sexual fantasies and became a very easy way for us to make love while doing no such thing physically.

I did take her to lunch a couple of times in London over the summer but, as we were in restaurants, physical contact was restricted to heavy petting in alleyways, car parks or taxis.

By September, we were hopelessly in love with each other. Probably, this was increased by the restrictive nature of our relationship.

So, I met her at Heathrow, and we flew back together to Malta, stayed the night in the Phoenicia Hotel in Valletta before flying out to Sicily for a mad mid-week break.

She was very slender and enchanting, but appallingly untidy. Her dress in the Phoenicia had ended on the floor in the excitement of it all. Later, I hung it up in a wardrobe for her. She, now dressed in jeans, promptly forgot it the next morning as she wasn't used to having clothes hung up in wardrobes!

We went to Catania and spent two days there. She wanted a baby, and I wanted it to be mine. However, I was still very much in love with

Christine and in October, we went on a pre-arranged trip to India together to visit Delhi, Agra, Jaipur, Udaipur, Goa and Mumbai.

We had a marvellous time. I rode a horse for miles across the desert, couldn't walk the next day and so discovered Jodhpur by mistake as I was unable to ride – it remains my favourite Indian location still twenty years later. We went across a lot of India by taxi and listened non-stop to the new album by McCartney, 'Chaos & Creation', which was every bit as good as any Beatles album.

I was now very confused. When I arrived home, I determined that this all had to get sorted as I was becoming an emotional wreck travelling between the two and loving both.

I loved Christine for all the right reasons. We got on exceptionally well together and, except for Aston Villa, skiing and horse riding, we liked all the same things and shared the same views.

On the other hand, Natalie was an untidy socialist who really thought that Princess Diana had been a good-looking Mother Teresa. They say love is blind.

Moreover, Natalie was beautiful, trusted me and somehow combined the love I had always had for Christine, and Marianne before Christine, with the passion that I had felt for Hazel Fewtrel in 1979.

Nevertheless, it couldn't go on like this. I arranged to take Natalie to the Malmaison Hotel by Smithfield Market on my return from India. I had decided to tell her it had to end. However, during a magical dinner, I realised that I just couldn't do it. Then she got pregnant but lost the baby.

Then Christine discovered the affair, and an immensely tense and confusing period followed culminating in her becoming pregnant – something that we had discussed but had assumed wouldn't happen given her age. She was by then 42.

## This Life In Death

Soon Natalie was pregnant again and this time kept the baby. She was ecstatic when she first found out. I took her to the restaurant 'Fifty Cheyne Walk' in Chelsea, overlooking the Thames and we sat next to Michael Caine and his wife. Natalie wanted to tell them, but I urged caution. The last thing I needed was a 'Mr. Death up to his usual tricks' headline. Moreover, Caine looked very grumpy, so I don't think she would have got the reaction she might have expected from him.

Nevertheless, grumpy Caine must have wondered why Natalie was going to the ladies every five minutes. I knew. She just wanted to check that she was still pregnant.

Next, J found out that both Christine and Natalie were pregnant and was utterly horrified. He had never wanted me to marry again but had accepted it eventually. He certainly did not want Christine to become pregnant and was appalled when he found out that both she and Natalie were.

So, just as I was getting my business career back together, I had managed, once again, to throw my domestic life into total confusion and misery for many by my widespread and apparently insatiable love of women.

The months of pregnancy were difficult for all of us. Christine understandably blamed me for having an affair and Natalie for stealing a married man. Natalie blamed Christine for not leaving me and me for not leaving Christine. I blamed me for everything, rightly as I had set the ball rolling and was the chief architect of this misery. Therefore, I dedicated my life to trying to keep everyone happy.

Moreover, one shouldn't have children unless one is prepared to love them with all your heart and look after them for ever. I had always adored having my children and loving them all, they are my life, and despite this awful malaise that I had caused, I was so excited to be a father again, just when most of my friends were becoming grandparents.

Moreover, I knew that I would see us all through this difficult period, because although I understood both women's pain, I also knew that, soon, like me, whatever happened, they would never regret having these two children.

Natalie was then rushed into hospital when she nearly miscarried. I stayed the night with her before driving her car back to her flat, checking that it was OK and having a bath there as I had been up all night.

Her car was best described as the most unsafe and untidy vehicle that I had ever been in. Worse, when I let myself into her flat, I was horrified to discover that she had been burgled. However, on closer inspection, I discovered that she hadn't but had let two female friends stay and they had vacated the place in a ransacked state.

On my return to the hospital, I went with her to have a scan. She declared that she was having a boy and pointed at the screen.

"That's an arm you clot", I pronounced as a father of four, who knew about these things.

The lady doing the scan asked if we wanted to know the sex. We both nodded. "It's a boy". We were both ecstatic.

Horatio Flite Christopher Howard Hodgson already looked like his mum even at this early stage of his development. He was to add her ballet dancing skills to my tenacity on the football field and was to become a most accomplished footballer as a result - but that is for the future.

Soon afterwards, Christine also had a scan, but when I was back in Malta. She called me and, as I spoke to her, I was walking in our garden by the swimming pool, but also on the edge of the bastion, as was my habit, because I got a buzz from looking down.

"Do you want to know the sex?" she teased.

"What do you think?"

"It's a boy."

I exploded with joy again and nearly tumbled off the bastion and down 150 feet into a vineyard below.

George Paul Anthony Howard Hodgson was to arrive with his mother's academic brain, thank God for that, and looked like her, but also like me. At last, I had a child who looked like me.

On 24th November 2006 Christine gave birth to him, with good encouragement from an ever present me.

Then, she was moved to a private room after some dinner and fell into an exhausted deep sleep. This left me to sit in a rocking chair with my latest son in my arms while watching Ian Bell score fifty in the first of that 2006/7 winter's Ashes tests in Australia.

I knew that what had happened had been wrong in the words of the bible. I knew that I had caused both women serious emotional stress by my refusal to choose one of them. They had both wanted me to choose one, provided it was them. I remembered how Philip Dunn's mother had told me that it must be wonderful to have two women fighting over me back in 1979. I knew then, as I do now, that this was rubbish. It was an emotional rollercoaster where I didn't want anyone to be hurt but knew they would be. I was emotionally exhausted by it all but knew I had no right to complain, because I had caused it all.

However, with this little bundle of love in my arms, I felt a warm, no raging hot, love for all my children and thanked God for every single one of them. This latest addition, who even looked like me, was no exception.

## This Life In Death

Soon it was Christmas, and this was a much easier one for Christine than Natalie, as she proudly showed off George at Stratton Audley Hall to Marianne, Michael and the rest of the extended family, who welcomed him with a huge and wonderful amount of love. Meanwhile, Natalie was still pregnant and without me being there for her.

However, on 28th January 2007, Master Horatio Hodgson made his entrance. He was born by caesarean section after an extensively long labour where his mother had been extremely brave, but Horatio couldn't make an appearance by the natural route and after over 30 hours of trying, it was decided that the caesarean option was the best.

I dressed him in the delivery room and the nurse remarked that I had obviously done this before.

My love for Horatio was as complete as it had been for George, and despite all the heartache, pain and exhaustion to Christine, Natalie and me, none of us would have changed anything once we had these babies in our lives.

One of the first visitors to see Horatio was Dink. She was still at drama school in Tring. She had asked if she could have time off to visit her newborn brother. The headmistress sent for her.

"Davinia, do you think that I was born yesterday? You asked only 2 months ago to do the same thing. Was this a twin born 2 months later?"

"Miss, I believe you have met my father. Perhaps, I could explain."

Kindly, she was allowed to come and meet Horatio, one of my two new million-dollar babies. For this whole episode was to cost me a fortune. However, I have never resented a penny of it and consider that I was extremely fortunate to have fathered these finest of fine young men, instead of thinking about my forthcoming retirement – as most of my friends were. And thank goodness because my best business achievement ever was still mostly a concept in my head.

At the same time as Horatio was being born, so was 'Charles the Man who will be King' published by John Blake Publishing Ltd. It was to receive excellent reviews, and the 'Mail on Sunday' even dedicated a whole page to its review that carried many quotes from the book and some pictures.

As part of the publicity campaign organised by John Blake, I did some TV chat shows and radio interviews. Some of the latter were 'phone-in' shows. These often-attracted hostile female Diana fans, who had believed every word of the late Princess's propaganda, saw her as a saint, and therefore, me as a villain.

However, while they behaved mainly like ranting fanatics, they lacked knowledge, accurate facts, and were easily defeated by a calm me who was never rude, nor raised my voice, but just presented the irrefutable evidence.

While I know I won every single discussion with every single caller, I don't believe I changed many of their opinions. They clearly wanted a fairytale as opposed to the truth. However, the book was not only most fair on Diana, and a lot less forthright than I knew a lot of hard evidence could have dictated it to be, but it also extolled the Princess's achievements.

Once out of hospital, I needed to find a place for Natalie and Horatio to live. She owned two apartments in Clapham and one in Camden. However, we decided that none were suitable for us to bring up Horatio in.

Christine understandably did not want Natalie living close to our new King's Rd home in Chelsea, which had been purchased by us, as we had decided that the King's Rd apartment was too small to house George, Christine and, because she was still a very successful career woman, a nanny.

She suggested I took Natalie to live in the 'Castle' in Malta. Marianne told her that this was madness, as it was giving Natalie the best of my properties to live in. However, Christine was certain, and Natalie liked the idea as she had already stayed there in the year before Horatio was born, and loved Malta too, which she had known since she was a child.

So, in February 2007, Natalie, Horatio and I flew out of Heathrow bound for 'Bastion Charles' in Mdina. It was agreed that I would split my time there with the King's Rd house as much as my Maltese tax status allowed.

In the meantime, I had also sold 'Belvedere House' in Sandbanks and replaced it with a nearby apartment in Salterns Marina overlooking Poole Harbour and Brownsea Island.

I had achieved these moves myself, as both girls had been in late pregnancy at the time and packing and cleaning would have been dangerous for them.

I hadn't sold the King's Rd apartment but let J move in, where he happily spent the next five years before buying it off me. J by now was enjoying a good career at Accenture, where he was working in capital markets and had sold $25million worth of business in a relatively short period.

XXXXXXX

Despite this truly monumental upheaval in my homelife, I had managed to keep focused on Memoria and from the end of 2005 and the beginning of 2008 we had opened Memoria Sherwood Forest, Memoria Charnock Richard and Memoria East Lancs.

Moreover, we had won further consents at two sites and were now building both. These were at Memoria Wear Valley, Bishop Auckland, County Durham, which opened in early 2008 and Memoria Three Counties, Braintree, Essex, which opened in the spring of that year. This gave us now five crematoria that had been consented, built and opened in four years. Moreover, we had a list of over 60 sites we were looking at and 4 of which where we had asked Mercia to take options on land which we had identified and negotiated with the owners.

So, Memoria was now steaming along, and prospects were looking good. However, and while I was very pleased with the combined efforts of Michael and Chris at finding sites, Mercia at gaining consents and building them, and their appearance inside and out once they were open, I was less pleased with the staff performance.

Recruitment and management of staff had been Chris John's responsibility. I felt that Chris was very busy with Michael finding and gaining options on land where we wanted to develop and that he lacked both the discipline and the force of personality himself to recruit, train and manage staff to the level that I required and had envisaged. I wanted the standard of recruitment and the level of training to produce dedicated staff who would always, 'do unto others as they would have done unto them.'

I wanted men and women who understood that, while they couldn't take away the pain of bereavement, they could be as polite, kind, respectful, considerate and efficient as humanly possible to help bereaved families at their time of grief.

I understood that correct recruitment, extensive training, good reporting lines and leadership by example were the only way to achieve this.

I didn't believe that Chris Johns, despite his many other excellent qualities, had the judgement or man management skills to achieve what I wanted. So, I had replaced him with myself in the spring of 2007. I was completely at home in this new role. It was like going back in time to Hodgson & Sons Ltd of thirty years earlier.

In 2007, I also became very concerned by the state of the world economy. I believed that the world was living beyond its means and had been doing so perhaps by as much as 6% or even more per annum for a decade.

Michael and most other people believed the financial press instead. They did not share my view. However, in 2008, this granting of unsustainable credit raised its ugly head initially with sub-prime debt in the US but quickly exploded into a worldwide banking crisis.

This caused Matthew and Nick at Brackley to panic. They could see that they were unlikely to receive decent banking facilities going forward and that if this recession was to cause Memoria to go down then they would be left with five crematoria too.

I really don't know who approached who, but I suspect it was Mercia who approached my old company Dignity and offered to sell them the freeholds of our crematoria.

A deal was duly struck without us knowing anything about it until I got a call from Peter Hindley, the Dignity CEO, who had replaced me some 17 years earlier in that role, to inform me that they now were our landlords, and that, as they were also crematoria owners, we could not force them to renew our leases, and therefore we must sell to them now.

I replied that our leases were thirty-year leases and that, as I would be dead by the time they ran out, I wasn't bothered. However, I really was because I also knew that the crematoria values would fall rather than increase, as the years left on the leases reduced, and, as I had worked so hard all my life to recreate the Hodgson family wealth and pass it on to my children, I knew I had to react.

Anyway, you don't fuck with a Peaky Blinder. So, I called Michael Hackney and Chris Johns and set up a meeting in London at the Carlton Towers hotel in Belgravia.

Both men were less well off than me by a long way. Therefore, I thought that I must listen to what they wanted to do.

I also realised that Dignity could be pushed by me into making an exceptionally generous offer for us as it was not a property company but a funeral and cremation company and needed to operate like one.

This was because, now that it had been re-floated on the stock market, I knew that investors would not understand it buying five crematoria just to remain the landlords. They simply had to buy us out even at a silly price.

I asked both chaps what they wanted to do. Chris Johns understandably thought this was a great opportunity to have a payday that he had never seen before and may never see again. Michael was also tempted but, loyally voted to go with what I wanted.

It was clear to me that the 'Memoria Beatles' were now broken, and that any disagreement at this moment could cause a serious rift. Such a discord would mean that things couldn't be just glued back together. Therefore, I had to keep us united going forward.

I also knew that we had no right to stop Brackley from selling the freeholds of our sites and that their lease values would reduce as the years passed now that we had lost our automatic right to renew them.

I thought for a few moments and then announced that I would agree to sell if I did the negotiation.

"You don't have any negotiating experience and want to sell. I have loads of negotiating experience and don't want to sell. Therefore, I will get us a much better deal," I told Chris.

This was agreed. There was no split decision. We would sell and I would deal with it, while consulting both to ensure that we were all still 'singing from the same hymn sheet' as matters progressed.

Nevertheless, I would hate to give you the impression that I was happy about what had happened because I was not. I was devastated. We had put in a huge effort to build a business that had managed to successfully navigate those awful start-up years and was now becoming a very decent vehicle which I could ensure became as successful as Hodgson Holdings had twenty years earlier.

Indeed, this seemed to be a downturn in my fortunes which was 100% not of my doing, and that the past ghosts of 'Sir Jack' and Philippe de Margerie had been replaced by Nick Owen and Matthew Roberts as the pantomime baddies who had been sent from somewhere to destroy my dreams and the belief that I had one last and the best funeral business success left to create even if I was approaching sixty.

Nevertheless, I started the negotiating progress with a call to Peter Hindley.

Matthew Roberts and I were no longer on speaking terms. However, he still talked to Michael and informed him that if we were lucky, we might receive several hundred thousand or even a million each in a smug voice.

"Well, we will have to wait and see," I exclaimed when this was reported to me.

I played a very tough game. I wanted to retain the company Memoria; I wanted the right for it to operate freely in the market going forward with zero restrictive covenants; I wanted a very decent figure for goodwill associated with the five sites, despite my first two demands; and I wanted a backlog of expenses to be paid out of the operations they were buying and hence I wanted to remove the cash from all the sites as a result.

In addition, I insisted that Tony Walker, who you will recall had found us a lot of prospective sites on the promise of so much a cremation on those that got built, be included in the deal and his arrangement honoured by Dignity.

All in all, these demands were excessive and were initially resisted. However, I refused to budge and without too much of an argument Dignity agreed to meet all my demands.

This meant that Michael, Chris and I shared a sum not far short of what Dignity had paid Brackley for the developed sites, while the latter had borne all the development cost of all five sites, and we had received close to £3 million each for fresh air around five sites, one of which had been open only two days and another for only two months when their businesses were bought from us by Dignity.

Moreover, it should not be forgotten that 4 years earlier Dignity, in a fit of madness, had given us two sites to build, one consented and the other certain to receive a consent. Now they were paying us a fortune to take back what could have been theirs anyway.

Had we done well? Yes, we had done very well! Did I feel sorry for those two old pantomime dames Matthew and Nick? You can bet I didn't!

Dignity knew they had seriously over-paid and perhaps feared the fact that they had given away two of the five sites might come to light too.

So, they inserted a gagging clause into the agreement preventing 'Mr. Death' from celebrating his success in the press.

I readily agreed, as I no longer wanted personal media coverage, but only as long as my old chum Richard Oldsworth, who was still

Dignity's PR representative, got Memoria a decent article in the Sunday Times or Telegraph in exchange for our silence. This he duly did.

Around this time, we were approached by Andrew Sells, formerly of Nash Sells, a venture capital firm that owned Westerleigh, the second largest cremation operator in the UK and whom Michael and I had been interested in buying before we had started Memoria.

Andrew had fallen out with his partner John Nash, now Lord Nash, and left the business. However, he had originally nurtured the Westerleigh concept, thought the idea of building a national chain of crematoria had great possibilities and now wanted to invest in Memoria. He had demonstrated considerable foresight in this regard.

This was timely as Memoria MK II would need funding and, with bank finance out of the question due to the banking crisis of 2008, as alluded to earlier, we would need private funds to gain consents and build sites – as we were certainly not going to venture down the road of turnkey leases again after the Brackley experience.

The banking crisis itself also drew a recruit to Memoria MK II. This was my 3rd son Jamieson. He had started out running his own travel business whilst at university in 2001 before doing well in the city with the Capital Markets division of Accenture with staff under him in both the UK and India. However, like many others in his profession saw the current chance of large job losses in the banking and IT sectors as high. His opinion seemed confirmed when two banks disappeared overnight. He concluded that it was time to get back to entrepreneurship and set up a new consultancy business. Michael and I knew he would be a good addition as 'Business Development Director' and Andrew and Chris accepted this.

Then another piece of outrageous news came to our attention. The pantomime dames, Matthew and Nick, refused to hand back the four pieces of land that we had asked them to take options on under the terms of our previous agreement for them to build sites for us.

It was bad enough that they had sold our leases to Dignity, but now, in an act of complete spite and fury that we had done such a good deal ourselves with Dignity, they sold these options on land which we had had spent years finding and which they only had because of their contract with us.

This would also mean that these four sites would be built to the 'Memoria design', which we created on Michael's breakfast room table and then been commissioned with our architect Phil Baldry.

I was very angry indeed. Now we had to make a very important decision. Brackley had a contract with us, and we had given them these four sites under those terms. So, as they would not sell them back to us, should we sue them?

This would be time consuming, expensive and without 100% certainty of winning.

Alternatively, should we conserve our funds to concentrate on building new different sites from the possible list of still circa 60 which we had originally made some five years earlier.

We decided to move forward and not look back in anger – and we were right as you will see.

## This Life In Death

Chapter VIII

Great Expectations and Exits

2009 – 2014

So, initially there were going to be four directors, Andrew Sells, Michael Hackney, Chris Johns and me. We had also asked Jamieson to join us as an independent consultant, the only one of us to be paid on a £24,000 a year retainer, that was a considerable cut from his Accenture take home pay. He had also negotiated an equity per successful delivered planning consent up to a maximum of 10% for up to 10 sites – which we will hear about later.

We wanted to keep overheads very low to conserve cash for development.

The four directors would own 25% each and we would all commit to putting £1 million into the Memoria coffers to get us off the ground, as we knew bank debt would be very hard to come by.

Then, not altogether a surprise to me, even if it was to the others, Chris Johns pulled out.

Why wasn't I surprised? Because to re-invest over 33% of his Memoria MK I windfall and to go on working under my direction, who had removed him as Operations Director and had since recruited Jamieson to deal with planning applications, were big clues as to why he had taken his decision, and the fact that Andrew Sells terrified him was perhaps the final straw.

Chris decided to become an industry consultant, we accepted the position and engaged him as our contracted consultant. This meant we now only had three directors, each with 33% of the equity and each of whom had agreed to invest £1million.

Then it came to my attention that Dignity had relinquished one of the four Brackley options back to the pantomime dames as they considered it to be too close to their Exeter & East Devon site.

Nick had given the option to Chris Johns to see if he could place it for them and instead of Johns bringing it to us, who had retained him as a consultant, he sold it to the Southern Co-op instead.

What on earth had happened to decency, honesty and honour in this profession?

I was furious and determined to sue him. The case ended up in arbitration somewhere in the South West and so Justin Mason, our lawyer, and I trudged off to a rural hotel, where Johns plus lawyer and Justin and I were kept in separate rooms, while the arbitrator journeyed between the two.

This went on for hours and until after dark. Eventually, it was offered that Johns would pay £100,000 in compensation to Memoria rather than risk a court case. I agreed, as a bird in the hand was worth two in the bush, and frankly, we could do without the distraction of this case.

Justin and I retired to the bar for a beer before he was due to drive back to Birmingham and me to Dorset. We were joined by Chris Johns.

To show that there were no hard feelings I offered him a beer too. He accepted. He took a sip and then asked if I would accept less than £100,000 as he wasn't a rich man.

I had given Chris Johns 33% of Memoria for nothing. Thanks to my negotiating skill, this had turned into nearly £3 million. He had then become our contracted consultant having gone back on his MK II deal and had followed this by seeking to cheat me. Now he wanted my charity.

I just squinted my eyes as I stared into his. You don't fuck with a Peaky Blinder.

XXXXXXX

Meanwhile at home, my nomadic lifestyle continued as I journeyed between Christine and George in either London or Poole and Natalie and Horatio in Mdina, Malta.

George and Horatio were both turning into delightful little boys whom I adored and was grateful to be their daddy when I should have been thinking about becoming a grandfather – which I now was.

In 2006, my eldest son, Howard, had married the 3rd saint to have entered my life after Marianne's mother, Raymonde, and Christine's father, Tony.

She was the beautiful, intelligent, kind and altogether wonderful Lorraine. They quickly had two children, a boy and a girl. The first born was a boy. Howard asked my permission, sensitively, to call him Charles. I had always insisted that my late son Charles would be the only Charles of that generation. However, this was a different generation, and I happily agreed.

The little girl was christened Harriet. Both she and Charles have grown up to be talented, intelligent and sporty personalities that the whole family are extremely proud of.

When Charlie was a baby, his attempt to say 'grandpa', came out as 'baba'. I immediately seized on it and adopted it as my 'family' name as I wasn't altogether sure that I wanted to be called 'grandpa' anyway. Seventeen years later and now with three grandchildren, I remain 'Baba'.

So, while I had become 'Baba', I was also bringing up two young sons in different countries with different mothers, who had completely different personalities. So did the boys. George, was studious and quiet, Horatio was a natural athlete and a cheeky little chap. The big difference between them and their mothers was that, while their mothers, understandably, despised each other, the boys loved each other and became great friends.

This was very important to me, as was that my three surviving children from my first marriage all accepted George and Horatio – which they did – and that Horatio was treated 100% as much of a Hodgson as any of my other children – which he was with the exception of my mother, who thought out of loyalty to Christine, that she would not consider him to be 'one of us.'

However, Horatio won both Christine and my mother over and the latter's will left a legacy to all her grandchildren of equal proportion – Horatio included.

It was around this time that Natalie, who has always tended to see the grass on the other side of the hill as being greener, decided that she wanted to move back to the UK. However, she didn't want to return to London but decided she would prefer the Cotswolds instead as she wanted to be close to Marianne and my daughter Davinia, both of whom she had become friendly with.

However, in the end, she opted for a charming cottage, further to the southwest in a village called Lockridge, near Marlborough in Wiltshire.

She had one friend who lived close by but none of her family or other friends lived within a hundred miles. I considered this to be a risky choice as a result. However, she was adamant.

So, the 'Mason's Arms,' as it was named and indeed had been a village pub at one time, was duly purchased by me and Natalie and Horatio installed.

## This Life In Death

Now I could be found in Mdina, as I still had to spend my days there for tax purposes, or Poole, where I had an apartment, or London, where George and Christine lived in the week – along with his nanny Sonia, or in Wiltshire, where Horatio and Natalie now lived.

Of course, this was all my own doing and if I wanted to blame anyone for this 'gypsy' style of life, I only had to look in the mirror. However, looking back, although I was by now sixty, I was very young for my age, had huge energy, was determined to build my biggest business success to date and was delighted to be the father to my five surviving children.

I also realised that I had caused the events that had given rise to this nomadic life and had no right to complain. In addition, by both Natalie and Christine living in England, I had time to return to my wicked ways while alone in Malta, which I did with great gusto.

Therefore, out of this chaotic domestic existence I managed to create order, discipline and contentment. I would work twelve-to-fourteen-hour days on 'Project Memoria' and then dine with either George and Christine, when in London or Poole, or with Horatio and Natalie in Lockridge, or entertain a host of different girls when in Malta.

So, I yet again found a way of dealing with my completely contradictory characteristics and juggle them into a workable formula upon which to build more success – and indeed my greatest creation was yet to come.

Around this time, Christine, who was now involved with 'The Prince's Trust' and 'Business in the Community' on behalf of Capgemini, where she had risen to the heady heights of CEO UK, took a table of corporate guests to a fund-raising dinner at Buckingham Palace. I went along as 'Mrs. Christine' and duly stood back so her guests could be presented to either HRH Prince of Wales or his wife, HRH Duchess of Cornwall, dependent on which of the two lines they walked down.

"Sorry darling, Charles is going down the other line of guests," Christine whispered over her shoulder.

"Not to worry. I have met him several times but never the Duchess," I whispered back.

This was true. When Prince Charles had learned that I was writing a book about him and that this would include an account of his relationship with his first wife, the late Princess of Wales, he had discouraged close friends to co-operate with me. A very dear friend of the Prince had explained that this was to protect the image of the late Princess Diana for the sake of his two still young sons. I had replied that I considered this to be a very selfless act by HRH, when one considered how she had made several attempts to destroy his reputation and even prevent him from becoming King.

However, the friend of Prince Charles was right and now I had been denied access to people like his second wife, Camilla, Duchess of Cornwall as a result. Nevertheless, while the future King Charles III had thwarted my attempts to get interviews with such people, he had failed to prevent me talking to many Palace staffers.

It had been as hard for me to find any of these people to say a good word about Diana as it had been for the same folk to say a bad word about Camilla. Therefore, I was now intrigued to see her in person – even if I was unlikely to exchange a few words with her because I was not in the front row of guests.

At last, the future Queen Camilla, arrived in front of the Capgemini party and while passing a few words with Christine and her guests, she looked up and noticed me in the second row.

"Aren't you Howard Hodgson?" she asked.

"I am indeed Ma'am," I replied, completely flabbergasted that she knew who I was.

## This Life In Death

"You have written the best book about my husband that I have ever read. You have captured him perfectly."

I can't remember my reply to that. I just knew, at that moment, that I was grinning inanely and, for one never short of words, I was now stumbling for them. However, I recovered enough to ask her if Prince Charles had read my book.

"No, I don't believe he has. But that is because, other than work related matters, he reads nothing," she replied with a warm smile.

I subsequently sent her a signed copy of 'Charles the Man who will be King'. She sent me back a delightful thank you note. Sadly, and unlike my letter from the Prince of Wales, which is reproduced here, this was lost when we moved out of our house on the King's Rd, London.

Nevertheless, the moment was captured on camera and is reproduced here, where you can see for yourself my wide grin of appreciation to a wonderful woman who has helped His Majesty King Charles III follow so successfully in the footsteps of his mother.

A year or so later I was to be back at Buckingham Palace and this time was presented to Prince Charles once more. He seemed to remember who I was and was duly very friendly.

I asked him if he had read my biography about him.

"Why would I want to read a book about myself?" was his reasoned reply, which was caught on camera.

"Because you might learn something," was my uncharacteristically rude reply to a man that I admired so much and would follow to the end of the earth. Worse, this was blurted out while I pointed my figure at the future King of England. This was also captured on camera.

So, this was a deja vu moment, and I had crossed swords again with the saintly prince. If you study the photograph, you will also observe, a nervously smiling Christine, who was clearly thinking that I had just buggered up her chance of getting a gong for all her good works by mere association with her 'Peaky Blinder' husband! She needn't have worried as she was deservedly awarded a CBE in the New Year's honours list of 2020.

xxxxxxx

In September 2009, Michael Hackney with the help of our planning consultant Kris Mitra secured our first planning consent under the Memoria Mark II banner. Jamieson was still learning the ropes at this stage and was subsequently not yet heading up our planning campaign, which he was to do so very successfully as we shall see.

However, Dignity who were building a site introduced to them by the 'Pantomime Dames' not far away in the village of March, were set on stopping us and placed a judicial review on Fenland District Council, who had granted the consent. This was successful and our consent was squashed in the summer of 2010.

However, Jamieson, who had taken over the obtaining of new site planning consents as part of his business development role by then, successfully won a re-application in April 2011 and secured the consent. However, by that time March was built and so it made no commercial sense for us to build even though we now had a consent to do so.

Nevertheless, it enabled me to approach the new Dignity CEO, a likeable man by the name of Mike McCollum, and secure £175k from him to ensure that we wouldn't build. This was welcome income and, along with the £100,000 that I had taken from Chris Johns, ensured that we could meet J's salary and other costs, without Michael, Andrew or I having to put our hands further into our pockets.

## This Life In Death

In the meantime, a decent man and Cardiff City Councillor by the name of Jonathan Bird approached J, having read the article in the Sunday Times about me building a new crematorium business and offered us a site he had between Cardiff and Barry in South Wales.

Michael and J went to look at the site while I was in Malta. On my return the three of us met Jonathan, his brother and sister at his home and an agreement was reached.

Jonathan also obtained planning permission for the site in November 2009. However, once we had secured the land, we had to take the consent back to the planning department to remove several outbuildings and move the position of the crematorium itself as the cremator chimney was too close to a line of trees at the bottom end of this impressive 20 acre site.

This all took most of 2010 to resolve, along with other time-consuming pre-commencement planning conditions such as newt surveys. However, construction started in late 2010 and finally, on 24$^{th}$ October 2011, just over two years after the 'pantomime dames' had attempted to destroy us, Memoria's first new crematorium in the 'MK II' era opened.

It had the facility to play personally chosen music, recorded eulogies or show as many photographs of the family's choosing as they wanted.

This was because I had always known how important it had been to personalise the service of my son some 30 years earlier and now technology made such a 'celebration of life' service so personal, affordable and easy to achieve.

However, I had to run the gauntlet of the Church of Wales. I was bombarded by countless messages, phone calls and even one visit to urge me not to do this as there was no room for such distraction in a religious service. In essence, their message to me was that a funeral service was about God and not the deceased.

I disagreed. I stood my ground, even when told that the Church of Wales would not recommend our new crematorium. I was nervous but knew I had to resist these threats.

This was because, Memoria Cardiff & Glamorgan was also to open with a mission statement, which I had written and was determined that it would become our 'Apostles' Creed' and that this would set us apart as offering an unrivalled standard of service in facilities which were second to none. It read:

'Memoria – Cardiff and Glamorgan Memorial Park has a mission to provide exceptional standards of service, facility and products to the bereaved families that use its funeral directing services, crematoria, cemeteries, gardens of remembrance, financial & legal services or online retail store. This is because it is not only commercially sensible to do so but also because it is an essential act of human decency towards people who have just lost a much-loved member of their family or friend. Bereavement is the price we must all pay for the joy of loving and being loved. The loss of a loved one is the most stressful, unhappy and traumatic experience that we will face in life. We at Memoria realise that we are unable to eradicate such pain, but we also know it is our responsibility and duty to be as efficient, kind, respectful and polite as humanly possible to our clients at their time of grief, and thereafter when they need to conclude estate matters for their cherished relatives or friends. Therefore, it is our aim to provide immaculately clean and tidy facilities in tranquil and beautiful surroundings attended by people who are sincerely dedicated to our mission, and who take a great pride in their work as a result.'

How could I be true to this statement while denying families the technology that was readily available to help them really say 'goodbye' in a way that they wished to.

Yes, this was the start of the very best company ever created in the field of bereavement. Its standard of service and facility were second to none before or since. It was born and grew successfully out of the unique concept of 'do unto others as you would have done unto you' and its pride was that and not profit, nor stardom or acclaim, but instead pure client appreciation and gratitude.

Indeed, in 2024, some 12 years later Memoria's independent review commented, when reviewing 1,000s of five-star reviews:

'Memoria Limited is highly praised for its excellent service, beautiful locations, compassionate staff, and modern facilities. The most frequently mentioned topics in reviews are the quality of service, the peaceful and calming locations, the professionalism of the staff, and the comfort of the facilities.

Overall, Memoria Limited provides a comforting and supportive experience during difficult times.

The staff at Memoria Limited receive high praise for their compassion, professionalism, and helpfulness. Reviewers frequently mention the positive impact of the staff on their experience, highlighting their ability to provide comfort and support during difficult times.'

One reviewer mentioned that their special needs granddaughter was able to visit the crematorium and look around a few days before the funeral, highlighting the accommodating nature of the staff.'

This was all created because I had always known from childhood that was what 'Hodgson funeral businesses' should be doing. This is what I had learnt on the knee of my father. This was why I had written the 'Mission' in 2009 and why it became our Apostles' Creed.

I had also understood that, with Hodgson Holdings plc, trying to maintain this level of excellence, while building size by acquiring companies with no such aim or desire, and being under pressure to produce profits for the plc shareholders did not allow you either the opportunity or the circumstances to achieve this to the level that I wanted.

But now I had no such constraints and could afford to 'get rich slowly', to quote John Gunn, and to do so by the virtue of excellence.

However, none of this would be possible if it was not for one brilliant, and unusually human and entrepreneurial, banker called Gary Johnson.

Gary worked for the Royal Bank of Scotland, who had dropped the name of their English acquisition, NatWest, until 'Fred the Shred' Goodwin's' activities along with the resulting carnage, came to light – when they sensibly restored it in England at around this time.

Getting any form of new bank debt was very difficult in these years and for many years to come after the 2008 world banking crisis, even if you owned an established company: if you were a start-up like Memoria, it was almost impossible.

However, Gary, who was introduced to us by our supplier and friend Justin Smith of Cemetery Development Services, came up with a loan of 50% of the build cost and this was for a start-up! What a man! This would not be enough to get us to where we wanted to go but it was one hell of a push down the road.

However, although this did allow us to conserve cash, it would not be enough to allow us to build a second site or meet the considerable planning costs associated with gaining a consent.

So, we would need to find another form of funding if we were going to expand at the rate which I believed that we must in order to capture the country's few remaining sites before they were either swallowed up by either Dignity or Westerleigh or even the Co-op.

Then, as is often the case, a chance encounter changed the course of history.

They say you 'make your own luck' – and I'm sure that 'where there is a will there is a way' is true; however, while the second statement is almost copper-bottomed, the first is more open to the wheels of fortune.

A few years earlier, I had been commissioned to write the film script to 'Six Feet Under' by Carlton Films. They had optioned the film rights and renewed that 'option' several times. They wanted a film based on the book. But it couldn't be called 'Six Feet Under' due to the deal that I had with HBO about their American TV series.

Despite their enthusiasm, they never quite got the finance together, and I really did not like their chosen producer Philippa Braithwaite, the wife of the actor Martin Clunes and a highly successful film and TV series producer of hits such as 'Sliding Doors' and 'Doc Martin' among others.

This was nothing personal. It was because she understood nothing about funerals or funeral directing and would not listen to someone who did.

However, eventually the 'option' lapsed and the producers of 'Mission Impossible' at Pinewood decided to pick it up and were very keen to secure the script and decided that I should entitle it 'Stiff – The Movie'.

I duly did. However, things were still moving very slowly, and I was becoming, as usual, impatient.

Then Christine mentioned the script to Nicola Horlick. Nicola had enjoyed a very successful career in finance and banking since I had first come across her as an institutional buyer in the eighties.

Originally, she had made her clientele a lot of money by buying Hodgson Holdings stock. She had remained a fan of mine and was keen to help finance the film as a result.

She was Chairman of a company called Derby Street Films. I met her with Christine at 'Windows on the World' at the top of the Hilton

Hotel in Park Lane, London. We discussed the storyline and then she asked me how much I was prepared to invest to back my own work.

"Nothing."

"Nothing? Well, why should investors put their hard-earned cash into a film that the rich writer won't sink a penny into?"

"Because, I need every penny I have to invest in Memoria," was my reply.

She hadn't heard of Memoria. I explained all. This brought back memories of her early success when she had backed me as CEO of Hodgson Holdings over twenty-five years earlier.

"I am Chairman of a company that provides investment cash to companies like Memoria," she announced enthusiastically.

We started to talk about Memoria instead of film finance. It was a very important moment.

Indeed, this was a gigantic turning point that pointed to the stars for those of us astute enough in business development to see the opportunity. She was chairman of a company called Rockpool.

Michael, J and I were very keen to meet Rockpool. We realised that unless we were able to gear up to meet both the cost of winning consents and the considerable sums needed to build those sites our various individual expertise would be worthless as we would still only have one site, while our less capable competitors, who did have access to cash would build the remaining sites left in the UK.

Moreover, I believed that if the cost of that cash was 10% or less, we would be more profitable than Memoria MK I had been with Brackley Builders.

In addition, I also realised that we were not going to get any terms whatsoever from a bank unless it was a very small percentage of the amount required. Therefore, such a route was a complete non-starter as collectively we were either unwilling or unable to find the funds personally to fund two or three sites let alone our target figure of ten.

On the other hand, Andrew Sells took a different view. He was a 'venture capitalist' (private equity today) by trade. He was completely disinterested by the development, construction, or running of the business. He seemed only marginally interested in the P&L, and this usually centred on the cost of things.

However, he was very interested, as many private equity guys are, in the balance sheet and the articles of association, which were of secondary concern to the three working directors.

Moreover, while he brought neither wit nor wisdom to our board meetings, he was never slow to criticise anyone else's performance, even though he had provided zero ideas, work or even financial introductions to help create a future for the company.

It had become apparent quite early on that Sells was a difficult man. Indeed, we had received many warning calls from people who knew him, and had advised us to steer well clear of him, while we were forming Memoria MK II. More than one of which had reported that Andrew and John Nash had come to blows in the Nash Sells board room.

I didn't know if this story was true or not, but we could not afford the luxury of turning Sells away in any case, when he came knocking at our door with a million pounds in his fist.

This was because the state of the world economy was very bad following the crash of 2008 and beggars could not be choosers. So, I had determined to try my hardest with Andrew, as, for one, needs must, and, for two, in fairness to him, I also realised that I wasn't the easiest of men to get on with when I came across men like him.

## This Life In Death

So, life with Sells had been difficult enough from the beginning, especially for Michael, who Sells bullied whenever he could at board meetings.

However, my view on wanting to explore what Rockpool had to offer and Andrew's view that we should wait until we could raise bank finance at around 5% or less became a catalyst for increasing disharmony.

Andrew believed we should wait until the world economy improved, interest rates fell, and banks were willing to lend again and at reasonable rates.

Whereas, I believed that if we waited for these ducks to line up, there might not be any decent sites left to develop; we would be losing money by having only one site to support our current overheads and we could afford to borrow at up to 10% interest from other avenues rather than joint stock banks who perhaps were never going to lend us the funds we needed even if Andrew's ducks eventually did line up.

So, in my view, which was shared by Michael and J, if we didn't find an alternative funder, we simply had nowhere to go and the wonderful creation of Memoria would remain an 'if only' in my mind and the pot of gold, at the end of the rainbow, would remain exactly that for ever.

Therefore, even though I had tried hard to accommodate Sells previously, I now knew this was time to have one of my 'you don't fuck with a Peaky Blinder' moments. I booked an appointment for Michael and me to go and see Matt Taylor and Andrew Green at the Rockpool offices in Pall Mall and did so despite Sell's opposition.

We had a good meeting. We liked them. They appeared to like us. They seemed like people whom I felt that I could trust, and they were associated with Nicola, whom I had known for over a quarter of a century.

My feats as the 'enfant terrible' of funeral directing had not yet become a dim memory to them or their investors either, and so we appeared to be a decent prospect for them to invite their potential investors to invest in.

Moreover, unlike Sells, they seemed keen to understand, just like Gary Johnson of NatWest, how the business worked.

Even more importantly, their desired return of investment appeared to be around 6.5% to perhaps 7.5% per annum and this was something we could certainly afford, and I hoped to reduce even that when we came to negotiate final terms.

However, Andrew remained unconvinced. So, I invited him to talk to Matt Taylor himself, while Christine and I took my mother on yet another cruise up, and then down again, the Nile – but with a young George now in tow too.

This resulted in Andrew not only being extremely rude to and difficult with Matt Taylor but also in both phoning me several times a day as I meandered up and down the Nile.

Nevertheless, on my return, and under a considerable amount of pressure from me, Andrew eventually agreed that I could negotiate just one deal, subject to the Memoria board's final approval.

And we had that one deal in mind. We had a large list of targets as you are already aware. However, there was one that J felt he and his team of planners could get over the line quite quickly. This, we hoped would become Memoria Kirkleatham.

However, we had to secure the finance as they were achieving this so that in the end the securing of the consent and the finance were running in tandem.

The Rockpool offer meant that their investors had a small percentage of voting A shares, which would be swept up in their eventual exit, but their investment was mainly held in guaranteed dividend bearing B shares, which carried a coupon of just 5%. The A shares would be purchased as a bonus at the same time as the B shares were redeemed. However, the B shares coupon increased to 7.5% if all shares were not redeemed on the due date.

These terms were excellent for us to be able to fund Memoria Kirkleatham, if J and co could land the consent. More importantly, it was a blueprint that we should be able to repeat time and time again. Michael, J and I were delighted. Sells was not but decided to honour his word to agree to the building of this one site.

The Kirkleatham site had first been earmarked in 2008 by Redcar & Cleveland Council. This was very pleasing as most councils sat on their hands at best and were fierce opponents at worst, when it came to planning consents being granted, for there are few constructions as locally contentious as a crematorium.

By 2010 J had taken 'planning' under his wing and set up building a team of third-party professionals to support him.

I really believe it is both unfair and unhelpful for me or anyone else to try and evaluate who did what in the tremendous success story which is now about to unfold. It was truly a team effort.

Without Michael's knowledge of finance or banking or keen understanding of land suitability, Memoria would have been so very much the poorer.

Without my vision of what Memoria should be, my knowledge of funerals and how to treat the bereaved, and my ability to lead the Memoria army and negotiate with anyone, the same would be true and Memoria probably may not have happened and certainly would never have become such a theatre of excellence.

However, here, I am going to single out J's role re business development and obtaining planning consents. For, if he hadn't built his team so carefully and led them so well, we would never have won the long list of consents that were often obtained against all the odds and set planning precedents in this most difficult of difficult fields.

As a result, I have asked him here to explain how he and his team performed so outstandingly and how he evaluates their impact on the growth of Memoria.

*"The most important reason for our success was our total commitment to the projects. We managed to put together a team of consultants who were as committed as if they were a Hodgson – fighting for their own future. The board support for our activities was crucial too – especially in the early days when we were totally unproven. To this end, HH showed an unbelievable level of confidence in my abilities to come out on top.*

*In planning, when you have commercial challenges as well as objector pressure, matters become very personal and mostly determined in the court room. At times, it felt as though the world was against us, but we all realised very quickly that the trick was attention to detail in everything that we did from site selection to the ability to cope with detailed cross examination. Our core team was made up of Ian Ponter (planning barrister), Kris Mitra (planning consultant), Brian Duckett (Landscape Architect) and Ian Roberts (highways engineer). Every single one of these men fought for Memoria like it was their own business. I was also able to install that belief in them that they were fighting for a worthy cause – a family business who were building public service facilities for the benefit of the local community in the face of massive commercial and local opposition. We fought multiple battles and won over 90% of them – remembering that before this team, success rate at appeal was less than 40%. I am immensely proud of those achievements as they were highly challenging and if we had lost just one or two of the early battles, Memoria would not have been able to grow to even 50% of its eventual size."*

So, by 2010, while Michael was now running finance, land purchase and central administration; I was supervising the building of the Memoria Cardiff and Glamorgan site from Malta but with flying visits to stay with Natalie and Horatio near Marlborough before dashing across the Severn Bridge and on to the site; J was now entrusted with planning.

He took the site's application forward with key council employee support and spent £40,000 preparing a planning application that year.

However, and unbelievably, the Council changed its mind about the site that it had selected and, in a pre-application meeting, made it clear that, despite having chosen the site, it was no longer of a mind to support our application.

I was furious. £40,000 of our money had been wasted on this council's say so. However, obviously having a tantrum about this was not an option either at that moment.

So, we had to source a new site, which Michael did and secured it in 2011. Then, with the help of an apologetic council, planning was secured in August 2012, despite a unanimous majority of 7 to 4 after many rejections were received from local residents, who did not appear to be that 'local.'

The site was then built to a new and specially designed smaller footprint, with many 'green' features and in a new partnership with the French cremator manufacturer ATI and their English building partner Needham's and so our second site opened on 2nd January 2014.

xxxxxxx

In December 2012, I returned from Malta to Sloane Street, London for my annual medical. I had no intention of trusting any Maltese doctor with such a responsibility.

## This Life In Death

Peter Wheeler, who had been our family doctor since Anthony Ashe had been relieved of this duty in 1992, due to him being the brother of my ex-lover Caroline and having brought her to dinner in Wilton Place on that fateful 'sliding doors' night in 1992.

Peter's letter with the results duly arrived a few days later. As usual, he remarked that he was amazed that my liver was functioning so well given the amount that I drank. Indeed, I appeared to be in rude health.

However, he mentioned that my PSA had risen since my last medical and that I should have another blood test with that in mind perhaps in three months' time.

I did not know what PSA was. Therefore, I decided to take another one the following week. To everyone's horror, it had doubled again in the three weeks since the last test.

PSA stands for prostate specific antigen. Basically, if it is going up one could be suffering from prostate cancer.

Now I was sent by Peter to see a top Harley Street prostate cancer surgeon by the name of Bijan Khoubehi. He felt my prostate gland in that most uncomfortable, unpleasant, but unavoidable of ways. He said it felt soft. This was a good sign. However, he thought that I should have a biopsy to be 100% certain that there were no tumours there.

I was due to go skiing with Natalie, Horatio and Davinia in the Three Valleys in January 2013 and said I would have the biopsy on my return.

It was a very happy trip; Horatio was by now able to ski with us after morning ski-school. Davinia was a good skier and together we helped Natalie improve – and she was, with her ballet dancing skills, a good and willing pupil.

However, all the time, the forthcoming biopsy was hanging over me like the sword of Damocles. When I returned from France, I went into hospital, had a general aesthetic, the biopsy was done, and I managed to do the only presentation that we ever needed to do to Rockpool investors that evening.

The results came back quickly, and I went to see Bijan to learn my fate. J insisted on coming with me. So did Dink. I warned her she may have to listen to an awkward conversation.

I knew, in my heart of hearts what he was going to say before he said it. But it was still a shock when he did. I could see his mouth moving but I could not hear the words as my brain was racing away to try and deal with the fact I had cancer, could be terminally ill, which meant death and who was going to look after my family in the event of that – especially my two youngest sons.

I had had cancer before. I had had a lucky escape in 2002 when I had been referred to a dermatologist re a patch of hard skin. It was nothing at all in fact, but she had discovered a malignant melanoma on my chest during the investigation. A biopsy had been performed and it had confirmed her diagnosis.

A second operation the following week was undertaken to ensure a larger area around it was also removed and soon after that I had been told that the melanoma had been caught before the cancer had entered my bloodstream and that my life had been saved as a result. It had been a harrowing but a relatively short time.

However, this was much worse. I now had prostate cancer. But was that all? Had it already escaped from the prostate and therefore spread elsewhere. I had been suffering from pains in my back and now I suspected the worst.

Bijan also seemed concerned and immediately arranged for me to have various scans the next day. Christine was in India with Capgemini; Howard was in Dubai; Natalie, who had decided by this time that she didn't like rainy Wiltshire, was back in a new house that I had bought her in Malta.

J and I took George out for supper. I appeared as cheerful as I could muster and determined to put a brave face on matters.

Feeling sorry for myself would not make anything better and this was a time to demonstrate the qualities of bravery and leadership to all the family that I had always preached as taught to me by both my parents when a child and had attempted to demonstrate by example all my adult life. This was going to be a tougher test of my mettle, but I knew that I must live up to what was expected of me.

At that meeting in his consulting rooms, I had managed to hear Bijan tell me that I had four options. These were: do nothing; have directed radiotherapy; have general radiotherapy; or operate. He advised me to think about it. I replied that I didn't have to. I knew that I wanted these offending tumours removed from my body as soon as possible.

Bijan replied that I must realise that if I went down this road that I would never be able to father any more children. I replied that I was approaching sixty-four and had fathered six already and believed that my responsibility was to them rather than having more.

He replied that we could discuss dates for the operation after the results of the additional scans were known.

That first night I lay in bed alone exhausted by the fact that I could think of nothing else. However, the next morning that cloud had lifted. I felt serene. I felt amazingly not frightened of dying. My thoughts were pure, and I seemed to have become a saint over-night. If there is a God, then this was his doing and certainly not mine.

I spent the day alone in or around Harley Street having scans. I was on top of the situation.

Next it was back to Bijan's consulting rooms for the results. By this time Christine was back from India and she and J came with me. It was good news. There were no signs of cancer elsewhere. Nevertheless, Bijan would not be able to tell if it had escaped from the prostate until the operation was done.

However, for now it wasn't showing elsewhere. I was so elated that for several hours I even forgot that I still had got prostate cancer. I phoned Howard in Dubai to give him the good news and then went to have a decent lunch with Christine and J, during which, Christine, in a very charitable act, suggested that I should give Natalie the good news too.

Bijan had arranged for the operation to be performed at the London Clinic on the first possible date - Saturday 16th March 2013. Initially, I hadn't thought too much about this as I was so happy to know that I wasn't riddled with cancer.

However, over the weekend, this started to play on my mind. I wanted the operation to be sooner. Marianne suggested that I get a second opinion. She told me a friend of Michael's was also suffering from prostate cancer, was being treated by the very top man in Harley Street and had had his operation arranged in days rather weeks.

J and I duly trapsed off to see this illustrious surgeon. He had a very fine clinic. I was shown round, watched a video and then asked by him:

"When would you like to be operated on?"

"As soon as possible," I replied.

"How about next Tuesday?"

I was delighted and arrangements were made. However, I knew that I really liked Bijan and trusted him. So why was I able to be operated on in this clinic next Tuesday but not by Bijan for over a month? I decided that I must ask Bijan the question.

"Because, Howard, you strike me as a man who wants to be continent and continue to have erections and so enjoy a good sex life."

"Of course I do," I replied indignantly.

"Then I can't do the operation until six weeks after your biopsy to allow the swelling to go down. I would be doing the operation by robotic surgery ten feet away from you. I need there to be no swelling if I am going to succeed in joining everything up again so that it all works. If you want to have the operation sooner. You will have to go elsewhere."

"Bijan, baby, you got the job."

He performed it on Saturday March 16th 2013, as planned. He was successful and I was to enjoy my first orgasm on 17th April. Thank you Bijan.

xxxxxxx

I had determined that no one other than Michael and J should know about my illness at Memoria and had even dealt with the Memoria Cardiff & Glamorgan nightly reports while in hospital and feeling extremely unwell.

This site was working well, Memoria Kirkleatham was soon to start construction, the Cameron coalition government was doing a good job all round, and I had survived an unpleasant operation for a killer illness. Life was looking up again.

## This Life In Death

While I had been ill, I hadn't been frightened of dying and had become an extremely nice and considerate person. Now that I was cured, I became frightened of death once more and reverted to my normal 'Peaky Blinder' self. Life had returned to normal.

And of course, while all this prostate upheaval had been going on Memoria's search for sites and its quest to build at least ten of the limited number of new crematoria sites left in the UK had remained at full steam ahead.

The next big planning exercise appeared initially to be a failure. Indeed, an expensive failure. However, as the greater picture was to reveal itself, it was anything but that.

J had been pursuing a site in Vale Royal in the county of Cheshire. Our application had become the subject of one programme in the series 'The Planners' made by BBC 2.

Jamieson had fought against very stiff opposition from locals who were not only vocal but organised protest marches in the village and even staged a car crash to influence the planning committee.

This was further complicated by Westerleigh pursuing their usual policy of seeing where we were applying and then attempting to find an alternative site and launching a second planning application in the hope that we, as a much smaller company with limited funds, would withdraw.

Richard Evans, their CEO, was neither a likeable nor trustworthy chap. In particular, you could rely on his word being his bond with about as much certainty as a Birmingham City supporter could rely on their team not getting relegated. However, he was not stupid either.

He had realised that it was likely that we would withdraw rather than either waste our valuable cash on a failed application or risk building a crematorium which would never be profitable if both applications were granted. Westerleigh had wisely selected a less contentious site than ours which was only three miles away.

Our application was denied. This was J's first setback and we knew that public inquiry appeals had previously only about a 35% success rate and cost over £100,000 which we could ill afford to risk.

Nevertheless, I decided that we had to show more mettle when it came to Westerleigh or they would just trample us under foot at future locations by using the same tactic.

Therefore, we had to hope we could win the appeal and that this would discourage Westerleigh from making an application, which they hadn't yet as they were some distance behind us in the planning process.

Accordingly, J was given permission to extend his planning team and launch the appeal.

This he did and against high odds they won it. The news came to me the night before my prostate operation that the day had gone well, and this cheered me as did the Villa, against QPR, win which I awoke to ask about after the operation.

However, and most unfortunately, the victory was not announced until June 2013 and by that time our competitor had obtained a consent and more crucially had started to build. This could not prevent us from building but we knew that the area did not need two crematoria and that we could not possibly build ours if it was to be loss-making as a result of this.

Therefore, the outcome seemed to be a bad one. We had a consented site which we could not afford to build, the application had cost us circa £50,000 and the appeal more than double that and yet we had nothing to show for it, while Westerleigh had a new crematorium under construction. However, apparently every cloud has a silver lining and certainly this one did.

Andrew Sells, who had reluctantly agreed to the Rockpool funding of Memoria Kirkleatham, had remained adamant that funds could be raised at a cheaper cost from banks. I knew this was complete nonsense. However, the Memoria Board gave him six months to prove his point. Unsurprisingly to me at least, he completely failed to get us into a discussion with anyone let alone sign any loan agreements.

However, despite his failure, he was still intent on blocking any more funding deals with Rockpool. He had the ability to do so given the existence of a shareholders' agreement Michael and I had signed with him in 2009.

Then the Vale Royal circumstances told him that, in his mind, J had been outmanoeuvred by Richard Evans and that, due to a much smaller size and lack of access to cash, we were unlikely to expand beyond two or perhaps three sites with the much bigger Westerleigh and Dignity as our competitors.

Consequently, he wanted out. We were delighted because we wanted him out. He was preventing us from having access to Rockpool cash and at the same time brought in neither alternative funding, nor wit, nor wisdom, but just manic and unhelpful distraction and rancour to our board meetings.

Without all the usual trouble associated with Sells, a deal was agreed. He was pleased with it and could hardly contain his glee as he left the meeting.

So, Andrew Peregrine Sells had just consigned himself to become our Pete Best of the Beatles. He was now due to miss the train which took us across the rainbow to the pot of gold, but unlike Pete Best, he only had himself to blame.

I had little sympathy for him then and even less when he bemoaned his fate years later as if it had been our fault.

So, thanks to Rockpool's funding and J's planning team – I now had great expectations. But I had also happily survived two essential exits – my prostate and Andrew Sells.

# This Life In Death

## Chapter IX

## The Wonder of it All Baby

## 2015 – 2020

With the negative, truculent and unproductive Andrew Sells removed mainly from our lives, for he still had his shares in Memoria Kirkleatham as part of his exit deal, and me now able to negotiate funding for each new consented site, we looked to have a much brighter future. And so, it proved to be.

They say you can wait ages for a bus and then four turn up. This is what happened to Memoria – except they were consented sites rather than buses.

In fairness, we had known about one for some time and had used it to pay off Sells. This was Memoria South Oxfordshire in the Vale of the White Horse. It had been agreed that part of his exit would be this consented site, which we would manage for him for an annual fee.

Indeed, a relatively simple planning application had been approved in April 2012, even before Memoria Kirkleatham had, by 10 votes to 1. However, it was subjected to a Judicial Review challenge by my old company Dignity as they owned the old municipal crematorium in Oxford and, quite rightly, feared that a brand-new state of the art crematorium run to my standards and by me, would hold serious implications for their site. They had a point.

However, I knew that Judicial Reviews were not decided on such issues. I knew the site was in the right location and that we had proved the local need for it. Therefore, I believed that J and his team would win. However, I also knew that this would be time consuming, a major distraction, and potentially expensive. Moreover, there was no guarantee that we would win.

Therefore, I decided to approach the Dignity CEO, Mike McCollum and offer him a way out for both of us.

Mike was a decent man, and I could accept his handshake on a deal, which was becoming increasingly rare in a funeral industry, where an ever-larger percentage of the industry was held by large corporations that were run by career businessmen, who understood little about bereavement and cared even less about it. Moreover, their word was certainly not their bond.

My plan was that if Dignity would drop their challenge, I would agree not to open our new facility in the Vale of the White Horse until the 1$^{st}$January 2015. Mike agreed. We were both as good as our word. He withdrew the challenge and so construction started in February 2014 and the site didn't open until 2$^{nd}$ January 2015 as I had promised.

However, by that time, two more consents had been won. Both had been very hard fought; by local opposition in one case and massive competitor competition in the other. Perhaps the winning of these two consents was the biggest challenge we had faced to date, and these victories gave us an impressive track record. Thus, NatWest and Rockpool now had further comfort to believe what I had always known, Memoria was going to become the leading bereavement service brand in the UK.

Firstly, there was the application for a site in Amber Valley, Nottinghamshire. This was a crucial battle. Initially, I had thought that I would be able to secure the site from the landowner by charm. He had phoned me in Malta, and I had taken the call while hovering over the bastion edge as usual.

"Is that Howard Hodgson?"

"It is,"I replied.

"The good looking one, who looks like Robert Redford?"

I never like answering 'yes' to this commonly posed question as I think that it is an arrogant answer and, anyway, I want to be recognised, while not being disrespectful to Mr. Redford, as Howard Hodgson instead.

So, I answered rather non-committedly, "The one with fair hair – yes, that's me."

We got on very well and I thought that I would be able to convince him that I would be able to offer him the best price and, with a small commission per cremation once a certain number had been reached each year, and he wouldn't receive a better offer.

I was wrong on all counts. We were up against my old friends, the 'Pantomime Dames', amongst others and the owner decided, having spoken to us all, that sealed bids were called for.

However, I was not deterred. This was another Ann Bonhams 1981 moment. I knew we had to win. I was determined to win. We were going to win!

J brought Michael and I the necessary GIS demographic analysis for the site. Together we built not Michael's usual budget, but the most positive one we could believe in – so we could see how high our bid could be. We then shared the figures with NatWest and Rockpool.

Armed with their approval, I posted our sealed bid. We won.

Now it was over to J and his trusted team for the planning battle. This was not going to be a placid affair like Memoria South Oxfordshire. Indeed, it was even going to make Vale Royal look like a walk in the park.

The level of public objection was enormous. Over a thousand objections had been received by the council. Moreover, this had been accompanied by many demonstrations from local residents outside the proposed location.

Our application was for a site that was on a protected green wedge, and this made objectors feel that they had a strong case.

I am an extremely keen green supporter of His Majesty the King, as you have already realised. However, the description of this field on a hill in front of a busy dual carriage way, next to a petrol station and a hotel, while being surrounded by housing was as utterly preposterous as describing Margaret Thatcher as a communist.

However, they still felt that they needed to employ 'bully boy' tactics to such an extent that there was a police presence at the planning committee meeting to ensure law and order were maintained.

Jamieson was subjected to constant verbal abuse when he spoke during a three-hour debate. Worse, the application failed by 7 votes to 4. The objectors were jubilant.

However, Michael and I had enough confidence in J and his team of planning advisors that we decided to back a public inquiry appeal.

When this eventually was convened in June 2013, it was to last for 5 days. J was cross examined for four hours on need and his defence of our position was as admirable as it was telling. So were the performances of other members of our illustrious planning team but none more than the star of the show, barrister Ian Ponter, who caused outrage with our opponents sitting in the gallery, as he destroyed their witnesses one after another with his meticulous and unforgiving cross examination, mixed with quick wit and the occasional hilarious observation. We were so grateful that he had been batting for us rather than the opposition. For, in these situations, decisions often depend on a performance like his.

As a result, in July 2013, this, the most senseless of senseless fights over a piece of useless scrub land, came to an end. The decision of the public inquiry was announced, and that announcement told both sides that we had won.

This resulted in two very significant additional points. Firstly, Jamieson and his team had set a very useful precedent for the acceptability of crematoria on protected green land. Secondly, it resulted in a young man applying for the groundsman's job. His car broke down on the way to the interview and he had to run the last mile if he was to make it on time. He did and came in sweating profusely and looking like a beetroot. I was impressed. J and I decided to employ him.

I saw a lot of hidden talent in this young man. He was not to disappoint me and over the next decade was to rise from the role of gardener on £16,000-a-year to over ten times that annual sum as a main board director as he lived the dreams that I had planned for men and women who wanted to join us in creating something really special – a creed, a religion and a dedication to service, compassion and excellence. His name was Carl Clamp.

The site was to open on the same day as Memoria South Oxfordshire – 2nd January 2015 and now Memoria MK II had built and opened four sites in four years, but this was just the start of things to come.

xxxxxxx

The second battle was over a site in Countesthorpe South Leicestershire, and was one of the most challenging and toughest that we were ever to face. Westerleigh had previously tried to win a consent for a crematorium on council owned land in the same small town, only to withdraw it following massive and hostile public opposition.

Michael, undeterred by this, then found a small but well-located piece of land less than half a mile away also on the edge of the same village.

J submitted our application on the 13th May 2013. Once again, local opposition erupted and the application was refused, 11 votes to 1 in November that year.

Meanwhile, only six miles away in Harborough, the Co-op lodged an application to build a crematorium. This was also refused in December 2013.

I was, at this stage, more worried about 2 or more crematoria being built rather than none as I knew outside these local areas there was widespread support for a new crematorium on the grounds of need and choice as the only crematorium for miles around was a very old, decrepit and austere municipal site in the city of Leicester itself. Therefore, both Michael and I were keen to support J's appeal.

Both Memoria and the Co-op submitted appeals as a result. They were heard by the same inspector, and both were won by written representation, instead of public inquiry, in March 2014.

So now, and despite the blood curdling rage of the objectors, there were two sites granted within six miles of each other.

However, Westerleigh, in an act of cavalier piracy, probably motivated by their Vale Royal experience, and believing if they got a consent that we would not be able to finance our build, submitted a third application in the village of Kilby just a mile away from us.

Moreover, at the same time, they also submitted a section 288 challenge – which was the same as a judicial review – to our appeal win. Their logic being if they could hold us up, while they got a consent, even if we won the 288 challenge, we would not risk developing our site.

I thought that this act by Richard Evans made the 'Pantomime Dames' and even Andrew Sells almost look like reasonable folk.

The three of us discussed this complicated situation at a board meeting at the table in the basement kitchen of my King's Rd London house. We reviewed the options.

If we were to build regardless of the 288 challenge to our site; the chance that the Kilby site might also get a consent; and not forgetting that the Co-op already had a consent just 6 miles away; we would be taking a massive gamble.

Of course, the prize could be winning the 288 challenge, that Westerleigh was refused a consent a mile away, and that my Memoria operational team was good enough to take more than our fair share of 'battleground' cremations from the poor Kilby site in Leicester and the proposed Co-op site in Harborough, which now seemed certain to be built.

However, we also had to consider the downside risk too; if we built and lost, we would be forced to rip down what we had built to date, and worse, pay for the site development that far and pay back 100% of the money borrowed from Rockpool investors to build the site.

Our planning lawyers and the barrister, Ian Ponter, gave us a 70% chance of winning the 288 hearing. This still left us a 30% chance of losing and then there was no guarantee that the Westerleigh site would not be consented or that we could beat the Co-op site into a poor second over the wider area.

I was by now, thanks to Sells departing, a 51% holder of Memoria. Therefore, I realised that the decision was mine. Initially, I elected to halve the risk.

So, I left the meeting and phoned Mike McCollum, the CEO of my old company, but now competitor, Dignity PLC and offered him a half share in our site. It would be run by me, but he could have an option to purchase if we ever wanted to sell.

Mike listened patiently as I made him aware of the whole story. When I had concluded, he took no time to wish me good luck and decline my offer saying that he would watch my latest 'Houdini' act with interest.

I closed off the call and re-entered the kitchen. My mind was made up. We were going to go for it all on our own. You don't fuck with a Peaky Blinder, and I had enough confidence in J and our planning team to go ahead.

They say fortune favours the brave and we were, not just me but Michael and J too – especially Michael as he was risking everything and was unbelievably brave at that moment.

Next, J managed to assist in the Westerleigh scheme being refused in June 2014. Naturally, they appealed and had a hearing set for November. Meanwhile, our 288 hearing had been set for October. This was not a time for the faint hearted as we continued, much to the amazement of everyone but ourselves and Andrew Green of Rockpool, to build our site.

Then around came October and J, backed by our planning team, including the very important Ian Ponter, went to the Royal Courts of Justice. The Judge listened very carefully but didn't decide on the day and instead said that he would take the evidence away for further consideration. This seemed to be a cruel twist of the knife to me at the time, but I kept that opinion to myself.

Next, the planning team were engaged by J to get the Westerleigh appeal for Kilby rejected. Thus, they were able to contribute to the very important rejection of the appeal that Westerleigh duly suffered.

Then finally on the 16$^{th}$ of December 2014, just before my eldest son, Howard's 41$^{st}$ birthday, and with the site now 90% built, J received the news, while interviewing staff for the new Memoria South Leicestershire site at the Leicester Marriot, that Westerleigh's 288 challenge had also failed.

He excused himself, went to the gents, where he burst into tears, and then phoned me.

I'm usually more inclined to tears than J. However, on this occasion, I was in my poolside lounge in Mdina, Malta, and I just stared into the mirror with a clenched fist and thought that Richard Evans shouldn't have fucked with a Peaky Blinder. But he had and he had lost.

The emotion caused by this nine month adventure had been highly challenging for all three directors.

J, obviously as a non investing director and owning few shares at this point, stood to lose the least financially. However, he had become exhausted by the emotion of fighting these battles, which he and his team had won. This was completely understandable.

Michael's courage was enormous as the loss, if we had failed, would have wiped him out financially and left him probably dependent upon Marianne for the rest of his life as he was now 64 years of age – not a good time to become penniless.

I would have taken the biggest financial hit - but, I would have hopefully survived, even if a lot poorer as a result.

However, those of you who have read Volume I 'The Struggle' and now Volume II 'The Madness', know only too well that throughout the struggle and the madness of this life, my huge motivating force had always been to re-build the family's station and wealth. If I had lost here, I would have dented both badly.

So, this might not have been as big as the flotation of Hodgson Holdings in 1986 or the Ingalls deal of 1987, but the risk was every bit as big as buying Hodgson & Sons Ltd in 1975 and the acquisition of Ann Bonham & Son in 1981.

Westerleigh, after licking the wounds of their crushing defeat here, secretly bought the Co-op site in Harborough, as the latter had decided, rather foolishly in my opinion, to come out of the cremation market and sold their other crematoria to the once again enthused Dignity.

We had no chance to bid for Great Glen, as it became known, as we were not made aware of the sale, even though the Co-op had contacted us and asked us to supervise the build and run the site for them. I was furious with this tardy deception.

However, I need not have worried, as over the next decade, the Great Glen site, which opened in June 2016, failed to make the vaguest dent in our numbers. This was because I knew how to deliver exactly what bereaved families wanted and they didn't. Indeed, the service levels of the two crematoria remain miles apart today.

Memoria now had five operating sites which had opened in just over four years. However, just like the early Hodgson & Sons years, we were still under most people's radar, except for those who, like Dignity, Westerleigh or now the 'Johnnie come lately' firm Horizon, were our competitors.

Happily, the wicked 'Pantomime Dames' were by now deservedly falling by the wayside. This was entirely their own fault. They could have had a brilliant ride tailgating us, but their poor judgment and greed had prevented this.

As McCartney had written about Lennon in his 1971 composition 'Too Many People':

'You took your lucky break and broke it in two, now what can be done for you.'

Not much would be done to help the dishonourable 'Pantomime Dames' going forward and I for one shed no tears.

xxxxxxx

# This Life In Death

The next consent happily lacked any such drama or cause for sleepless nights. This was a wonderfully stress-free application compared to Amber Valley, South Leicestershire, Vale Royal, and even Kirkleatham or Cardiff & Glamorgan. Indeed, along with South Oxfordshire it became the easiest to date.

The site was in Waveney on the Norfolk, Suffolk border in the east of England.

Planning was easily achieved by 8 votes to 2 in July 2014. Indeed, it gave us some cheer in the middle of the South Leicestershire wrangle.

J was even able to engage in some wit when he called me to announce his latest success.

"I've got some very bad news for you."

"Oh fuck", I replied as my heart sank at the prospect of more bad news in the middle of our massive fight with Westerleigh in South Leicestershire.

"You are going to have to make that dreadful journey to Waveney for many years to come," he announced triumphantly.

This was a reference to the fact that I hated the hideous car journey which had to be endured to get there.

The site was opened on 2nd November in 2015. It was our 6th site in less than 5 years and our 4th during the twelve months of 2015. This was more than any firm, despite most being much bigger than us, had or has achieved before or since.

Moreover, given the complexity of 2 of them, it was a great reward for Michael and my nerve and the ability of J and the planning team.

Perhaps now with 6 sites being operational Michael and I could contemplate drawing a salary, which we had never done over the last 12 years of running Memoria MK I and MK II. This was a sign of our complete dedication, especially by him, as I had investment income to sustain me, whereas, he had to live off the Memoria MK I proceeds and little else before that.

In 2014, I had introduced one hour time slots for all Memoria services. Most crematoria had 30-minute slots, some 40, and a few still only had the 20 minutes, which had been the norm in the 1960s when I was a young funeral director.

My thinking was that I must allow more time for families to express themselves while still coming and going without seeing another funeral cortege, as this turned the whole affair into a depersonalised conveyor belt, rightly, in their minds.

And because I had introduced so many aids to make a funeral service a personal celebration of life such as eulogy screens, where personal photographs could be run at either a point in, or throughout, the service; personally chosen music of any kind and by any artist; and free of charge mood lighting for the committal and a single large photograph above the catafalque which encouraged this personalisation more and more; I became increasingly aware that this could not be fitted into the 40-minute time slots that we had operated under in Memoria MK I. Hence my decision. Moreover, for only an extra £200, a family could reserve a double slot, which gave them access to two hours on site.

Initially both Michael and J were horrified as both were convinced that, by cutting our slots from 12 to 8-a-day, we were bound to lose bookings due to reduced availability.

However, they acquiesced to my belief that this extra time was essential if we were to deliver the standards of service and facility that I demanded that we offer.

I was proved to be right, and cremation numbers rose towards the 5-year maturity figures and beyond with a marked acceleration at all sites as market penetration analysis showed we that were gaining markedly not only in our core areas but also in the battleground areas where clients could easily choose another crematorium instead of ours if they so wished.

Indeed, within a year, a trickle of non-Memoria sites adopted one-hour times and within three years this became a flood.

Also, in 2014, I had introduced direct cremation at Memoria Kirkleatham in answer to a request from a funeral director from Whitby, who wanted to have his funerals 'committed' in the hearse at the end of a church service in the town and then deliver the coffin to us the next morning for an unattended cremation with no committal service. This was to enable him and his bereaved family not to have to make the long journey to the crematorium.

Unwittingly, this was probably the start of direct cremation, which has now risen to circa 20% of all cremations in the UK as, in the following decade, the Anglican Church finally lost any remaining hold on funeral services and families demanded more freedom of choice.

However, the real reason for the growth of direct cremation was the explosion of television advertising by companies selling pre-arranged funeral plans from around 2017 onwards as we shall see.

This drive towards better standards of service and facility, that I had been so fanatical about since the 1970s, meant that I was also becoming increasingly interested in moving Memoria up the 'food chain' to having earlier direct contact with the bereaved families that my crematoria served.

My motivation was three-fold: I wanted to ensure that these services were properly explained to people who had suffered a bereavement and I did not believe that all funeral directors did this and it might involve them in a longer journey to a Memoria site – so I had to do something about these guys putting their interest before that of the family; I wanted to expand our activities into financial services and funerals consequently; and lastly, I knew that I could easily do both.

This was because I remembered that I had introduced pre-arranged funeral plans into the British market over twenty-five years earlier and I also knew that I had never met a more creative or better funeral director than me.

However, I also realised that we had to stay focused on crematorium development and gain as many of the increasingly small number of remaining decent sites that might be consented.

Moreover, I knew that I could neither devote resource or cash away from these goals to buying funeral directors whose acquisition prices remained at an all-time high due to the price inflation that Dignity had introduced into the market, and which had been copied by the various Co-ops and private funeral directors alike to the point that funeral inflation was running at five times the average national annual inflation rate and had made funeral directing a desirable occupation to such an extent that the number of private firms had increased by over 33% since the Millennium.

So how was I going to be able to introduce a pre-arranged funeral plan product and at need funeral operation into the group on a shoestring?

I decided that I would write the pre-arranged funeral plan myself and get it underwritten by a life assurance office and that I would set up an online funeral business offering both direct cremation and traditional attended services nationally and serviced by a combination of our own funeral hubs and accredited funeral partners to cover areas which were out of our economic travelling reach.

Therefore, we would not only make a profit on the sale of pre-arranged funeral plans, but we would be storing up both future funerals for our funeral division and cremations for our cremation division which would help both of their future profitability and so the 'back book' created would have a significant value.

Moreover, to make choice simpler for the clientele, I decided that both funeral plans and at need funerals would be available in easy-to-understand fixed price packages.

Therefore, those who wanted to spend more could and those that didn't needn't – but everyone would receive five-star standards of service and facility whatever they chose.

I also intended to offer an extended range of other financial services and legal products associated with bereavement, that I had talked to the press about nearly 30 years earlier, but these were not to be introduced until 2021 as it turned out.

Therefore, I was kept extremely busy, and was unusually well-behaved women wise, in 2015, as I was still in charge of the construction of crematoria, the running of 6 crematoria and now the creation of 'Low-Cost Funerals' which encapsulated both our financial service division and our funeral division.

When we had opened Memoria Amber Valley, I have already mentioned how Carl Clamp had come to my attention. I had also noticed a young man when we were engaging staff for Memoria Kirkleatham in 2013.

His name was Paul Reed, and he had taken a £5,000 pay cut to join us from being a local municipal cemetery superintendent.

Normally, I never seriously considered municipal employees as they generally lacked work ethic, motivation and dedication. However, here was a lad who was willing to take a 20% pay cut so that he would have a chance to better himself with Memoria.

He became the Memoria Kirkleatham manager and made a good team with his appointed assistant Gill Johnson, who had got her appointment despite opening her job interview, before she even sat down, with the words:

"So, it's true, you do look like Robert Redford," as she flashed her eyes behind batting eye lashes.

She had applied for the manager's role but Paul had pipped her to it and so she had had to settle for the number two slot.

However, I was now going to need someone to help me build both the financial service division and the funeral division. I knew Paul would be the perfect choice and so he started his 5-year ascent to the main board in 2015, while Gill got to be the Memoria Kirkleatham manager as she had always wanted and became a very good one too.

Around this time, I was approached by two organisations. Both were to have a very positive effect on our new fledgling funeral division and our already robust cremation division.

The first came from the CWS. I got a call from an unusually pleasant and capable woman high up the Co-op, whom I had got to know quite well when she had wanted me to run Great Glen for the CWS before they decided to sell it to Westerleigh instead, much to my already recorded annoyance.

She had heard that I was starting a funeral division and that it would be offering direct cremation. The CWS intended to offer direct cremation too, but as they no longer owned any crematoria, she wanted to know if I would give her a special price for direct cremation.

We had lunch in London and a deal was agreed. The CWS were prepared to pay £450 for a direct cremation. These would be booked in with LCF, our funeral division, who would then decide to which crematorium the CWS should deliver the deceased.

We agreed a five-year contract after all the usual CWS messing about which took months and gave a clear picture that the organisation had, if anything, got even worse since I had struck that famous Ingalls deal with them in 1987, nearly 30 years earlier.

This new CWS scheme was offered by their 1,000 branches only and not advertised for fear of it adversely affecting their traditional funeral business.

However, it became an immediate hit with those CWS clients who were short of cash while funeral price inflation was still raging at this time.

The result was excellent for us. The cremation division started to receive around 2,000 additional cremations per annum as a marginal cost business paying them £320 for each, while the funeral division bagged an amazing £130 on every occasion for making a couple of phone calls. That is quite a lot of revenue when 2,000 cremations are involved, in fact it is £260,000, which was not too bad when the corresponding outgoing was so very small.

Of course, I could have given the cremation division more and LCF less. But I had designed it that way so that I could get my hands on the generated cash as both Michael and J were very nervous about my plans to start advertising both funeral plans and funerals on TV.

Therefore, this deal alone had secured the future of LCF and allowed it to have its own cash to invest in its own expansion in both in the funeral plan market and the at need funeral business.

The CWS deal was therefore very significant and as important as some of the much more highly publicised Hodgson Holdings plc deals in Volume I of these memoirs.

Indeed, given that LCF was to be acquired for £33 million in less than 5 years from its penniless inception, it was perhaps a lot more important.

Moreover, as I had allotted 33% of the shares in LCF each to my two fellow directors, despite it being my idea, design and work that achieved that value, I like to think that when they kneel beside their bed each evening, they remember me in their prayers.

The second organisation to contact me was a husband-and-wife team by the name of Bryan and Catherine Powell. Bryan had been a chauffeur in the 1980s at Hodgson Holdings plc's Erdington hub in Birmingham.

Some years later, he had met and married Catherine and now together they had started an online direct cremation business called 'Pure Cremation.' It was becoming successful. However, they had a problem. They had an arrangement with Worcester Crematorium whereby they were only allowed to bring two cremations each morning.

This held obvious problems for them. It meant that they had to remove from wherever they were instructed in the UK back to their Redditch mortuary and then were limited to ten cremations-a-week.

So, they contacted me now in the hope that I would allow them unlimited early morning access to our 6 crematoria for either direct cremations or a short, limited attendance service.

Naturally, I agreed as this was more marginal cost business that Memoria's funeral and cremation divisions would not have otherwise received.

All three companies businesses, Pure Cremation, LCF and the Co-op, especially with the advent of Covid, grew rapidly, which meant that before too long, LCF was handling around 5,000 funerals-a-year in total, with circa 2,000 of them being our own, which also added 5,000 additional cremations to Memoria's crematoria.

Eventually, the CWS awarded their contract to Westerleigh in 2021 at a hideously low price, which we would not have contemplated accepting; and Pure Cremation went on to develop their own crematorium at Andover and so cremated for themselves.

However, the great boost that both contracts gave to the fledgling Memoria Funeral Division in the years between 2016 and 2021 was enormous and for which I'm very grateful.

The CWS funeral operation seemed thereafter, as has always been its fashion for decades, to stumble from one crisis to another but while always surviving as even it still performed better than their other divisions.

Whereas Bryan and Catherine Powell sold out for tens of millions in 2023 and retired to live in Monaco. Very well done them.

xxxxxxx

While all these exciting times were exploding like some American film drama at Memoria, life domestically remained much the same.

Christine's career continued to flourish by her polished and largely non-confrontational board performances, unlike her more controversial husband, and her charm as an operational officer at Capgemini, where she was promoted despite being English and a woman.

Those two facts weighed heavily against her. However, miraculously, and to her great credit, she had become a member of the Capgemini Group executive board and was their UK CEO. A very significant achievement.

Moreover, thanks to the fact that she was rubbing shoulders with the great and the good a lot of the time to bring in new business and doing a lot of work in the community, instead of just running the UK operation, she was making both good contacts for her future and ensuring that Capgemini was paying for her to get the CBE which she richly deserved. But this was exactly how the system had always worked and still does today.

At home in London on the King's Rd, George was growing up into a charming young man whom the whole family adored, although I remained a little concerned that he was turning into a modern-day Bertie Wooster as his nanny Sonia was indeed Jeeves and catered for his every whim.

Meanwhile, in Malta, Horatio remained a delightful chap who was liked by one and by all for his outspoken wit and cheeky charm.

His mother, Natalie, continued with her nomadic life of chasing the greener grass on the other side of the hill.

She always seemed to want something badly, but when she got it, she seemed discontented ever more quickly on each occasion. The fact that I was still sitting on the fence about choosing between her and Christine obviously had something to do with this.

But I was not solely responsible because it had been a recurring theme in her life before she ever met me.

Nevertheless, I did understand her position and tried my very best to keep her feeling loved and secure.

I bought her a very substantial property in Mellieha Bay. It had five bedrooms, four bathrooms, four reception rooms and two kitchens set over two spacious and well-appointed floors on a split level.

However, the architect, one of the most famous in Malta, had failed to consider that half of the house's foundation was built on rock and the other half on clay.

## This Life In Death

Clay contracts when it dries out in the summer and rock doesn't. Therefore, half the house moved, and half didn't. This caused it to crack from top to bottom and rendered it unsafe to live in.

I instructed lawyers, took the architect to court, and following several adjournments and a house visit by the judge and both legal teams, the matter was settled out of court in my favour and to my satisfaction as all my purchase price and legal costs were recovered.

Next, and while the battle of South Leicester was being fought so courageously by Memoria back in England, I rented the wandering Natalie a house in Gozo, which had a pool and was extremely homely and cosy. Initially, she seemed very happy but soon fell into a depressed malaise about the place once she worked out that it would mean getting up very early five mornings-a-week to get Horatio into school on time back on the main island of Malta.

So, we just stumbled on, me wanting nothing but to supply the warmth and love needed for a young lad being brought up in Malta when all he seemed to want was to live by Villa Park, in Birmingham B6, UK and her wanting to do equally the best for her son, while keeping him in Malta, where she was happy and far from the depressing pressures of finding work in her chosen career of being an actor.

Nevertheless, she would have to do something with her life and so we considered the idea of opening a boutique hotel in Valletta, which was becoming an increasingly popular all-year-round weekend break location due to its fantastic history, beauty and pleasant climate.

However, as neither of us really had the essential drive and determination to make such a project work, the idea was dropped, and I could see that we were starting to drift apart.

In fairness to Natalie, she had waited ten years for me to leave Christine or Christine to leave me. Neither had happened and she now realised that perhaps neither of us would ever leave the other.

## This Life In Death

To many people it must have seemed like I just wanted my cake and eat it. However, neither of my two little sons wanted me to leave their mother and I just wanted to keep them and their mothers as happy as these stressful circumstances would allow.

But, now after a decade of this exhausting existence, it was coming to a painful close because, while I knew that Christine and I were better suited, I had loved Natalie a lot, and we had nurtured and brought up a wonderful son together and had enjoyed many magic moments over these years.

Natalie, when she was happy, could be as delightful a little girl as she could be completely the opposite when she was not.

But now it was over. She moved back to Brighton. Her father and I bought her an apartment there. Horatio went first to school and then college there and she remains there today.

Horatio throughout these years has remained as extremely close to me as my other children. We speak daily. He visits me in Monaco every month. We ski and sail together throughout the year. He and George are also very close. He is adored by the whole Hodgson clan and that includes Christine, who says her life is richer for having Horatio in it.

He is every bit a part of our family as anyone else in it. Natalie and George are also fond of each other, and I remain friendly with her and Valerie her mother. Sadly, Chris, Natalie's father, passed away in 2021 after an illness borne with his usual grit and fortitude.

Natalie and I, and Christine and I, have done a very good job in bringing up two fine young men. My world is a better place with them in it. So, what happened in 2005 might have been wrong in many people's eyes, but I make no apology to them and would not have changed any of it.

xxxxxxx

Meanwhile, the Memoria express was still roaring along. The new funeral division and financial service divisions were developing nicely, as Paul and I were gaining valuable footholds in both markets, much to the usual rumblings of the older funeral directing generation, with their lament, “It’s that man again”.

Moreover, the six crematoria which I was now running were more than meeting everyone’s expectations in both standards and returns on investment.

Moreover, J’s ‘SS’ style planning team was still ‘hot to trot’. Denbighshire had originally been on Memoria MK I’s target list. However, the Pantomime Dames, especially Matthew, hadn’t felt too comfortable about its prospects.

Nevertheless, after their split from us, they had attempted, but failed, to bring a scheme forward. Whereas, now free of them, we were also keen to have a go ourselves and decided to go for it.

Michael spent many thankless hours searching for a site and happily, for a change, was assisted by the council, as well as a decent local developer, Glyn Pritchard-Jones, who knew my long-time lawyer, the ever-present David Mandell.

Once Michael had found and secured a site, Jamieson submitted a planning application in early 2014.

As usual, there was significant local opposition. This is always to be expected, because while a community usually wants a crematorium, as it needs one, it still believes that it should never be built near it.

Of course, this defies logic – because how can a crematorium serve a local community if it is not local. But such is human nature when it comes to these issues.

This opposition gained further support from a local funeral director, who was objecting because he wished to promote an application for his own crematorium in neighbouring Flintshire.

There was, in our opinion, a need for both sites to be built as there was a huge gap between the existing crematoria in Wrexham, Chester and Colwyn Bay.

The Denbighshire application was refused, despite a very supportive recommendation to consent it from the planning department, in May 2014. J and his team appealed, and a hearing was set for November 2014.

Meanwhile, the local funeral director, who had done so much to put a spoke into our wheel in Denbighshire, seemed to be getting a free ride in Flintshire. The council issued a statement saying that they were mindful to support his application, even though it was for a crematorium to be built on green belt land, if a better application was not received within three months.

You don't fuck with the Peaky Blinders.

J and Michael set about a furious schedule. A site was found, optioned and an application submitted within the schedule. So now we were English people fighting for two sites in the notoriously anti-English North Wales. The odds didn't look good. However, as Volume I and much of Volume II have told you – when the going gets tough the tough get going.

After an extremely gruelling 5-day inquiry, and against ferocious opposition, Memoria won the appeal. The site was opened in May 2016 and was the last time that I supervised the building of a site, as the Memoria cremation, funeral and financial service divisions were by now taking this youthful sixty-six-year-old at least twelve-hours-a-day to manage. Michael took over supervising the builds going forward and did an excellent job.

But now, we had to face an even more difficult set of circumstances in Flintshire. Had we bitten off more than we could chew?

This was to become the most vicious two-way fight we were to face. It may not have been as crucial for our survival as either Amber Valley or South Leicester, but it was a truly brutal fight with all the local emotion being against us. We would have to use the unemotional logic of what was best for the community and planning precedent to have any chance.

In the Welsh corner, a popular local funeral director who had a lot at stake. In the English corner, the Mohammed Ali of crematoria, Memoria. In the middle, the referee, the completely inconsistent council planning committee.

In fairness to the council planning officers, they had recommended one site for acceptance and that was ours. This was because they had rightly accepted the planning precedents of our case.

However, the planning committee thought with their heartfelt loyalty to the local man against the English. If his site could not be consented, then why should ours being the 'cock-eyed' logic employed despite the very real need for a crematorium to serve the local community.

So, in the end both sites were refused. Yes, refused – despite the Flintshire Council having declared that there was a need for at least one site to be built only a year earlier.

We decided to appeal. This needed a two-week inquiry and that needed to be rearranged three times to suit various people's diaries. This only added to the tension. It finally went ahead in July 2016. We got the decision in August, and, against all the odds, J and his team of 'Ali' wonder men had pulled it off. We had won yet again and yet again on appeal.

The local FD also launched an appeal following his refusal, but perhaps wisely, withdrew it, as his site was on green belt land after all. However, instead, he issued a 288 challenge to our appeal victory in the hope of stopping us from building and thus keeping his slim hopes alive for a future second application on his own site.

Unlike at South Leicester, this time we didn't take the risk of starting to build. Instead, we waited. The challenge was eventually heard in March 2017 and – yes, as you have no doubt already guessed, J and co won. The site was eventually opened on 25th June 2018. It meant that Memoria now owned three sites in Wales and were, as a result, Wales's largest operator.

This marked the end of two very long and at times bitterly fought battles for these two sites. We had won. Michael and I had backed J and his team. They had delivered both results.

These battles had not only been won because of reliance on facts and planning law, but also by sheer endurance. J had received several death threats over these years of roller-coaster emotion.

But, like father like son, you don't fuck with the Peaky Blinders.

By now Memoria had eight crematoria, some with cemetery facilities, and quickly expanding funeral and financial service divisions. The group was very profitable, had gravitas and needed expert management.

This was provided by the three directors heading up well-trained and wonderfully dedicated executives to manage every aspect of the business.

I oversaw all operations. This meant that I ran the Memoria Cremation, Funeral and Financial Service Divisions. I was ably assisted by Carl Clamp, Mark Reath and Richard Todd. Carl was my number two in the MCD. He looked after operations, specialised in cremator matters, and was ably assisted by Mark over front of house operations and administration systems, while Richard looked after all funeral director relations.

Paul Reed ran the MFD, and which included our own funeral operation and those all-important fulfilment contracts that we held with the Co-op and Pure Cremation amongst others.

I had, by this time, also recruited a Communities Director by the name of Frank Meilack to build relations with local communities wherever we operated.

Together these five men made up a very powerful team which ensured that standards of service and facility were excellent at every level in every part of every Memoria division.

It also meant that we were listening to the needs of both our funeral directing partners and the religious and ethnic communities which we all served when their members suffered a bereavement.

This exclusively funded genuine concern was also to prove to be money well spent as market penetration figures showed that our Trustpilot 5-star reviews were being reflected in our locally increased market penetration. This made me pleased and feel that my determination to live by our 'Mission Statement' was not only 100% justified, but also improving profitably.

This was a warm feeling. More profits made by doing good, rather than ripping people off made me feel very content and realise that I was achieving what I had set out to do.

At this time, Michael oversaw land acquisition, building and finance, where he was ably assisted by his assistant Julie Huggins. These were key areas of the business which were ably managed by him.

Jamieson, not only headed up the 'Mohammed Ali' planning team – but by this time he supported me in Operations by doing 50% of the site visits and site management meetings. He also took over all recruitment and set up our HR function as we grew as a company. An endeavour where he was ably supported by Jacqui Peirson. He created a number of useful Operational Performance tools (like market penetration reports) which linked GIS software back to net performance. This aided our decision making over our competition which was useful. Once his planning duties started to calm, he went on to lead the company's response to the CMA investigation – but we will get onto that later.

Next on the trail blazing hit list of our new site targets was North Hertfordshire. Michael found an excellent site near Hitchin and Jamieson submitted a planning application in April 2015. Amazingly, the council, despite developing plans to build a crematorium in their own local municipal cemetery, approved our scheme at the planning committee on 15th December 2015 and the site, where Michael had supervised his first build was opened on 17$^{th}$ June 2017. However, around this time and much to everyone's surprise, the council suddenly announced that they intended to resurrect their plans to open their own crematorium. Frankly, this was a ridiculous idea and, potentially, a scandalous waste of public money.

As Mrs Thatcher had said nearly forty years earlier, "There's no such thing as government money. It's your money and we spend it." And in this case intended to 'waste it.'

In North Herts, there had been a need to build one crematorium. The council planning committee had granted a consent to Memoria to develop one, and we had used our own money to build it.

Now these foolish people wanted to waste several million pounds of the local public purse to build a second, which would never make a profit but would also put our investment at risk by splitting the market – as there just wasn't enough population living in the area to support two crematoria.

So, yet another long-running and arduous battle, that gave rise to a couple of sleepless nights, had to be fought over the next three years, until eventually the council saw sense and dropped the idea.

Now Memoria had nine sites and only one, Memoria Waveney, had been a relatively simple affair to develop. In Memoria MK I, Chris Johns had always said, never proceed without the planning officer's recommendation for the council to approve an application and if you then lose forget about appealing the decision.

Well, if we had listened to that advice and hadn't rid ourselves of the short-sighted Henry VIII personality Andrew Sells, I might have been, by now, running one crematorium as a hobby rather than nine instead, along with funeral and financial service divisions, and the three of us being on our way to a multi-million-pound fortune.

However, life had to get easier – didn't it? Surely, there would be cases coming up that were not going to fully test our nerve and determination and the ability of our planning team every time we applied for permission to build. Don't bet on it!

The 10th site was every bit as challenging as any of the previous ones and had a lot more to do with our old enemy Richard Evans the CEO at Westerleigh than the local planning committee.

We had identified Worksop as a potential site over a decade earlier in the early days of Memoria MK I. However, no land owned by willing sellers had ever been found.

Then Michael found two sites which were both suitable and both had owners willing to sell. One was in Barnby Moor, situated between Worksop and Retford, the other at Babworth, a little over a mile away.

Michael selected Barnby Moor as the better site and took an option on the land. We should have taken an option on the Babworth site too. We didn't. This wasn't Michael's fault as it would have been a new policy and would have needed board approval to option two sites so close together. So, it was a collective fault – and an expensive one.

Why? Because the owners of the Babworth site, having warmed to the generous offer made to them by Michael, decided, upon his selection of the Barnby Moor site instead of theirs, to offer their land to our old chum Richard Evans of Westerleigh.

Naturally, Richard wasted no time in biting their hand off and so a race to be consented started just as it had done at Vale Royal some years previously.

The sites were only just over a mile apart and there was not a large enough population to support both crematoria. So, it seemed likely that a sensible planning committee would approve one but not both.

However, if this chapter has taught you anything, it has taught you that local government planning committees are nothing if not inconsistent and often absurd. So, both sites were consented at the same meeting in late 2017.

J, immediately tried to negotiate a sensible commercial deal with Evans. The latter, as usual, promised much but delivered nothing. He obviously felt that if Westerleigh built, we would not dare to and so a second Vale Royal result would land him a victory here too.

I had other ideas. I realised that if I let Evans get away with this on a second occasion, he would simply just follow us around the country, like a Komodo dragon does its injured prey, and pick us off one site at a time by using the same strategy.

So, I determined that we had to build. However, I also realised that we were only likely to undertake a maximum of 500 cremations per annum if we proceeded due to there being two sites in the same area. This would not be enough to even get close to a financial break even. This was also bound to be a major concern to our backers Rockpool and NatWest as well as our own board.

However, I also realised that I had something incredibly valuable that Westerleigh didn't possess. I had started our funeral division some three years earlier. This meant that we were by now cremating some additional 5,000 people per annum from areas outside where we owned crematoria. This was my secret weapon which I was to use to save the day.

Paul Reed, on my instruction, found a suitable site for a funeral hub in Retford and consequently decent numbers of Memoria's funeral division direct cremations and those from the CWS contract were delivered to our Retford mortuary which ensured that Memoria Barnby Moor undertook some 1,500 cremations in its first year of 2019 and so was immediately profitable.

The site had had to overcome more pre-build planning conditions than Westerleigh's and so opened about four months later than they had.

However, given that our standards of service and facility were superior and the staff a lot more accommodating to the local funeral directors, it soon started to take a better percentage of the local traditional market as well.

Once more 'mighty midget Memoria' had refused to be intimidated and had won yet another Napoleonic struggle to gain an opportunity to prove yet again that its concentration on service to the bereaved meant that, once a Memoria site was open, the public voted to support it over other crematoria, whether private or municipal. Making money by providing excellent service is not only an honest and decent thing to do but it is sustainable as it is built on rock solid foundations.

This is where we had the opposition by the short and curly ones. We understood about bereavement and funeral directing and they didn't. We made money because we cared about bereavement and funeral directing while they were purely playing for money.

## This Life In Death

The 11th site on our list was Memoria North Oxfordshire. There was a man called David Wilson, who owned a natural burial site some twenty miles away from Memoria South Oxfordshire on the north side of the city, close to Blenheim Palace.

David wanted to gain a consent to build a crematorium in his not yet opened cemetery. He had attempted to achieve this twice and had failed.

I knew that it was my duty to Andrew Sells, the owner of Memoria South Oxfordshire, as we managed the site for him, to either prevent the build or at least win it for Memoria as we would act honourably towards South Oxfordshire in a way that another operator might not.

J believed that, if Mr. Wilson got better advice on making a planning application, he would win. Therefore, it seemed obvious to me to buy the site from the ageing and unwell Mr. Wilson, rather than allowing Westerleigh the opportunity to do the same.

Consequently, with not insignificant help from J and his 'Mohammed Ali' planning team, David won his appeal and planning consent for a crematorium was granted.

David might have been elderly and not in good health, but he still drove a hard bargain and the land cost us £6 million. Therefore, by the time the site was completed in October 2020, it had cost over £10m to develop.

Nevertheless, as the picture in this book shows, it is resplendent, with not only all the usual wonderful Memoria facilities, but also the magnificent 'Churchill Pavilion' where families can hold post service receptions.

Indeed, when by mother passed away in December 2020 and my brother in April 2024, I chose this crematorium to hold both of their 'celebration of life services.'

So, while it had been a delicate and expensive negotiation, it had delivered a 'king of kings' site and had been, nevertheless, a less stressful route to opening than most.

This could not be said of the 12th site. Memoria Doncaster & South Yorkshire threw up a surprisingly complicated planning situation. We had applied in July 2019, but within 3 months, two separate competitor firms submitted rival planning applications.

The first came from Horizon. Their site was located to the southwest of the city. The second from Dignity. Their site was located to the northwest. Our location was to the northeast.

All three applications were set to be determined at the same planning committee with J speaking to promote our scheme over the other two.

Michael had done a very good job in finding a site which was not on green belt land. This gave our site a crucial advantage over the other two and after eighteen months of manoeuvre, deliberation, legal claims and counterclaims, on 21st December 2020, a day after my eldest son, Howard's 47th birthday, the celebrations for which had been tempered by the death of his beloved grandmother earlier in the month, we were granted a consent while the other two were refused.

However, the champagne had to stay on ice until 2021 as Dignity appealed, which we opposed and sent the 'Mohammed Ali' planning team into battle.

J was our star witness and in a three-hour cross-examination at the public inquiry, managed to impress the inspector enough on the key argument of lack of need for the Dignity site, that he refused their appeal, and we had won perhaps the last 'really big' site left to build in the UK.

Indeed, the site was to open on 2nd May 2023 and became an immediate success – as I always knew that a marriage of 'real need' with 'Memoria service' would be.

In 2024, it will undertake some 1,300 cremations with hardly any support from our own funeral division. Success like this doesn't just happen. It comes about because of the care and attention that goes into the building of a site, the maintenance of a site and, above all, the training of the staff that operate that site.

It is their selection and training to the aspirations of our 'Mission Statement' that makes all the difference. And that is why I have dedicated Volume II to the Memoria staff – because without them we would never have believed that we could succeed or indeed would have succeeded.

However, without the exploits of the 'Mohammed Ali' planning team and their tenacious leader J, the 'Mighty Midget Memoria' would never have had the opportunity to put these plans into action throughout the UK.

And so, to the last planning consent in this chapter. Number 13 was Memoria Faversham & Mid-Kent. For once, from a planning perspective the site Michael had selected was straightforward and we had submitted an application in May 2020.

As usual, there was an extensive amount of communication with the planning officer. However, we managed to win all the key arguments, and the application was consented in May 2021. Too good to be true? Yes, of course!

Once again, our old nemesis Westerleigh appeared from nowhere to follow us into the area and were promoting a new scheme. This despite having promised not to if we gave them some cremations from our CWS contract, now that the covid-19 epidemic was upon us and the death rate was soaring. Richard Evans had fallen from grace and had been replaced by one Neil McCausland, who apparently wanted to re-build bridges of goodwill with Memoria as a result. We had taken him, rather foolishly, at his word.

The Westerleigh scheme was only a ridiculously close eight miles away, and if granted would cut two key areas, Canterbury and Herne Bay off from us.

Despite, the lack of need, their scheme also received a consent in July 2021. Our site opened first and, largely thanks to the additional cremations our funeral division could deliver has remained profitable.

'My word is my bond' was something my father taught me. He kept to it through the good and the bad times during his life as witnessed in Volume I of this saga. It became my mark too, as a result of his teaching. I might drive a hard bargain. However, I never go back on my word.

In the last fifty years I have sadly seen an ever-decreasing attitude towards good ethical behaviour in the funeral industry.

Some of this has been caused by a 33% increase in the number of funeral directors, most of whom had no funeral tradition, in the UK since the millennium. They became funeral directors because the profit per funeral had been boosted so much by the Dignity price inflation that two or three funerals a month were enough to survive on.

However, this was then followed by the CMA investigation into the price of funerals, and the rise of direct cremation. Both factors caused funeral price deflation.

Nevertheless, some of it has had nothing to do with the 'little man', but the big operators, who have been controlled since before the millennium by men, who have no natural funeral culture, and few business ethics compared to the small traditional funeral director. I will return to this point when dealing with the changing face of funerals in the final chapter.

# This Life In Death

Chapter X

The Really, Really, Big Deal

2020 – 2021

During the 'Wonder of it all baby' years, life within the Hodgson Clan had remained unusually and very happily stable, perhaps, because I had quite enough to do in the running and building of Memoria and so had little time to consider pleasures of the flesh and therefore there was little to no disruption apart from an occasional one-night stand with any woman that I came into contact with at an estate agent or bank and that got sometimes suspected or discovered by 'Sherlock' Christine.

She had remained a saint to live with me. Some people have a drink addiction; with some it is cocaine; but with me it was sex that I ran to for distraction, reassurance or just comfort.

Indeed, it always had been from the age of seven and my desperate need to run away from who I perceived myself to be and the need to crawl back into any possible womb – even if for only a few moments and only once.

The outer me has a tough exterior; wants to be perceived as fair, strong and a good example of a decent father and boss.

However, this protective suit of armour has never allowed anyone, not even my wholly and utterly adored children, to see any sign of weakness, despair or mental frailty.

So, the truth is that when they say, whoever they are, 'No man is an island', they forgot about me. I have always been an 'island' and have remained one since punching the boy Lister on the nose at West House School in 1958.

Was this a demonstration of exceptional strength? No this was caused by an exceptional lack of self-esteem and a fear of showing any weakness in case I drifted back into being or perceived as being that 'Milky Bar Kid' weakling that my parents had been so despairing of in the 1950s.

Meanwhile, Christine's career continued to flourish exceptionally and deservedly well, while George and Horatio had turned all too quickly into teenagers, via magical years where I had treasured seeing them growing up and watching them discover each other and life and their rite of passage to have pet dogs.

These were domestically wonderful years. Perhaps my calmest and favourite. I had 5 living children of various ages, and I adored them all.

Horatio had a Portuguese water dog when he was only 9 years of age. He called him Otto. He was, and still is, adorable. This was followed by George getting a cockapoo which he named Oscar. These two chaps, along with Ossie, who was also a cockapoo and arrived from Swansea in the covid lock down of 2020, became adored by the whole family, along with Howie's three dogs – which meant that we now had a-six-dog-family, and we were all the better for having them. We all loved them, and they all loved us back.

As for me, I truly loved all of them so much, but Oscar, was to become my life-long and important friend, in the way that Scamp and Syd had done when I was first a lonely and useless boy, and then again, as a middle-aged man in his crisis years of going nowhere.

Howard, my eldest son had developed, along with his angel wife Lorraine, a wonderful family and a very successful recruitment business for chefs, assistant-chefs, waiters and carers, where applicable in care-homes, hotels, pubs and restaurants; as well as a corporate entertainment arm, which supplied huge numbers to Ascot, as well as other national sporting events – including the hospitality suites at my beloved Aston Villa.

Naturally, I would go there, whenever in England and take my sons, and on occasion, even my aged mother, where we would have lunch and reminisce with 'Deadly Doug' in 'Directors' before the match. Doug and I had by now forgiven each other for our actions against each other concerning the future of Aston Villa.

I had forgiven him because I had realised that we had gone out of the frying pan and into the fire with his sale to the American Randy Lerner, who was a poor owner compared to Doug.

He had forgiven me because I was his adopted son, and for no other good reason. Bless him.

In the years following the Millennium, Davinia had grown up to become a very good looking, attractive and intelligent young woman. Nevertheless, she had to survive some quite appalling relationships on her right of passage to womanhood.

The first was with an imbecilic bon viveur, the sort of 'Hooray Henry' that gives public schools a bad name. The second was a cold-hearted selfish snob, who gives them an even worse name. The third a cocaine addict who liked to beat up women when he was as high as a kite. He gave humanity a bad name.

I had little to do with the first two. However, I did have something to do with the third. When I found out, from J, that this guy was encouraging Dink to snort cocaine, I went round to their apartment in Chelsea and told her to pack her clothes as she was coming with me.

He asked to explain. I replied that I wanted no explanation – but told him instead to keep away from Davinia in future or I would put him in hospital.

I had no idea that he had already put my daughter in hospital himself. The Hodgson family had conspired to ensure I was not told of this in case I killed him.

She came home with me and became my PA. She wasn't the most brilliant I have had, but she was the best looking – as the photographs in Volume II prove. Indeed, as we already know, her easy charm and good looks had drawn favourable comments from many including Terry Venables and Eric Clapton.

Eventually, she met a very decent man, called Richard and he and Davinia fell in love. He was older than her and had been a boyfriend of Roger Moore's stepdaughter previously.

Richard and Davinia got married in 2019 and then in were blessed with a daughter in 2021. She was christened 'Alexandra' but nicknamed 'Lady Mary' by me as she reminded me of the 'determined madam' of the same name in the very successful BBC series 'Downton Abbey.'

As this little baby grew into a beautiful little girl, she became more and more fascinating to me. Her looks, her character and her fearless attitude to everything and everyone, reminded me of someone I had loved so very much forty years previously.

I do not believe in reincarnation. But this wonderful child's similarity to Charles Alexandre Howard Hodgson was spellbinding to both Marianne and me.

XXXXXXX

Memoria had by now had become the third largest cremation provider in the UK; the most successful and innovative; with the best trained staff and was producing extremely high levels of client satisfaction and gratitude.

It boasted 12 crematoria, and a 13th where the very successful J planning team seemed likely to win a consent.

In addition, I had developed, with the assistance of Paul Reed, a new, innovative and very successful online funeral division, which was by now well supported by two funeral hubs – one in Nottinghamshire, close to our Barnby Moor crematorium and the other in Oxfordshire, on site at Memoria North Oxfordshire.

Now we were suddenly faced with a new challenge. The appalling Covid-19 pandemic, which caused a national lockdown, and among many strict restrictions, came a limitation on the number of people who could attend funeral services.

This had been set by the government nationally, after consultation primarily with me, at a maximum of 30, and meant that bereaved families were set some heart-rending decisions about who could and couldn't attend their family funeral service.

Worse, many unionised municipal crematoria set lower numbers and, in some cases, dictated no attendance was allowable at all, in what they claimed was a defence of their members' lives.

This was inhumane exploitation of the bereaved by lazy and undedicated staff in my opinion. This was not the attitude of Britain's fighting spirit as so wonderfully portrayed in the London Blitz, but more man's inhumanity to man, with an 'I'm alright Jack' attitude to the crisis.

When I had set the number at thirty, I had devised a detailed plan of cleaning the chapel, foyer, toilets and other areas in between services. This wasn't a monumental task for our wonderful staff because they had always cleaned this way before the pandemic. To them I had only added disinfectant to the procedure.

## This Life In Death

Our plan worked perfectly. Indeed, during the first lockdown, not a single member of our staff contracted covid and only two did ever – until the first injections were issued and when we ensured all our staff were immediately vaccinated as priority health workers.

We had suffered no fatalities and yet we had done a magnificent job allowing bereaved families the chance to say goodbye to their loved ones despite very real health dangers of the pandemic.

Our staff were a credit to Memoria, our 'Mission Statement' and themselves. I was extremely proud of each one of them.

Naturally, the pandemic saw a natural rise in non-attended direct cremation due to the restrictions, some people's fear of attending a service and the fact it was cheaper than an attended service.

This had meant that the CWS direct cremation contract exploded into very significant numbers as did those being booked online with our own funeral division. Both dramatic increases meant that the Memoria Funeral Division was now flushed with cash to use on advertising and Trustpilot testimonies to tell the world how good we were.

Moreover, the pandemic made the UK public, especially those over 65, completely aware of their own mortality. As a result, our pre-arranged funeral plan sales shot up too, under the management of Paul Reed and assisted by the very capable, if somewhat hard to work with, Sally Howarth.

To cope with the expansion in the funeral division, we hired a very capable girl from the CWS, where her talents had been largely ignored while being recognised by me. Her name was (and still is) Kirsty Lowther. She was to prove to be a very good signing.

Moreover, as we also needed to deal with a landslide of increased business in the financial services division as funeral plan sales rocketed, I took on a guy called Ronnie Waite, who had recently been let go by the Glasgow funeral company Fosters, who were owned by a London-based private equity firm.

Ronnie had made his name in the funeral plan business at Golden Charter, before falling out with their funeral directing owners and moving on to Fosters, where his blazing trail there initially delighted their owners before his quick-fire plans brought in more cost than revenue. Therefore, he was once more released.

Of course, his hundred-mile-an-hour attitude was there for all to see, and I was not blind. However, I believed that he was like dynamite – if used carefully, he could blow up the competition. If left out in the sun he could blow us up instead.

Nevertheless, I thought that he was worth the gamble. Memoria had worked as Foster's English funeral director to conduct redeemed funeral plan funerals for the last two years, and I believed that I could see his strengths and weaknesses.

I invited him to come to dinner in London and discuss what he could bring to Memoria with Michael and Jamieson. He came, they listened to him and were duly impressed. So, he was added to the team and initially, and under strict supervision from me, things got off to a dazzling start.

Then out of the blue Michael, now aged 68, announced that he wanted to retire. J and I were taken aback. Things were going so well. The three of us had created a huge success and J and I were really surprised.

Worse, Michael did not just want to retire but he wanted to sell his stake in Memoria. J and I knew that it would harm the profitability of the company by having to service the debt created, even if we could raise the cash for Memoria to purchase his 39% stake.

Moreover, it would have been impossible for us to do so personally without securing such loans with every asset we possessed and that included our Memoria shares.

J and I were understandably annoyed and thought Michael was being selfish. Of course, he could retire, was J's point, but to cause he and I to have to sell was unfair and not in the spirit of the three musketeers especially as it had been J's consents and my building of the group which had created and underwritten his share value.

Ultimately, Michael had a right to sell if he wanted. Then I explained that as J and I owned 64.5% between us, we could veto any sale unless the price was right.

"Let's take a leaf out of Villa's book regarding Jack Grealish. Jack can be released from his contract and go if the price paid for him is £100 million. And who is going to pay that?

"Let's set the price at 20 x EBITDA and sell if we get offered that. If we do, then we should sell. It would be crazy not to and we will all be extremely wealthy. If we don't then we shouldn't and you and I will be happy and Michael can't complain," was my instant plan to deal with this latest crisis.

After a short conference call with Michael, all three of us agreed to go along with this plan and were happy. Moreover, I was very relaxed as I knew that I controlled the destiny of my baby as I held 51% of the voting shares.

A price to the closest million was worked out at 19.66 x EBITDA based on the expected earnings for 2020.

The buyer would also have to take on the NatWest bank debt and possibly buy out all the Rockpool investors B shares in all crematoria except Memoria Kirkleatham, where Memoria already owned them, and Memoria Cardiff & Glamorgan, where there weren't any.

It should also not be forgotten that what was on offer did not include the A shares for Memoria Kirkleatham, which was owned by Hodgson, Hackney and Sells privately and was not part of Memoria, or Memoria South Oxfordshire, which was owned by Sells alone. Both sites were branded and operated by Memoria but not owned by it.

Only 4 big hitters and investment houses were contacted, and appointments made for us to present the Memoria story.

Initial front-runners appeared to be Montagu, who owned a funeral conglomerate called Funeral Partners and Westerleigh, our long-term rival.

Both were fans of Memoria and appeared keen to buy us. We had already been courted by both. In particular, the new Westerleigh Chairman, Neil McCausland, had been trying to persuade me to sell to them for the last year, as I had developed things that they didn't have and wanted – namely a funeral division, a contract fulfilment division and a financial services division.

These new marginal cost businesses had both seriously increased our cremation numbers but also moved us up the 'food chain' and thus closer to dealing directly with bereaved families, who could thus choose what they wanted rather than what a funeral director told them they needed – which wasn't always the same thing.

Dignity had by now got themselves into such a financial mess that they were not serious contenders. The CWS, who had engaged a charming but ineffective lady funeral CEO, were also in no position to act as they were, as usual, busy trying to fix their own financial disasters by yet another murderous cull in their usual annual 'palace revolution.'

We held meetings with the two front-runners, separately, in a private dining room on the top floor of a Chelsea pub.

Both presentations went well, and I really enjoyed the one with Westerleigh as I got to meet their CEO, Roger McLaughlan at last.

We had become firm friends during the covid pandemic, when I had enlisted Westerleigh's help to deal with the huge upsurge in CWS direct cremations. We shared common interests in cricket, football and wine. However, lock-down had meant that we had never met. But when we now did, I was not disappointed by this wonderfully joyful and giving man. Perhaps, the first decent thing I had to show from any association with Westerleigh.

Unfortunately, not long after this Rog was to retire due to illness, but our friendship was to blossom from this first meeting, and he remains a very special and close friend today. Our livers take a beating when we meet in an explosion of appreciation for each other's pure zest for life.

Both front-runners were keen acquirors but neither seemed willing to make the first offer as they thought the asking price was too high, that we wouldn't get it in any event and so wanted to see what the other was going to bid first.

Then J suggested that we should talk to Darwin Bereavement Fund. They were a unit trust fund that had been set up to invest in bereavement related companies and had already made acquisitions in this sector. I agreed.

They visited our brand-new flagship crematorium, Memoria North Oxfordshire, where the three of us showed them around before going on to have lunch at Stratton Audley Hall.

Darwin was represented by two men called James Penney, their CEO, and James Welsh, their senior finance officer. I liked both but immediately identified with James Penney as a CEO to a CEO.

After lunch they left and Michael, J and I agreed that they would be better custodians of the Memoria brand than anyone else we had presented to. Therefore, the name, our wonderful staff that had made that name and the bereaved clientele who had bought into that name would be better off with them.

However, we all doubted very much they would come up with the best offer sadly.

xxxxxxx

While all of this was going on, my mother, who was now ninety-four was diagnosed with breast cancer. She refused to have an operation understandably at her age.

It seemed that her life would now be limited to months rather than years. I don't think that I really accepted this at the time. After all, my mother was indestructible and made Margaret Hilda Thatcher look like gay liberation rights for lesbians in the socialist republic of Lambeth, London.

I had spent most weekends since I was thirty, when I was in England, with her. Moreover, she had come several times a year to visit me in Malta.

Even though we could, as very strong opinionated and wilful personalities, fight like cat and dog, especially as she believed everything printed in the Daily Mail and, in particular, if it was about the late Diana, Princess of Wales. Nevertheless, I really enjoyed her company.

In addition, I secretly harboured a serious guilt in my heart that I had loved my father much more than her when I was a child and her favourite child at that. This guilt drove me in adulthood, especially as she got older, to make this up to her in every which way I could.

## This Life In Death

But now we were coming to the end of the line, and I was devastated, but knew that, as usual, I must be strong and set an example to the family.

The end came very quickly. She held the last of her famous cocktail parties in mid-November 2020, took to her bed two weeks later and died within a week.

My sister and I had fallen out over the Natalie affair years earlier but were now happily reunited at our mother's bedside.

On that last day, a Sunday, my mother clung onto life with the tenacity that she had lived it, she finally allowed that death rattle to echo up her throat with Horatio and I holding her hands, Christine, whom she loved as a daughter, stroking her forehead and George massaging her feet.

I jumped up when I knew she had gone and walked out on to her balcony overlooking Poole Harbour, Brownsea Island and the Purbeck Hills in the December twilight.

There I stood alone and wept. I let the tears flow silently, for fear of anyone hearing me, but with very much heartache for the loss of a mother however old she was.

I dried my eyes and called Kirsty Lowther. Within thirty minutes my mother had left her home for the last time.

This was something that I had organised tens of thousands of times before but now it was a very personal occasion because it was my one and only mother. A woman who had adored me but had never quite been able to show me that in those early 1950s days.

A mother, whom I had never quite been able to show her how much I loved her through my rampaging days of the 1960s and then my love for Marianne's parents in the 1970s.

However, if she and I had often messed up how we should show each other affection in a very British Empire way, this was not true of my mother with my younger brother.

She had loved him and, along with me, financially supported him, all his life.

Russell, my brother, as you will recall from Volume I, was academically gifted but lazy, mentally very fragile and extremely selfish.

He blamed all these failings on his mother's departure to South Africa when he was fourteen. Indeed, this experience and that of being left in the care of a lazy, drunken and wicked stepmother must have been dreadful.

However, many folks have had to put up with far worse and not failed at everything attempted for the rest of their lives as a result.

He would be pleasant to his mother when he needed money; once it was in his account, he would ignore her until he needed more.

She would respond by waiting in her car, even in her nineties and in the winter, outside the apartment I had lent him, in the hope of seeing him.

However, he would drive past her, ignoring her very presence until he needed more money, and then would turn up, like a bad penny, smiling and being concerned about her well-being.

On one such occasion, when the prodigal son had returned and I had elected to have dinner with mother and him rather than go to my eldest son Howard's house to watch Villa play West Brom on TV with George and Horatio, Russell criticised my two youngest sons' absence from the dinner with their grandmother.

Given Russell's heartless treatment of the very same woman, over several years, I could not believe my ears. I exploded. An argument ensued and to my eternal shame a left hook from me floored Russell.

My mother, God bless her, jumped up and bashed me on the back of my head, in defence of her lame duckling. Moreover, when the red mist lifted, I also apologised to him, because I had behaved no better than he.

All my life I had looked after him. I had kept my promise to my father to protect him and even now my love for him and the promise I had made to my father, meant that I would always forgive him.

Then came the week of her death. He lived less than half-a-mile away from her. He arrived on the Tuesday in a drunken state and was very aggressive with our sister, Denny. He hardly spoke to my mother and clearly had caused her distress by his actions. Then he was gone.

Christine, Judy, who was Russell's loyal and long-suffering girlfriend, whom he had added to the 'support me financially' list of donors, George, Horatio and I took it in turns to sit with and chat to her.

My eldest son, Howard sent a carer from his agency. The guy was black and was brilliant at his job. Nevertheless, I was worried knowing my mother's 1920s racist attitudes. I need not have worried. She adored him and even let him take her to the toilet.

We come to the Friday evening, and I'm holding her hand and chatting to her.

"You do know I haven't got long," she said calmly.

I nod with as much of a reassuring smile that I could manage.

"Where is Russ?"

"Oh, he's coming. He's been busy doing a boat deal." I smiled as I stroked her hand.

He didn't come. Nor did he the next day when she asked again.

He hadn't answered his phone to me all week after his argument with our sister Denny. I called Judy and asked her to tell him that his mother was dying and asking for him.

She called me back with the words, "He told me to tell you that he said his goodbyes on Tuesday."

I was furious but Christine said that I would forgive him. I didn't. We never spoke again after her funeral until days before his own death.

I did love my brother and had shown him how much all his life, but I could never forgive his selfish cowardice in not being brave enough to sit with his mother who had done so much for him and demanded nothing of him in return but had just wanted to see him one more time.

My mother died on Sunday 13th December 2020. She was 94-years-of-age. Michael told me he had never known anyone still to have a mother at seventy years of age like me. Of course, he was right, and I had been very lucky, and I knew it.

However, all bereavements of loved ones provoke a very difficult time, and no two deaths evoke the same emotions in us.

xxxxxxx

In the middle of this usually explosive Hodgson domestic drama, the sort I had been trying to erase from our family since even before my parents had split up in 1970, but seemingly, in hindsight, I had caused more of than anyone else since, Sonia, George's nanny, placed a letter on my desk. It was from Darwin.

I read it. Surely this couldn't be right. I read it again very calmly, very carefully and very slowly. I had read it correctly the first time. Darwin Bereavement Fund were offering us the asking price for the Memoria Group.

This meant that they would have to invest close to £200 million to buy all Memoria A and B shares and to cover the NatWest overdraft, and I personally would get to add over £61million to my personal and not inconsiderable wealth.

I was stunned. But I was not happy. I had not wanted to sell. My 'Grealish' stunt had not worked. However, I had given my word, and the price demanded had been met by James Penney in this letter.

Michael was naturally delighted. J was more reticent. Like me he had not wanted to sell. However, when we talked, we both agreed that our word was our bond and therefore, the sale must proceed. Moreover, we both understood that the price was very full and made all three of us very financially secure for the rest of our lives.

However, as is often the case when money is involved, the three of us were not to agree about how the cake would be sliced. Why?

The offer was for the Memoria Group and did not differentiate between Memoria Ltd, the crematorium division or Low-Cost-Funeral Ltd, the funeral and financial services divisions.

This was a problem and a problem of our own making. The three of us would need to face it together and agree a united approach.

Jamieson, surprisingly and perhaps not so surprisingly, was keen to advance the value of Low-Cost-Funeral Ltd.

Surprisingly, because he had never thought it would become that successful and other than sit on the board and run its HR function had had little to do with its success for the five or so years it had been invented by me.

Not so surprisingly, because I had gifted both him and Michael 33% each in the company when I had first conceived the idea and set the company up in 2016.

On the other hand, Michael and I argued that Low-Cost-Funeral, while being a very valuable marginal cost business, had considerations that could not be ignored.

For example, the online funeral and financial service divisions depended on getting leads from expensive TV advertising; the margin on the first was low and lapses could seriously dent the profits on the second; the cremation division was charging artificially low prices for cremations to these in-house divisions; and the highly profitable CWS fulfilment contract only had around two years to run – and we could lose it or be forced to reduce prices seriously, if we wished to keep it.

Whereas Memoria's cremation division was cash and asset rich, served a largely captive audience which was larger than might be expected due to the extremely high standards of service and facility we provided to the bereaved.

Indeed, it was because of J's 'Mohammed Ali' planning team and my ability to develop and operate these sites, the jewel in the Memoria crown was the cremation division and its value was solid and very significant and to promote the other divisions at its expense made no sense on many levels.

However, it was also not lost on either Michael nor I that he owned 37% of the cremation company, I, 48% and J only 15%. Therefore, J, by promoting the value of LCF, was seeking to elevate his share of the spoils.

## This Life In Death

The fact that J had been gifted his shares in both companies and had always been paid albeit a small retainer while Michael and I had put up a lot of risk capital and hadn't been paid at all in the first 14 years, was also not lost on either of us.

Potentially, this could have led to a 'Beatles type' bust up. It did lead to some harsh words but nothing too serious and we managed to resolve the situation – agreeing a final split of HH 44.5%, MH 35.5% and JH 20%. So we all remained friends, happy family members and kept up a united front.

Nevertheless, it still makes me smile four years on, that J received very nearly as much for shares in a company that he had 'poo-pooed' and had done comparatively little for as he did for one that he had done so much to make it the huge success it had become.

The understandably extensive due diligence then proceeded and was a lengthy affair. From our side this was handled by Michael, J and our chief lawyer Justin Mason, whereas I continued to run all operations while this painful administration progressed.

I had also decided that if matters were going to be expedited efficiently and without rancour that we needed to create a 'higher authority' to which disputed matters arising from the due diligence, warranties and indemnities or draft contracts, needed to be referred.

I suggested that this 'higher authority' should be James Penney for Darwin and me for Memoria. This was accepted by both teams and led to James and I having weekly calls to iron out any problems. This was a good idea as it prevented either sets of advisers from 'show boating' or creating expensive time-wasting stand-offs.

I had got caught in the covid lockdown in the UK and now that that was over, decided that I could not face returning to Malta.

The 'Castle' had been sold a year or so earlier and I had replaced it with a pleasant apartment in Portamaso, St Julian's, overlooking the marina where I berthed my sailing boat, Kendrick Baker. I rented the apartment out and decided to move to Monaco instead, as did Michael and J, although the latter decided to return to the UK in the end.

His departure was sad and made all the more so as his beautiful partner of several years, Emma, whom I had enjoyed having lunch with every day, left with him.

So, on the 22nd of March 2021, I boarded a private jet which was bound for Monaco.

Indeed, despite the usual last-minute dramas, the contracts were all signed in early May 2021 and the 'really big deal' was completed.

This meant that Michael retired while J and I stayed on as Group Deputy CEO and Group CEO respectively.

Memoria MK II was a remarkable success both pastorally and financially. I had fought back from the trials and tribulations of the previous two decades to become its father, figurehead, architect and creator.

However, I must also point out that without the devotion of Michael to arrange finance and run the administration – as well as finding some excellent sites, it would have been a lot more difficult.

Moreover, without J's amazing performance in building and then managing the 'Mohammed Ali' planning team, the outcome would have been wholly different. For without those consents, won against all odds, I would have had nothing to build and then operate.

When we set out in 2009, we hoped to get to build five crematoria. At the time of writing, Memoria operates fourteen.

The actual sale of the Memoria Group was not dramatic, except for the price received. It was not accompanied by a media frenzy in the way that the Ingalls deal had been in 1987, the Kenyon deal in 1988, or even my departure from PHKI in 1991. It had not even attracted the media coverage of most Ronson acquisitions in the 1990s.

We had not wanted it to. I had always wanted Memoria to be about what the company did and how well it did it rather than a media obsession with the trail blazing 'Mr Death.'

However, make no mistake, Memoria was not only my best creation, but it was also my most profitable and it increased my wealth by nearly ten-fold in a decade.

So, its sale really was 'the really, really big deal.'

# This Life In Death

## Chapter XI

'And In The End, The Love You Take Is Equal To The Love You Make.'

2021 – 2024

These were the last words written for the Beatles by James Paul McCartney, the 20th century Mozart, that I have been quoting throughout both volumes of 'This Life in Death.'

They strike me as a fitting description of what this last chapter sets out to do when summarising my life, my view of death during my life, and how either might influence your life – because I have sought to share my experience of life and death in these two volumes to demonstrate that if someone with my history can end up achieving what I have professionally, financially, and to make the glue that binds my family together domestically, then so can you.

My view of death must be two-fold – professionally and personally. Let's deal with these separately.

Firstly, professionally. When I was that inoffensive little 'Milky Bar Kid' of the 1950s the machinations of the funeral industry were very different to how they are some seventy years later.

Perhaps, no one has done more to change an industry, that had changed little since Queen Victoria was on the throne, than me spreading my gospel of change.

However, I only spread the gospel by acquisition. I hadn't designed that change. It had been written for me by my father.

Naturally, I wanted all the changes that I was making to every firm I acquired to be for the better and in the main they have been, because the changes I made were copied by local competitors and this helped raise standards as Hodgson & Sons Ltd became Hodgson Holdings plc and then PHKI plc and grew from one funeral home to 569 over a fifteen year period.

So, standards of service and facility received by the public today are undoubtedly higher than they were seventy years ago and Hodgson in its various forms did a lot to change funeral directing for the better by raising standards wherever it acquired.

However, the truth is that some spin-offs resulting from the building of the Hodgson empire brought in new and less welcome results too.

In the 1950s funeral culture and funeral service provision were very different to today. There were only two forces in funeral directing or undertaking as it was then commonly known. These were the various co-operatives throughout Britain and the local family funeral director.

The co-ops were really the only large businesses, and they weren't very good at providing compassionate service. They mainly offered impersonal production line funerals, which meant a cheaper alternative was available to the working classes.

These folk then were certainly poorer, had less disposable income and did not have the middle-class aspiration that Margaret Thatcher delivered to them thirty years later.

However, the co-ops were nothing like as bad as the local family funeral director would have had you believe.

The family funeral director had started to feed nasty rumours into their local communities about the co-ops from the 1920s onwards when the latter's success started to erode the former's market share.

In those days people mainly died at home and remained there. The coffin was made by the funeral director and brought to their home. Hence the caricature of an 'undertaker' with a tape measure round his neck.

The deceased was made presentable by the local 'laying out' lady and remained upstairs. Within 24 to 48 hours, the specially made coffin would arrive and the deceased would be brought downstairs and placed in it in the 'front room'.

Family and friends would arrive to pay their last respects, and the 'wake' often took place, or at least started, before the funeral.

## This Life In Death

The funeral service happened within three to five days of death and often sooner – especially in the warmer temperatures of the summer.

Funeral directors needed to own, or hire from 'carriage masters', a good number of limousines as few families had their own cars to follow the funeral cortege.

Around 50% of funerals had a church service, while the other half took place at the cemetery or crematorium. 90% of funerals were burials in the early 1930s and were still about 65% in the 1950s.

The poor were buried collectively in public graves, several at a time and down deep holes that might hold ten unrelated people.

All funerals were religious, most Church of England, and there was no celebration of an individual's life. Eulogies were reserved for the famous and noteworthy. There were virtually no immigrant funerals until the 1960s.

If the family elected to go straight to the cemetery or crematorium, the service would be taken by a 'rota' minister, who rarely mentioned the deceased's name and often got their sex wrong if the departed was a woman.

Service times at busier crematoria were 10 minutes and the chances of not seeing another funeral were virtually nil. Indeed, one might see several at a few of London's busiest crematoria and over a dozen if you were poor and could only afford a 'public reading time' burial – as several coffins were lowered into a mass grave one after the other without much care or concern by hardened and poorly paid municipal workers, who had little respect for the bereaved and even less if they happened to be immigrants.

So, there was a lot wrong with British funeral directing when I was a lad. However, the task of changing this industry from the state I describe here was started by my father, and men of a similar mind set like Morlais Summers, fifteen years or so before I took the helm at Hodgson & Sons Ltd.

These men went to the US and brought back the American way of death to Britain.

They imported coffin selection rooms, service chapels, private viewing chapels, multiple arrangement rooms, family lounges, and general mourners' lounges, all housed in what were to be termed 'funeral homes.'

They offered choice from a displayed price list. Those who wanted to spend more could, and those who didn't or couldn't afford to, needn't. But everyone benefitted from 5-star standards of service – even at a 1-star price.

They confirmed all arrangements in writing including the cost of their charges and the disbursements before the funeral and followed this with a detailed itemised account after it.

Moreover, they invested heavily in behind-the-scenes facilities such as mortuaries, embalming theatres, and refrigeration units.

We take all these things for granted now but they were revolutionary in 1960. Moreover, it took over twenty years for these practices and facilities to become commonplace by reluctant funeral directors because they required investment in their business rather than buying an apartment in Tenerife.

Hodgson Holdings by its devotion to this 'good practice' spread the gospel by its successful expansion all over England and so played a major part in this transformation.

This was because I was first and foremost a funeral director, and, thanks to my father, a very good one.

However, this got lost in all the media's obsession with my looks and 'enfant terrible' image and I did little to correct this as it was the closest I was ever going to get to being a Beatle and I liked the idea of that. Vanity and stupidity on my behalf.

Moreover, the journey that I led Hodgson & Sons Ltd on created PHKI and my resignation from there meant that my mission to look after the bereaved with kindness, respect and efficiency largely left the building with me.

As a result, I had created a vehicle that was to be run by men, who had no funeral culture, but had a great concern for financial results and little for the genuine care of the bereaved. This new monster increased prices year-on-year to restore lost revenue, caused by percentage market share falls, at a rate way above inflation.

This was because they needed to create a 'war chest' to buy back that lost market share, which would only be lost again, because they couldn't or wouldn't address the real issues within their business.

As they pushed prices up, these increases were mirrored by the various co-ops and the privately owned funeral firms in their wake.

This caused rampant funeral inflation and looked like a recipe for financial disaster as someone would surely introduce cheaper alternative services. I said so at the time from the 'sidelines.' I was wrong.

It wasn't until the advent of direct cremation and a CMA investigation into the cost of funerals some twenty-five years later that this nasty little merry-go-round was stopped.

However, by that time the free market had failed millions of bereaved families. Worse, as the profitability of a funeral had risen it had meant that a funeral director could survive on circa thirty-five funerals a year – rather than the two hundred plus when I was a lad. This had the effect of sucking hundreds of new entrants into the market.

Indeed, the number of funeral directors in England and Wales was to rise by around 33% in the first two decades after the millennium.

While most of these were decent men or women who had worked in the industry, some had not, were motivated by money, and did not possess the dedication of those generational family funeral directing business which had served their local communities well over tens or even hundreds of years.

So, in conclusion, Hodgson Holdings plc did change funeral directing for the better, but it also created a monster that had serious failings once it was run by money men with no other mission than profit.

Moreover, as it was grown by acquisition it meant that the bigger it got the higher the percentage of employees who lacked that initial Hodgson training and thus dedication to the bereaved. Therefore, the harder it became to maintain the staff standards achieved by Hodgson & Sons Ltd.

By comparison, Memoria is a perfect example of organic growth, which allowed time to hand pick and intensively train staff to operate to the clear aims of a mission statement, which I had written at its outset, but are enacted 100% perfectly every single day by the most dedicated and professionally capable staff ever created in any industry let alone the funeral industry and it is that consistent excellence that makes every bereaved family's horrid journey that little bit easier.

Therefore, this is the legacy that I am most proud of and wish to be remembered for rather than the media attention of the 'enfant terrible' years.

However, from 2017 onwards, the advent of direct cremation, linked to pre-paid funeral plans, which had never been regulated by the FCA, caused a further 'gold-rush' of new entrants into the 'death' market – and again, while some providers were very honourable people, some weren't and soon the FCA was following in the steps of the CMA down a road towards regulation.

However, while the CMA stopped short of a serious regulation of funeral directing, the FCA quickly (and correctly) decided that it had no option but to completely regulate pre-paid funeral plans.

The firms, which were eventually licenced by the FCA, such as Westerleigh, Memoria, Golden Leaves, Golden Charter, the CWS and others, soon saw that they had no option but to advertise heavily to protect their own future in the 'time of need' market share against the TV commercial onslaught on the 'oldies channels' ITV 3 and ITV 4 by Pure Cremation.

Additionally, while all of this was evolving Covid-19 struck and this limited attendance levels at most crematoria to 30 or even nil at certain municipal crematoria.

The combination of this with the sudden onslaught of incessant TV advertising of pre-paid funeral plans, which were being mainly bought by the person whose funeral was being bought and who did so with the attitude of 'you can put me in the wheely bin for all I care', saw the growth of direction cremation rocket towards 25% of all funerals by 2024 and this will be higher when living plan holders eventually die.

So, the combination of a serious increase in direction cremation and the CMA's warnings to the profession have caused funeral price deflation.

Is this good for the general public? Well in a price sense yes, but in a service sense and what is good for a bereaved family, no.

This is because they have been left with either a big bill for access to an attended service or a much smaller bill for a direct cremation with no service.

To not have a proper funeral service, be it a religious service, a non-religious celebration of life service, or a combination of the two, is inviting problems when coming to terms with bereavement.

It is essential to say goodbye properly and face up to what has happened. It is what has happened since mankind started to become civilised. Can you imagine the Queen, Winston Churchill or Princess Diana having just a memorial service?

Should we acknowledge our loved ones' deaths by going down the pub and having a few beers and some 'lovely sausage rolls'?

Of course not!

However, TV commercials try to tell the nation otherwise and that a memorial service will suffice.

Therefore, it must be cautioned that they are doing so because national direct cremation operators cannot provide families with local attended funeral services. Hence, they need to convince the nation that such services are not needed or even a good idea.

## This Life In Death

So, the public is currently left with the choice of either an expensive traditional funeral where they sit in one big black car and follow another big black car to the crematorium or have an unattended direct cremation instead.

Funeral directors have steadfastly failed to offer them anything else. Why? Because funeral directors are geared up to the traditional funeral and want to sell one first and foremost or will let folk reluctantly have a direct cremation if they insist on having one.

This is not only very bad news for the bereaved family. It is also disastrous news for the funeral director in the long term.

In years gone by, a bereaved family needed transport, and it could only express its love and respect by the type of coffin selected, the number of limousines hired, or the size of floral tributes bought.

Celebrating a loved one's life in a funeral service just did not happen.

Today, religious control of funeral services has all but disappeared and civil celebrants have largely replaced priests and vicars in the main Christian religious sects when it comes to officiating at a funeral service.

Families really do want to have local attended funeral services, but not all see the need to, or can afford to, pay for a traditional funeral with a lot of Victorian trappings which they see as wholly unnecessary in today's world.

I believe that the funeral market is failing much of the public currently in this regard.

I believe that every family in the land should have a choice of four types of attended funeral service: a traditional Victorian funeral service; a prime time attended service, where everyone collects at the crematorium; a selected time smaller attended committal service only or a direct cremation.

All should be offered by local funeral directors to their client to ensure that bereaved families have these choices and have them locally.

## This Life In Death

xxxxxxx

Secondly, my own personal experience of death has been well documented in these two volumes. I'm no stranger to this experience as you know, having lost a son of 3 years of age, a nephew when he was but 19, my father when he was only 58 and lastly my mother when she was 94.

These deaths were very different and not comparable, but all filled me with a huge sense of loss.

Charles's death was so devastating, it was far too tragic and serious to cry. I became a zombie on automatic pilot. I might never have returned to being vaguely normal, without the help of Michael Sullivan, who allowed me the chance to express my grief in the lyrics of songs we co-wrote.

My nephew Alex's death was a devastating tragedy made all the worse as he demonstrated the genetic mental frailty of Hodgson males, that my father had been forced to fight, and my brother, who had refused to.

My father's death overwhelmed me and filled me with a guilt brought about by the opportunities I had missed to tell him I much I loved him and was so grateful for his kindness during those first useless eight years of my life and my homesick years in Switzerland.

My mother's death finally cut that tie with where this 2-volume saga of over 750 pages, started. It was the final curtain.

However, in all cases, the grief that comes over you so suddenly and unexpectedly initially, goes from every few hours, to every few days, to once a week and so on before disappearing altogether and leaving you and your family with nothing but the fondest of cherished memories.

So, it must be better to have loved and lost rather than to have never loved at all in every single case. Such is life and we must therefore accept that bereavement is the high price that we must all pay for loving and being loved.

# This Life In Death

These personal experiences of family death made me more determined to ensure that people who were suffering the trauma of bereavement should be looked after with kindness, respect and efficiency.

We got very close to perfection in this regard with Hodgson Holdings plc, but we achieved it with Memoria Ltd.

xxxxxxx

The transition of ownership to Darwin was a seamless affair. Michael retired and was replaced by a Darwin nominee called Cate Gray. J and I continued in our positions and the cremation and funeral divisions continued to thrive under the leadership of Carl Clamp and Mark Reath at the former and Paul Reed and Kirsty Lowther at the latter.

The financial services division suffered from some unauthorised actions by Ronnie Waite, who allied himself post sale closely to James Penney and the new finance director, Cate Gray, in the hope of avoiding my strict controls on him and there was also the major task of dealing with FCA regulation at this division too.

However, all in all, life at Memoria continued pretty much as it had been before the acquisition until 2024.

Then in the spring things in my life were to change forever. One night I dreamt of Charles. This had not happened for forty-two years; I suspect as an act of self-protection against the bleak realisation that he was still dead upon my awaking.

I took this dream to be a warning and sent the whole family an email warning them to be very careful that day as a result.

Within hours, I received an email from Judy, my brother's partner. She reported that his liver was failing, he had been rushed to hospital and the doctors did not expect him to live many days.

## This Life In Death

Russell and I had not spoken since my mother's funeral. I had shunned any contact with him following his failure to visit her on her death bed.

For his part he had received his not unsubstantial inheritance from her and had replaced my mother and me with Judy for any other financial support needed and so there was no good reason to pick up the phone to me from his point of view either.

I had moved home from Malta to Monaco three years prior to this and from there hastily took a taxi to Nice Airport, a flight to Heathrow and a taxi to Poole Hospital. There I was shocked to see the state of my brother.

He still looked young for his sixty-seven years, but he was jaundiced, and his arms and legs were covered in horrible bruises. I could see instantly that he was extremely ill.

I had already consulted both my London doctor and a Harley Street specialist about getting him moved to London and the chances of getting him a liver transplant. I was politely, even kindly, but firmly informed that it was too late for either and that his organs were closing down.

When I arrived at the hospital, I was angry with myself that I still couldn't quite forgive him in my heart.

Moreover, he didn't seem particularly pleased to see me, but we were at least civil to each other. I spent an hour with him before making the return journey to Monaco and I was pleased that I had gone and had made human contact with him.

He never left that hospital private ward again and died a week later. When he did, it seemed like that mean and selfish adult had been washed away and I could only see in my mind that charming little boy that I had loved so much all those years ago. I wept.

We celebrated his life with a service at Memoria North Oxfordshire which acknowledged his shortcomings honestly but was full of love and genuine recognition of his sailing skills and undoubted academic genius. Now there was just my sister and me left.

## This Life In Death

Not long after, I was just about to watch Aston Villa play Arsenal away at the Emirates on TV in Monaco. I felt a pounding in my head, and a sharp pain in my left arm and chest.

I took my blood pressure. It was 199 over 125. This was serious. I abandoned the match and went to lie down. Villa won 0-2, secured 4th place, Champions League football and cost Arsenal the title. This delighted me so much that I felt better.

However, the pain returned the next day as my blood pressure soared again. Christine convinced me that we should go to the Princesse Grace Hospital. There, the accident and emergency unit informed me that I had had a heart attack, but they believed that it wasn't a serious one. Nevertheless, they were concerned that I might have a second and more serious one – as apparently that can happen.

Eventually, I was, after several confusing consultations with many doctors, allowed to leave wired up to a monitor.

Over the next few days things didn't seem to be getting any clearer, and my two doctors in London were diagnosing a different cause to the Monaco hospital.

As you will have gathered, if you have accompanied this seventy-four-year journey, I hate indecision. I jumped on a plane to London and Harley Street.

I was immediately given a heart scan and yes, I had had a minor heart attack, and this had caused every third beat of my heart to be irregular. I should rest and if I did and took all my medication when I was meant to, then I should make a full recovery in time.

J had decided to retire from Memoria at the end of the year. I did not relish life at Memoria without him. He had become an increasingly important part of the executive team, since we were no longer looking for crematoria consents, heading up HR, training, legal matters, and more recently, the cremation division.

So, I decided to step down as CEO too, but to stay on as a non-executive director and advisor to James Penney. My funeral career, which had lasted fifty-six years, was finally at an end.

## This Life In Death

XXXXXXX

In Volume I of 'This Life in Death' there is more social and political comment than in Volume II. This is because Volume I deals with matters which occurred a long time ago and need to be considered by you as they were the backdrop to my early years in a very different world than the one in which we live in today.

In Volume II we are increasingly approaching the present day and therefore there is no need to paint such pictures for you.

However, with Memoria no longer in my life for me to govern, and despite being told to rest, my attention turned to the world political stage, and I penned this article the week I retired:

'HASN'T HISTORY TAUGHT US ANYTHING?

The Bible predicts the end of the world and in so doing describes how things will be. It reads to me of something faintly familiar.

2 Timothy 3:
'The Dangers of the Last Days; You should know this, Timothy, that in the last days there will be very difficult times. For people will love only themselves and their money. They will be boastful and proud, scoffing at God, disobedient to their parents, and ungrateful. They will consider nothing sacred. They will be unloving and unforgiving; they will slander others and have no self-control. They will be cruel and hate what is good. They will betray their friends, be reckless, be puffed up with pride, and love pleasure rather than God.'

Does this sound a bit like the domestic life surrounding you? Have we been slowly drifting this way since the social revolution brought about by the baby-boomers in the 1960s? Have things gathered pace in recent years as the Wokes Society has pushed the pendulum too far in the direction of 'political correctness' to the point where we are now discriminating against people because they are young, white, male, and are not an ethnic minority but part of the indigenous population?

Are most television advertisements representative of British life? Are all cars driven by women? Are most families made up of mixed marriages or most parents gay? Are girls the only kids who play football? Why is it that unless white males are babies or old men, they are hardly ever seen in television commercials?

It is essential that everybody gets a fair chance in a meritocracy. There should be no discrimination against anyone because of their sex, colour, religion or sexual orientation.

However, we have become so obsessed by the idea of the over inclusion of every minority in our society that the majority are now excluded or hardly represented.

This is dangerous because if you ignore anyone you drive them away and in time will make an enemy of them. Why do increasing numbers of young white males spend their life on their mobiles laughing at misogynistic jokes or hanging on every politically incorrect statement made by Andrew Tate or Donald Trump?

Do we really want to make an enemy of these young men? Shouldn't we be encouraging them to play an important part in our future? Isn't their exclusion as morally wrong as was the exclusion of other sections that we have sought to correct?
Are we being led astray by the Wokes Society and are we sleepwalking into a place where the pendulum will violently swing back the other way and at some cost?

Remember, if the British, French and US had been more reasonable with their reparation claims made to the Germans at the end of the First World War, Hitler would never have been elected and so the horrors of the Second World War and the Holocaust avoided.

## This Life In Death

Throughout time each generation thinks it is wiser than the last. However, the truth is that while we benefit from invention and discovery, we hardly ever learn from previous generations' experiences and apparently almost never from their mistakes.
The Free World is led by the USA. It will have a presidential election later this year. The two main parties have their candidates: The Democrat candidate might have dementia and could be deemed to be unfit to govern in the next year or so. His vice-president, many knowledgeable Americans believe, might not be suitable to be a domestic home help.

The Republican candidate is charged with causing an insurrection where six people died and with stealing state secret documents. If convicted both charges carry very lengthy prison sentences. He is already a convicted felon, having been found guilty of 34 charges paying out hush money to silence someone whose claims might have altered the result of an election if heard. He is banned from doing business in the State of New York and received a huge fine for his irregular business practices, and he has been convicted of statutory rape.

He claims that all these charges are trumped up by the Democrats in government. Unfortunately, because the government in the USA controls both the legislative and the judiciary, a lot of Americans, who want to support the Republican Party like I loyally support Aston Villa, believe him.

In Britain we find this hard to understand because the government only controls the legislative and it is the King that controls the judiciary. While he holds this power, but declines to use it, no one else can and true democratic government is assured.
There is no evidence that the US government has tampered with the due process of the law in the case of Donald Trump, but their system of government is open to that sort of accusation by a man who should not be standing for election in the first place.

## This Life In Death

So, the leader of the Free World has decided to select either a man with one foot in the grave or a man with one foot in a prison cell as its next president. Is this the action of wise people? Does this bode well for the future?

Then there is Russia. It, having freed itself from the yoke of the tyrannical Soviet Union over 30 years ago, is now back as a dictatorship run by the mass murderer Vladimir Putin. Anyone who opposes Putin politically or even speaks out against him comes to a sticky end by poison, or a plane crash or dies suddenly in prison of an unidentified illness.

Meanwhile, Russia wages a wholly unjustifiable war against Ukraine, where tens of thousands of innocent women, children and elderly folk have been killed as well as 1,000s of young men on both sides. And yet millions of Russians believe the propaganda they are fed? Are they wiser than their grandparents?

The West let Putin get away with the invasion of Crimea. Didn't they learn anything from the experiences of Hitler's invasions in the late 1930s?

Elsewhere, Israel continues to insist that two wrongs do make a right as the mounting deaths of innocent civilians and their children in Gaza is disgraceful and completely inhumane. Have they forgotten how their forefathers suffered in concentration camps?
China continues to be a very dangerous player on the world stage; it has spent decades embedding its influence and control of developing counties in Africa and Asia by investing in them and so making their economies completely dependent on future Chinese support.

Its lack of honour in keeping to signed agreements, like that regarding Hong Kong, and its belief that honour is not about doing what it promised but how it 'saves face' when it doesn't is potentially a lethal combination.

But surely, after the Cold War in the 1950s and 60s we had learned how to prevent this? Apparently not.

I haven't even mentioned North Korea.
And so what about the UK? We also have a forthcoming election. The Tory Party is doing badly in the polls. The Government has been in power for 14 years. The public appear to want a change.
You must go back to the 1970s to see what having a real Labour Government meant. 'Tory Blair' was hardly a socialist and so neither were 'New' Labour's policies. However, while Starmer might be a little blue around the edges, the party he leads runs still Corbynista red beneath him.

In 1974, under Harold Wilson as the last 'red' prime minister, we as a nation paid ourselves 44% more for doing 4% less. Our currency was known as 'the spaghetti pound.' The German Chancellor described British debt as third world debt. Denis Healey was ordered off a plane by the IMF to stop a plummeting pound and hyper-inflation. We had become famous for trade union power, tea breaks and strikes. Everyone was saying that Britain had become the laughingstock of the world. And make no mistake, it was the poorest folk, in this union led shambles, who were the worst off.

Eventually, Mrs Thatcher was elected in 1979 by an electorate who had started to understand that a man, a family, a business, a multi-national company and even a nation, must earn money before it could spend it. It took years of pain before we arrived back as a truly prosperous society based on a meritocracy, incentive but with a social safety net.

Have we learnt from this history lesson? Apparently not. I might not believe that Rishi Sunak is a very good prime minister. However, I bet you within 2 years of a Labour victory you will look back and think of him as brilliant.

# This Life In Death

And in all this mayhem and potential for calamity, I watched last Saturday the Trooping of the Colour. There was so much comfort in this tradition, discipline and stability. God Save the King.'

I believe in these words and include them here, because it will be interesting in future years to see if my predictions come true.

Indeed, since writing the article in the spring of 2024, Trump was elected President of the United States in the November. How well he keeps his election promises remains to be seen.

Starmer did become the UK's Prime Minister in the summer but by Christmas his Labour government had slumped in the opinion polls as the public got its first taste of real socialism for over forty years.

Having a thoroughly dishonest government as well as one that has zero idea about either economics or human nature mean that the UK is truly 'Starmered'.

I predict that Labour's shocking mismanagement of the economy ensures that they will not get a second term.

This impending crisis will be made all the worse in the UK by them governing when a worldwide stock market crash occurs – which I predict will start in the bond market. We will have to wait and to see if I am correct.

xxxxxxx

In the autumn, my eldest son phoned me in Monaco to report that Paul McCartney was going to finish his 'Got Back' world tour in London at the O2 on 19$^{th}$ of December 2024.

I said I wanted to take all my children, their partners, and my older grandchildren as this might be the last time we would see him. It was perhaps the end of a sixty-three-year wonderful trip that I had been tailgating, and I wanted all twelve of us to be there at the end.

I took a box. He played for three hours, without a break and was wonderful. He could have put on another 4 or 5 three-hour concerts without having to repeat a single composition. He is unique. He has been playing the musical score throughout these volumes of this life. He is now eighty-two and his performance was eulogised about the next day as 'six-star perfect' by a press which now understood his value. When it was over, he announced, "See you next time."

I thought I would be very sad at the end. But when he announced that, I wasn't - because I believed him.

I flew home to Monaco but returned three days later to spend Christmas in Stratton Audley Hall with the whole family.

There I enjoyed the first family Christmas where every single one of us was there for a long time. It was magical and made perfect when at the end of King Charles's speech on Christmas day, the whole room burst into applause when he finished. This applause was spontaneous and took me by surprise. It was all the more impressive as it hadn't been led by me.

My faith in the King when he was Prince of Wales and had been so unfairly treated by the British gutter press, was now justified. He has become the very good King Charles III, as I always knew he would be. This fills me with national pride at a time when Britain seems determined to shoot itself in the foot in so many other ways.

Over this Christmas period, the usual collection of Second World War films was shown. These included 'Battle of Britain', 'A Bridge Too Far', 'Where Eagles Dare' and 'Sink the Bismarck.'

I hate the idea of war. However, as in the case of WWII, it can be unavoidable, as when appeasement has already failed, there is no alternative unless you would prefer not to fight to ensure good prevails over evil.

I watched them with interest, despite having seen them all several times before. However, I was now watching while being more aware than ever by the comparison of these men's courage, bravery and selfless sacrifice compared to the hypocritical adherence to the bleatings of 'Wokes Society' dogma by an 'I, me, mine' culture with no concept of selflessness and even less of courage or sacrifice.

I really don't believe Britain could have triumphed over the evil cruelty of Nazi Germany today in a society of positive gender discrimination against the young men who saved us in 1940 and onward until the job was done. Am I looking backwards? No, I am looking forward to see when the pendulum will swing back – as surely it must if we are to be saved from future destruction.

xxxxxxx

'And in the end, the love you take is equal to the love you make'. This is true. As is 'you get out of life what you put in'.

I have taken a lot of love, made a lot of love, but also, given a lot of love.

Moreover, I have tried my hardest to make the most of what meagre talents God gave me. Indeed, I have put a lot into my life, and I have had a lot out as a result.

For all my faults and failings, this is to my credit, as it will be yours too, if you follow my example.

You have accompanied me on this journey by reading these two volumes of my life. The struggle and then the madness.

The struggle was a struggle, and I felt exhausted just reliving it again. The madness of the early nineties was madness and is a lesson to all of us that we need to look in the mirror on occasion and give ourselves a good talking to if we are deviating from our goals or simply messing up our lives.

I have tried very hard to be as open, honest and objective as I could be throughout in the hope that I can give you the belief that if I, with all my limitations, could have achieved what I have then you, with a belief, a drive and a determination can be just as successful.

## This Life In Death

Therefore, if I am going to be wholly honest with you, I have one last thing to tell you about. This is a deep secret that only I really know much about, due to my own insecurity, but it must be shared, if this open-heart surgery is to be genuinely open.

As you know my father fought all his life from what Sir Winston Churchill termed the 'black dog.' This is debilitating depression. Sir Winston also struggled with it on occasion, as did my brother all his life.

Life can throw many slings and arrows at you, like the death of my son Charles in my case.

These horrible incidents will hurt you terribly and make you very sad. However, you're still on the bridge captaining your ship. You're still running your command centre. But, when depression gets you, there is no one on the bridge. There is no one in the command centre.

You know what you should believe. You know what you should do. But you don't believe it and you don't want to do it. Simply put, you are not the same you that is fighting against an outside foe, but a different you who is incapable of being the real you.

I never suffered from this debilitating mental illness when young and was very critical of both my father's and brother's mood swings and saw them as weakness and a lack of self-discipline. So, I showed neither of them much sympathy.

Then one day, in my mid-thirties, having survived the death of Charles three years before, I was hit by a terrible depression and suddenly realised what my father, brother and other sufferers were going through.

I had had no idea before, but now I had, and I could see the light. Luckily for me, my attacks were very few and far between. The next came when I was in my fifties and in my wilderness years. I sought to cure myself by writing lyrics and asking Mike Sullivan to write the music for me.

My thinking was that it might help me and even if it didn't, I would be able to write something that I couldn't have done when not depressed.

## This Life In Death

Here is an example of lyrics written when the black dog attacked me then.

*I feel castrated, locked with me inside*
*It's not this picture I want you to see*
*It's a schizophrenic Piscean me*
*Ordered convention has lost its hold*
*The art child won before I grew too old*
*Abdicated from responsibility*
*No flesh but drink don't you see*
*I need the time just for me*
*Yes need the time just for me.*

*Before I was so busy for you*
*Trying to win the race materially*
*Absorbing all responsibility*
*Absorbing all responsibility*
*But the strong have a sterile head*
*So I'm baring my soul instead*
*Going to write something great before I'm dead*
*Going to write something great before I'm dead*

*So I'm busy hurting inside*
*Exploring cultivation far and wide*
*To find a Cosmic solution I can ride*
*To find a Cosmic solution I can ride*
*Please God give me the possibility*
*To mend my broken family*
*I need it so badly for my sanity*
*To fix my dysfunctional family*

*Sunsets to remember*
*Divine fires – Look? Into the embers (repeat to end)*

You can see on the page and virtually feel the torturous pain going on in my head.

Mike had saved my life when I lost Charles. I had been holding everything together in the day but looking at the wall like a zombie at night. He had offered me a lifeline through lyrics.

Now I turned to him again for salvation.

## This Life In Death

The first time he had helped me get over the worst type of bereavement. The loss of a child. This time I was asking him to help me sort out my head – but of course I never let him know, or anyone else, why I had suddenly started to write lyrics again.

I was an island and couldn't admit to such weakness to him or anyone else. I simply didn't have the confidence to ask for help and didn't believe it would do any good if I did. So, the price paid would be high while the benefit would be nil.

Luckily, the writing lyrics trick worked, and with a new purpose, the captain reappeared on the bridge and the ship stabilised.

Then along came the Memoria years of hard work, purpose and planning for the future and the 'black dog' stayed away as he did with Churchill during the Second World War.

Then, after my heart attack and retirement, 'the black dog', seeing that I wasn't working flat out to ensure all bereaved families were being 'done unto as you would have done unto yourself' and plotting a course for the future, took me in his jaws.

I was suddenly struck with the idea that my fever of life was over, that my busy world was hushed and that I had nothing to look forward to. I was coming to the end of the line.

I felt very low. Then from nowhere, in a dream, a woman with long silver hair, which flowed behind her in the wind, dressed in a royal blue satin gown came to me and told me that I must learn to live for the moment.

I know that her name was Bobko and she was a mystical goddess. She appeared three nights running. I felt that she was a mother figure and was comforted by her as if I were a little boy again. On the fourth morning I awoke and 'the black dog' had gone and so had she.

Am I mad? Of course I may be, but the mind is very fragile, and we need to look after it carefully. Moreover, no man, not even a 'Peaky Blinder', can be an island. We all need to love and be loved.

We also need to appreciate when others suffer from an illness which we can't see or touch, that they are locked with a serious menace in their head, that their captain is not on the bridge at that moment, and their actions are not their own, and they need kindness and understanding.

These volumes are published by Chipmunka, the mental health publisher, and I am proud to be associated with them.

xxxxxxx

This now brings this seventy-four-year personal story almost up to date and I thank you for joining me on the journey. Indeed, I feel a little sad that we are getting to the end, and I will miss talking to you through these pages. I feel that we have become friends.

So, what am I going to do now? Watch ITV 3 and loads of those TV series I missed when running around doing all the things you have been reading about? Don't you even imagine that for a second.

I have taken delivery of an 80 foot 'Y' Yacht, named 'King Charles III', and I will sail her far and wide. I will ski like the wind. I will continue to ride. I will roar my F-Type Jaguar where it will take me. I will drink my wine, flirt with the waitress while I still can win that return smile, and plan – as I still have the last quarter of my life to live.

I have these two volumes of 'This Life in Death' to promote; then I will split 'Charles: The Man Who Will Be King' into two volumes and write the third about 'Good King Charles.' This will be followed by a biography about Paul McCartney, 'James Paul Mozart' and the 'The Project' about the re-birth of Aston Villa.

I have also stumbled on a young man with whom Michael Sullivan and I will write more songs. So, I really do intend to 'write something great before I'm dead' as 'Embers' says.

I will be positive and have a great zest for life. However, when looking at those 'sunsets to remember' and into those 'dying fires' I will be looking into the embers in the hope of catching a few glimpses of those memories that I have shared with you in remembering so many over such a long time.

## This Life In Death

And despite the struggle and the madness, it's been a good life, and when I eventually reluctantly leave it, I will be sad, as my family is my heaven on earth. Nowhere could ever be or ever feel so good as life with one's children and those very special people who love us and we love them back.

However, it's not over yet. Moreover, your life certainly isn't– so go out and make your dreams happen, because you can achieve anything if you want it enough and try your hardest to make it happen.

So, in the words of James Paul McCartney, "See you next time", when perhaps, if you want it enough, I might be reading about you.

# This Life In Death

## Book Index

# This Life In Death

# This Life In Death

# This Life In Death

# This Life In Death